DATE DUE

Demco, Inc. 38-293

A HIMALAYAN TRIBE

A Himalayan Tribe

From Cattle to Cash

Christoph von
Fürer-Haimendorf

UNIVERSITY OF CALIFORNIA PRESS
Berkeley   Los Angeles

UNIVERSITY OF CALIFORNIA PRESS
Berkeley and Los Angeles, California

1 2 3 4 5 6 7 8 9

Library of Congress Cataloging in Publication Data

Fürer-Haimendorf, Christoph von, 1909-
    A Himalayan tribe.

    Bibliography: p.
    Includes index.
    1. Apa Tanis.   I. Title.
DS432.A6F79   305.8'00954'163   80-10732
ISBN 0-520-04074-0

Printed in India

To

Clotilde Peploe

Preface

IN THE CAREER of most anthropologists there comes a moment when they have to decide whether to embark on new field research or to devote the rest of their days either to the analysis of material gathered during earlier investigations or to comparative studies, which can be done in any good library. Though my own preference has always been for fieldwork I have realized that after a certain age it is unwise to take up the study of an unfamiliar area to which one brings neither a knowledge of local conditions nor an acquaintance with any of the languages spoken. Faced with this dilemma I decided on a middle course which permits me to utilize experience acquired in past years, but which at the same time provides for stimulation springing from encounters with novel situations. In pursuance of this plan I have spent the last three years on the restudy of Indian tribal populations, known to me since the early 1940s, with the intention of recording and analyzing the social and economic changes that have occurred in the past 30 to 40 years.

The two main groups of tribes to be covered by this project are the aboriginal tribes of Andhra Pradesh such as Chenchus, Hill Reddis and Gonds, and the tribes of Arunachal Pradesh, the territory formerly known as the North-East Frontier Agency. The first result of my work among the Deccan tribes has recently been published under the title *The Gonds of Andhra Pradesh* (Delhi, 1979) and a comparative volume on the changing position of several tribes of the same state is now in preparation.

This volume, on the other hand, deals with the development of a single tribe of Arunachal Pradesh which I first encountered in 1944 and restudied in 1978. The fortunes of this tribe, the Apa Tanis of the Subansiri District, contrast sharply with the present situation of the tribal people of Peninsular India, and the recent transformation of the Apa Tanis' economic and social life, such as indicated by the subtitle of this book, deserves to be analyzed in a volume of its own.

Readers familiar with my earlier writings on the Apa Tanis[1] will notice certain deviations from the spelling of local names which I had then used and which subsequently were adopted in official reports and publications. As in recent years large numbers of Apa Tanis have become literate and have evolved their own spelling of the names of persons, social groups and localities, it seems reasonable to conform to those indigenous spellings, for any other policy would be confusing to readers in Arunachal Pradesh. There remains, however, one problem of nomenclature which I have been unable to resolve. When conversing in their own language Apa Tanis speak of themselves as Tani, and they say that the term "Apa" is a honorific used by other tribes as well as by Assamese when addressing Apa Tanis. I have posed to some of the educated Apa Tanis the question whether in print, and indeed in this book, the composite name Apa Tani should be replaced by Tani, which seems to be the genuine tribal name. While some of my friends favoured such a change there was no consensus on this tricky problem and other leading men took the view that such a radical departure from established usage would have to be debated at length by tribal leaders before a decision could be taken. As the elimination of the honorific "Apa" would involve adjustments in all government records and in the publications of the Census of India, there seems to be no likelihood of an early replacement of the tribal name familiar to speakers of English, Assamese and Hindi, and I am therefore retaining the composite form "Apa Tani."

Yet, other tribal names have been changed in recent years. The Apa Tanis' neighbours previously known as Dafla now object to this name and insist on being called Nishi. They dislike the name Dafla because in Assamese it has the derogatory connotation "wild man" or "barbarian." The adoption of the name did not come to me as a surprise, for in my *Ethnographic Notes on the Tribes of the Subansiri Region* I wrote as early as 1947: "Both the Daflas of the Panior region and the tribesmen of the Kamla region refer to themselves as Nisü or in some places as Ni, a word whose meaning is 'men', but which has gradually developed into a term applied only to the inhabitants of the hills" (p. 5). For the same reason

[1]*Ethnographic Notes on the Tribes of the Subansiri Region*, Shillong, 1947; *Himalayan Barbary*, London, 1975; *The Apa Tanis and their Neighbours*, London, 1962.

the old tribal name Abor has now been replaced by Adi, and other groups are pleading for the official adoption of the names used in their own languages.

Unlike some anthropologists who use in their writings pseudonyms for persons, clans and localities, a practice which greatly diminishes the future value of their works as historical documents, I am using the real names of the many Apa Tanis whose actions and fortunes have been described, and I am confident that none of them will object to seeing his or her name in the pages of this book. Their children and grandchildren may even welcome such information on the lives of earlier generations, a reaction similar to that which I encountered when in 1970 I returned after 34 years to the Konyak Nagas and heard young men, who had not been born at the time of my earlier fieldwork, expressing their pleasure of reading about their fathers and grandfathers in my book *The Naked Nagas* (London, 1939).

The entire project of restudies of Indian tribal populations extending from 1976 well into the 1980s could not be carried out without the good will and assistance of the Government of India and the officials of the concerned states. The success of research in Arunachal Pradesh, more than elsewhere, depends on the sympathy and cooperation of the members of the local administration. For in Arunachal Pradesh, which is normally closed to travellers, there are no facilities regarding transport or accommodation except those controlled by government departments, and official sponsorship is thus essential for any visitor to this Union Territory. I was fortunate in being granted permission to work in the Subansiri District and to benefit from the hospitality and help of officials from the Lieutenant-Governor Colonel A.K. Raja down to all the local officials at Ziro, the district headquarter. Not all of these can be individually named, but I would like to express my special gratitude to the Deputy Commissioner J.M. Syiem and to the Extra Assistant Commissioner Pau. Asistance of a special kind was extended to me by Lord Kojee, an Apa Tani member of the district staff, then working as Youth Coordinator. Not only did he give me a great deal of information on recent developments and the attitude of educated Apa Tanis to many problems arising from the current process of change, but he also went through my book *The Apa Tanis and their Neighbours* and annotated such passages as he considered outdated or inaccurate. The many hours spent in his company were among the most profitable of my entire stay at Ziro.

The warmth of the welcome given to my wife and me by Padi Lailang (whose name I had previously spelt Layang) and the hospitality enjoyed in his house in Reru was all the more gratifying as his whole family including the younger generation treated us as old friends. Among his sons Padi Yubbe, the present speaker of the Legislative Assembly of Arunachal Pradesh, is the most prominent and to him I owe an insight into the relations of modern politicians with their constituents. Even greater is our debt of gratitude to Padi Lailang's daughter Pume, known to her close friends as Nampi, and her husband Kuru Hasang, in whose house at Hapoli we spent long hours discussing over rice-beer or coffee numerous problems of custom and ritual. Two Apa Tani postgraduate students, Hage Batt and Hage Khoda, luckily at home on holiday during part of our stay, were also extremely helpful and so were some of the local politicians such as Bamin Kano, Tasso Gryayo and Hage Hale. To all of them as well as to Koj Murt, one of the *kotoki* attached to the Deputy Commissioner's office, I should like to express my most sincere thanks for all they have done to further our work.

Last but by no means least I should like to record my appreciation of the cooperation and companionship of B.B. Pandey, a member of the Research Department of Arunachal Pradesh, who left his headquarters at Along in order to accompany us to Ziro and assist our research among the Apa Tanis. As the author of a book on the Hill Miris he was well qualified to understand the problems of social change among tribal populations. By a lucky chance B.K. Shukla, who had been a research officer at Ziro when I stayed there in 1962, was able to join us for some days though his present posting as Deputy Director of Social Welfare is in Madras. Both from conversations and his unpublished monograph describing the Apa Tanis as he knew them in the 1960s I gained much information on those phases in their development which I had not been able to observe with my own eyes. Neither B. K. Shukla nor I myself would probably have been able to revisit the Apa Tani valley had it not been for the advocacy of our plan by Dr B.D. Sharma, then Joint Secretary in the Ministry of Home Affairs in Delhi, who exerted his very considerable influence to overcome bureaucratic obstacles and convince the Government of India that my anthropological studies were unlikely to involve any security risk. No less appreciated was the interest in my project envinced by M.L. Kampani, I.A.S., of the same Ministry.

During the diplomatic preparations of my visit to the Apa Tani valley I enjoyed the hospitality of the Austrian Embassy in New Delhi and it gives me great pleasure to thank my delightful hosts Gabrielle and Wolfgang Schallenberg, who did much to sustain my morale during the long wait for permission to enter Arunachal Pradesh.

Anthropological work requires not only the consent of the governments concerned but also the funds to meet the cost of air-travel to distant places and the expense of transporting camping equipment from one area of research to the other. In the case of my project of restudies in Andhra Pradesh and Arunachal Pradesh these expenses were covered by generous grants from the Social Science Research Council of the United Kingdom, the Leverhulme Trust Fund and the Wenner-Gren Foundation for Anthropological Research, while the administrative back-up was provided by the School of Oriental and African Studies. My thanks are due to all these institutions and to those who processed the grants awarded.

On my way to Arunachal Pradesh I had the good fortune of spending some time at Gauhati University, the North-Eastern Hill University and the University of Dibrugarh. To the staff of these universities and particularly to Dr C. Devanesen, Professor M.C. Goswami and Professor S.M. Dubey I am indebted for much hospitality and assistance.

My wife participated as usual in every aspect of my research and Miss Yvonne Turnbull earned my gratitude by typing the manuscript of this book.

School of Oriental and African Studies, University of London   CHRISTOPH VON FÜRER-HAIMENDORF

Contents

ARUNACHAL PRADESH

Introduction

THROUGHOUT THE AGES the Himalayas acted not only as a barrier between the peoples of India and their northern neighbours, but also as a refuge area where archaic styles of life and culture could persist in the isolation of secluded valleys uneffected by the march of progress in the rest of the Indian subcontinent. In the Central Himalayas and particularly in the Kingdom of Nepal tribal populations on relatively low economic levels overlapped and dove-tailed with representatives of sophisticated Buddhist and Hindu civilizations some of whose ideas and practices permeated to some degree even the tribal world. Along trade-routes traversing the Great Himalayas caravans of yak and of carrier sheep and goats linked Tibet with the markets of Nepal and India, and along these same routes pilgrims from both India and Tibet travelled in their quest for the merit flowing from visits to the shrines and sacred places located on both sides of the snow-ranges. Here the barrier of high mountains was not complete, though there were times of the year when snow covered the passes and blocked all contacts between Nepalese and Tibetans.

Very different conditions prevailed in the Eastern Himalayas, and specifically in the tangle of pathless wooden hills which stretches east of Bhutan as far as the extreme northeast corner of India. In this region, formerly known as North-East Frontier Agency and recently renamed Arunachal Pradesh, there are no through-routes and the precipitate gorges of rivers breaking through the Great Himalayan range never permitted trade depending on animal trans-port. Rainfall many times as heavy as that of the Central Himalayas sustains a vegetation discouraging all except the most intrepid travellers from the attempt to penetrate into an area where one may have to slog for days through dripping forests and jungles without ever catching as much as a glimpse of the surrounding country. Difficulties of communications rather than the nature of the neigh-bouring regions of Tibet and India would seem to be responsible

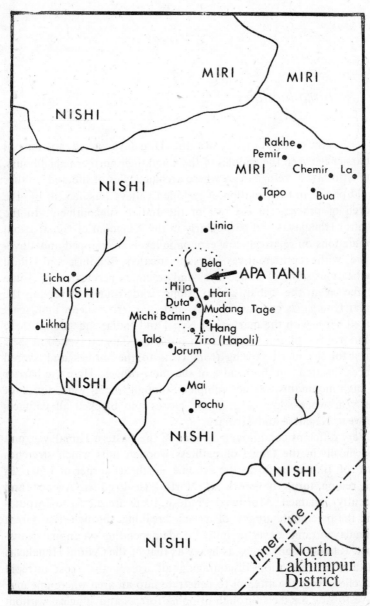

COUNTRY SURROUNDING THE APA TANI VALLEY

for the fact that the tribal populations inhabiting the mountainous tracts extending between Assam and Tibet remained for centuries if not millennia untouched by Hindu as well as Buddhist civilization. Their seclusion caused initially by physical factors persisted until the middle of the twentieth century because of political decisions taken by the Government of India in the days of British rule. The area situated between the northern fringe of the Assam plains, then as now covered by tea-gardens, and the crest line of the Great Himalayan Range, traditionally regarded as the border between India and Tibet, remained outside the administrative control of the Government of Assam. Its tribal inhabitants continued in their archaic style of life, unobserved and uninfluenced by outsiders. Until 1944 this tribal country was unknown to the Assamese of the plains no less than to the Tibetans beyond the Himalayan passes. It was inhabited by a number of distinct tribes of whose distribution and distinct characteristics the outside world was unaware. This region was nominally included in the Balipara Frontier Tract of the province of Assam, but only the southernmost parts were ever entered by government officials in the course of rare and generally rather ineffective tours, while most of the area remained unmapped and unexplored.

Towards the end of the nineteenth century, first H.M. Crowe and after him R.B. McCabe paid brief visits to part of the present Subansiri District, but though they reported the existence of a well-populated and intensively cultivated valley situated in the hills north of North Lakhimpur no steps were taken to follow up these explorations. Not until 1911 did the Government of India make any effort to survey the unexplored regions south of the notional border with Tibet. A semi-military expedition known as the Miri Mission was mounted with the avowed purpose of surveying the valleys of the Kamla and Khru Rivers, but difficulties in establishing friendly relations with the local tribesmen and a series of misunderstandings resulting in armed clashes compelled the expedition to withdraw without achieving the exploration of the regions of high altitude close to the snow-ranges. Yet, the published maps of the Survey of India covering the southern part of the present Subansiri District are based on the survey operation undertaken by the Miri Mission, and it is unfortunate that these maps found in the map collections of geographical libraries all over the world are the only topographical record of the region available to scholars, while the results of more recent surveys are withheld from circulation.

For 32 years there was no follow-up to the Miri Mission and the tribesmen of the Subansiri region were left to their own devices. A few of the Political Officers of the Balipara Frontier Tract visited some of the villages of the foothills, but there was no attempt to interfere in the tribal feuds and the periodic raids in the interior of the highlands. In 1914 negotiations between Britain, Tibet and China had resulted in the drafting of a convention which defined the international boundary, but this convention was never ratified because of a change of mind on the part of the Chinese government. Hence no action was taken to demarcate the frontier, but the course of the boundary as laid down in the convention negotiated on the British side by Sir Henry MacMahon has ever since been referred to as the MacMahon line. In this context it is not relevant that the uncertainties regarding this line which had never been established on the ground were among the principal causes of the conflict between India and China in 1962, but it is certainly strange that throughout the period between the two World Wars the Government of India took no steps to administer the submontane tract south of the MacMahon line which the draft convention had clearly allocated to India, but which successive Chinese governments continued to claim, though with varying insistence.

The dangerous situation on the borders of Northeast India, created during the Second World War by the Japanese invasion of Burma and the Naga Hills, stirred the Government of India to abandon its complacent attitude towards the tribal areas on its frontiers. Hence, the exploration of the still unchartered part of the North-East Frontier Agency was taken up as a first step towards the extention of administrative control ideally as far as the MacMahon line. It was then that an appointment as Special Officer Subansiri and Assistant Political Officer provided me with the unique opportunity of touring the hill-country southwest of the Subansiri River and of getting to know tribal groups which at that time had little or no contact with the plains of Assam. Many of the villages which I visited in 1944 and 1945 had never been entered by any outsider— European, Indian or Tibetan—nor had the villagers any conception of life outside their immediate neighbourhood. This situation gave me the matchless opportunity of observing the economic and social life of populations without any contact with modern life or indeed the political system prevailing in the rest of India.

The circumstances of my early work in the Subansiri region and specifically among the Apa Tanis, Nishis and Hill Miris have been described in my book *Himalayan Barbary* (London, 1955) and some of the results of my anthropological observations are contained in *The Apa Tanis and Their Neighbours* (London, 1962) as well as in *Ethnographic Notes on the Tribes of the Subansiri Region* (Shillong, 1947). The latter two publications have been out of print for many years, and the description of basic ethnographic facts will have to be repeated in order to make understandable the process of change which forms the main topic of the present book.

When my wife and I entered the Apa Tani valley in 1944 at the end of a strenuous and adventurous trek through the virtually pathless forests of the outer ranges, we found ourselves in a world different from anything we had experienced among other tribal populations. The people we encountered were friendly but clearly somewhat wary and suspicious and above all consumed by curiosity. We were the first outsiders they had ever seen, and for many days we were continuously surrounded by large crowds. Communications were difficult, for there was not a single Apa Tani who knew more than a few words of Assamese or indeed of any language other than the local dialects. Our only interpreter was a Nishi who was familar with the Apa Tani language as well as with Assamese which I spoke then with reasonable fluency.

The purchase of local food stuff was equally difficult, for the majority of Apa Tanis were unfamiliar with Indian coinage and all transactions had to proceed on a barter basis and for this we were ill prepared. The two commodities most eagerly accepted were salt and cotton-cloth, but tobacco and matches, whose use the Apa Tanis rapidly understood, could serve as small change. Self-sufficient in foodgrains, the Apa Tanis used their surplus rice to barter cattle and pigs from neighbouring Nishis, members of a tribal group far larger than the Apa Tani community, but noticeably less advanced in material civilization and the art of exercising social controls.

Neither Apa Tanis nor Nishis recognized any outside authority, and though they had vague notions of some powerful agency ruling over the plains of Assam, they themselves had never come up against a power concerned with events in their own villages. While Nishis were one of the few populations who lacked any mechanism of legal controls and resolved all serious disputes by force, the Apa

Tanis had a system of clan-heads forming village-councils with some judicial powers. In the absence of any alien administration it was thus possible to observe and gradually understand the way in which an entirely autonomous tribal society can conduct its affairs without interference by an outside political force.

Relations with neighbouring tribal groups vacillated between friendly trade-contacts and open hostility taking the forms of raids, kidnappings and even the killing of captives in cold blood. The absence of any superior authority or territorial organization allowed the play of conflicting interests full scope. Much of the energy and time of such tribes as the Nishis was taken up by internecine struggles, and going through my notebooks of the years 1944 and 1945 I find that a large part of my time too was taken up with the recording and, in the later stages of my work, also with the settling of feuds and disputes.

When we returned to the Apa Tani valley for a few weeks in the spring of 1962 the scene had begun to change. The tentative steps towards the establishment of an administration undertaken in the last three years of the British Raj had been followed up and greatly reinforced by the new national Government of India. The occupation of the previously peaceful and self-contained Tibet by the armies of communist China had turned the Subansiri region from a politically unimportant backwater into a strategically highly sensitive frontier area. The mounting tensions between India and China, which later that year led to the invasion of the North-East Frontier Agency by Chinese forces, had induced the Government of India to improve communications and station army units in the Apa Tani valley. An air-strip, taking up some of the cultivated land, served the provisioning of these units, and a fair-weather road linked the valley with North Lakhimpur. When the Chinese threat finally materialized, and some Indian frontier-posts were overrun, the Apa Tani valley was spared occupation by enemy forces. Yet the build-up of defences brought about significant changes in the economic and social climate.

By 1971, when I paid once more a short visit to the Subansiri region, the transformation of the Apa Tani valley had further progressed. The road linking Hapoli, the district headquarters, with the road-net of Assam had been greatly improved and lorries, jeeps and cars plied along this road throughout the year, bringing supplies from North Lakhimpur and taking tribesmen and their goods to the markets of the plains. Hapoli had grown into a fullfledged district headquarters and numerous shops, mainly owned by Apa Tanis, served the needs of the numerous government employees and such tribesmen as were hankering for imported goods. Education, started in the middle 1950s with the establishment of several primary schools, was beginning to make a significant impact and several Apa Tanis were already studying in universities of Assam and others of Indian states. A few years later I was to find several of them holding positions in the administration of the district as gazetted officers.

Arunachal Pradesh was never a region generally open to foreign scholars, and for seven years I hesitated to undertake the time-consuming and often frustrating task of trying to overcome the bureaucratic hurdles which stand in the way of one's entry into the promised land of Apa Tanis and Nishis. Research in Nepal, a country far more accessible to foreigners, kept me busy, and so I waited in the hope that restrictions on travel in Northeast India might ultimately be eased. However, a comprehensive research project concerned with the development of Indian tribal populations during the past forty years made it imperative to revisit not only the tribes of the Deccan, whom I had studied in the 1940s, but to observe also the economic and social changes which were transforming the conditions of the tribal populations of Arunachal Pradesh. Thanks to the efforts of enlightened officials in the Home Ministry in Delhi my wife and I finally obtained permission to spend six weeks among the Apa Tanis of the Subansiri District. We arrived in their country almost to the day 34 years after our first visit in March 1944, and the beauty of the broad valley lying between wooded hills at an altitude of close on 5,000 feet once again took our breath away. After the shocks we had received in Peninsular India where so much of tribal country has been ruined by deforestation and the invasions of alien land-grabbers we had feared that the same process might have destroyed the magic and the harmony of the Apa Tani valley. All the greater was our joy when we realized that despite many innovations the valley had retained its character. The wide terraced rice-fields were still surrounded by dark pine-groves and bamboo-gardens interspersed with fruit-trees just then breaking out into white and pink blossoms. Pastures studied with mauve primulae extended as of old on the fringes of the valley, and the sub-tropical rain-forest clothing the higher hills was interspersed with flowering rhododendrons.

Change had come in the shape of motorable roads now linking all the villages, and of the many pylons of electric and telephone lines which stand in the rice-fields and even more incongruously between the densely packed bamboo-houses of the seven main Apa Tani villages. Most dramatic, no doubt, is the change at the southern end of the valley where the hillocks once covered in bracken and pasture have been turned into the site for the sprawling modern settlement of the district headquarters. The local name of the site is Hapoli, but officially the name Ziro was retained for post office, bank, hospital and other public buildings when the civil station was moved there from the "old Ziro" situated in the northern part of the valley.

The large bazaar of Hapoli was soon filled with an excited crowd when on the morning after our arrival, we walked through its broad street. The news that Laling and Yelu, as we had been known to the Apa Tanis 34 years earlier, had returned to the valley rapidly spread from shop to shop and house to house, and Apa Tanis and visiting Nishis surrounded us by the hundreds. Though old people who knew us well were no longer numerous, others had seen us as children and had heard of us and our exploits in 1944 and 1945. They seemed to feel that a legend had come alive, and gradually we realized that entirely erroneously, but yet very persistently much of the modern development was attributed to the initiatives I had taken in the 1940s. Middle-aged Apa Tanis, who remembered seeing us when we first arrived, kept on telling that we had opened up the valley to the outside world, and that everything that had followed was the result of that first visit of ours. The Apa Tanis were, of course, completely mistaken for there can be no doubt that even if in 1944 the government of British India had not sent an expedition to the Subansiri region, very soon after 1947 the government of Independent India would have developed the area in much the same manner as other regions along the north eastern border were then being developed. Nor did my recommendations regarding the lines on which an administration might initially be set up go beyond the type of planning anyone familiar with the tribal people and their problems might have suggested.

Yet the Apa Tanis' mistaken belief in my role in the sequence of events which had led to present-day developments helped me greatly in re-establishing the atmosphere of intimacy and trust which had prevailed at the time of my earlier visits. Squatting by the fire in houses which have remained unchanged, and drinking millet or rice-beer of grades varying from excellent to barely tolerable, I myself felt transported back to the time when the Apa Tanis were still an isolated community and I a visitor from an alien world of which they had not the slightest idea. Yet, there were differences. In 1944 conversation was carried on laboriously through the medium of Assamese, which at that time I could speak and understand reasonably well, translated by a Nishi interpreter into Apa Tani, while now there were often some young English-speaking Apa Tanis present, or I could speak to Apa Tanis directly in Hindi.

The fact that nowadays some Apa Tanis are fluent in English made it possible to cover in six weeks a great deal of ground. Indeed the degree of sophistication attained by Apa Tanis is such that one of my friends, Lod Koji, was able to annotate my small book *The Apa Tanis and Their Neighbours.* Yet not only those educated in colleges and universities were aware of the modern world, but even ordinary and still illiterate villagers had greatly widened their horizon. This was demonstrated by the questions they asked us. They now know that there are time differences between different parts of the world, and I was often asked what time of the day it was in England or what the climate was in Europe in any particular season. The crops grown and the animals bred in my country were also matters of interest. Many Apa Tanis had been to some of the great cities of India, and would talk about the Taj Mahal or their encounters with such political figures as Jawaharlal Nehru and Indira Gandhi, who had visited the Apa Tani valley and had received delegations or tribesmen in Delhi. I could not help comparing this involvement in a wider world with the parochialism of many tribal people in states such as Andhra Pradesh where many villages remain almost totally cut off from modern developments and have hardly changed for the past half century.

The developments in Arunachal Pradesh are undoubtedly one of the success stories of present-day India, and one wonders why the astounding progress of the tribesmen of this region is being covered with a veil of secrecy while the far less creditable situation in the tribal areas of Peninsular India can be observed without any need for official permission.

Each of the following chapters combines a description of the traditional culture pattern as I found in 1944-45 with an assessment of the developments which I observed during my three revisits in 1962, 1970 and 1978.

ONE

Environment and Settlements

THE APA TANI valley is set in a landscape typical of most of the middle-ranges of the Eastern Himalayas. Densely wooded mountains, which rise from narrow valleys often as low as 1,500 feet to heights between 8,000 to 9,000 feet, form range upon range rarely broken by even a few square miles of level ground. The vegetation ranges from the luscious growth of evergreen shrubs and trees, giant bamboos and wild bananas well known from all the lower lying areas of Assam to the sub-tropical rain-forest of the higher hills. This more or less uniform tangle of hills stretching from the eastern border of Bhutan far east into the Adi and Mishmi country is broken by a single wide valley as different from all the surrounding country as the Kathmandu Valley is different from the rest of Nepal. Indeed there is a certain similarity between the much larger heart-land of Nepal and the broad Apa Tani valley, which is so flat that though surrounded by hills it is often mistakenly referred to as "Apa Tani plateau." Both these valleys stand out from all the neighbouring country, both topographically and in the nature of the civilizations which they have nurtured. In both places there are also traditions that the wide expanses now covered by intensively cultivated rice-land were once large lakes which were drained by legendary personalities or the forefathers of the present inhabitants. Viewed from the air there is even a slight similarity in the settlement pattern. Both Apa Tani and Newar villages are tightly packed aggregates of houses occupying rising ground in between terraced rice-fields.

In the case of the Apa Tani valley there is much to suggest that the valley was once a lake, and that the silt brought down by streams from the surrounding mountains filled out this lake and built up a plain whose fertile soil enabled the Apa Tanis to develop a civilization far superior to that of neighbouring tribes living precariously by shifting-cultivation on hill-slopes in country where rivers rush through deep gorges, and mountains sweep up to rugged crests with hardly as much as a ledge between river-bank and peak 6,000 or 7,000 feet above. The Apa Tanis tell that their ancestors found the valley filled with swamps inhabited by large amphibious reptiles known as *buru*. Nowadays Apa Tanis refer to crocodiles as *buru,* but according to tradition the original *buru* were of different shape, having small heads set on long necks rather like antediluvian saurians. No bones or other traces of these *buru* have been found despite the strenuous efforts of an expedition described by Ralph Izzard in *The Hunt for the Buru* (London 1951).

The early history of the Apa Tanis is shrouded in mystery. As in the case of other preliterate societies, legendary accounts of their place of origin and their migration to their present habitat do not entirely coincide, but the various stories all agree that even before the Apa Tanis reached the valley in which they are now settled they formed a society with a common ethnic identity. Most legends and the views now generally held agree that they came from a land vaguely located in the north, and that there they lived in a place known as Üpyo Supung. A place known as Mudu Burü also figures in several accounts, and it is believed that from that place, which lay closer to Tibet than their present location, the Apa Tanis brought a species of plum tree (*thakum*) of great ritual importance. Another tree thought to have been brought by the early Apa Tanis is *pinus excelsa*, the magnificent pine-tree so characteristic of the valley and the adjoining slopes but absent in the neighbouring Nishi country. In the area of the Khru and Kamla rivers there are various topographical features figuring in the migration stories of the Apa Tanis, the most prominent being Pij Cholo a peak between the Kamla and Sipi rivers, but there is not sufficient consistency in the various legendary accounts to permit a conclusive reconstruction of the tribe's early movements. In the region of Hure, in the Upper Kamla valley, there are marks on a rock which resemble footprints, and the local tribesmen, a group of Nishis, refer to these as "Apa Tani footprints" implying that Hure lay on the migration route of the Apa Tanis.

In Chapter 4 we shall discuss in detail the division of the Apa Tanis into three groups, whose formation is ascribed to the fact that not all clans migrated from Mudu Burü to the present Apa

Tani valley by the same routes. The people who ultimately settled in the villages of Hija, Duta, Mudang-Tage and Michi-Bamin crossed the Khru river between the present settlements of Mintlat and Buha, then stayed for some time in Tapal Tale (an area east of the main valley recently opened for colonization) and finally established their present villages. The ancestors of the villagers of Hari and Büla believe to have immigrated via Pepu Sela, an area due north of the Apa Tani valley, and the people of Hang, who now form a group by themselves, but were known as Nich-Nite, claim to have come via Nari-Anko, north-east of the valley. They are supposed to have crossed the Kamla river near the Miri village of Gocham.

A slightly different migration myth was recorded by Ursula Graham Bower (*The Hidden Land*, London, 1953, p.219) but such variations are not surprising in a society in which all traditions are passed on by oral transmission. The only relevant fact is that in certain rivalries between the various groups of villages reference is still being made to the divisions and groupings established—or believed to have been established—at the time of the original settlement in the valley.

Tribal tradition agrees that when the three batches of people arriving by different routes began to settle in the valley they were faced not only by huge swamps but also by huge reptiles, the *buru*, living in these swamps. At first the new settlers were so terrified that they barely dared to go out and collect firewood. Priests consulted omens to discover whether they should remain where they were or move on to other localities. The omens did not favour any further move, and so the Apa Tanis stayed on in the valley and pondered how to rid themselves of the *buru*. There are various mythical accounts of the destruction of these aquatic reptiles, but they all attribute its success to the magical virtue of two disc-like metal objects in the possession of two Apa Tanis who knew how to use them by remote control for the slaughter of the *buru*.

The destruction of the numerous reptiles is believed to have taken a long time, but when the swamps were drained the Apa Tanis established the present seven villages, and set about making the entire valley arable. Step by step they built dams and dug channels, and thus transformed the valley bottom into an enormous mosaic of carefully tended rice-fields, while on islands of higher ground groves of pines, bamboos and fruit trees were planted. A small river which may originally have meandered through the swampy bottom of the valley was forced into a more or less straight course between high dams, and numerous streams originating on the surrounding hills were used to irrigate the terraced rice-fields.

In 1944 there were seven Apa Tani villages, each occupying a site close to the rim of the valley. The social, political and ritual grouping of these villages will be considered in Chapter 4; here we are concerned only with the topographical setting. Hang, which in 1944 comprised close to 500 houses and was next to Büla the largest village, lies on the southern end of the valley and is built on a tongue projecting into the cultivated area. Hari and Büla ile at no great distance from each other on the eastern edge of the valley. Büla represents a special case in the sense that although one continuous conglomeration of houses, known by that name, it consists really of three villages (*lemba*) each known by a separate name, i.e. Reru, Tajang and Kalung respectively, and each constituting a separate social and ritual unit. On the north-western rim of the valley there are the four villages of Hija, Duta, Mudang-Tage, and Michi-Bamin. They form an almost continuous area of habitation, though the individual villages do not adjoin as closely as the constituent parts of Büla.

There is a certain uniformity in the configuration of Apa Tani villages and the lay-out of the surrounding land conforms to so definite a pattern that to visualize one village in its setting will give a fairly accurate idea of the traditional Apa Tani settlement pattern as a whole. An Apa Tani village is built on high ground that rises, like an island from the sea, above the level of the flooded rice-fields. The entire area of this raised ground is occupied by hundreds of dwelling houses, built on wooden piles but constructed mainly of bamboo. In the past the steep gabled roofs were invariably thatched with rice-straw, but we shall see that new techniques of house-building have brought about changes in this pattern. Space has always been limited in Apa Tani villages, and the houses stand wall to wall in streets and narrow lanes. Here and there a street broadens to form a small piazza, in the centre of which stands an open assembly platform known as *lapang*. Such platforms, raised some 5 feet above the ground, are made of enormous wooden planks often 20-30 feet long and about a foot thick. They are used for the performance of rituals and for public gatherings, for no Apa Tani house is spacious enough to hold a large assembly. *Lapang* serve also as workshops where in fine weather men may be seen making baskets, plaiting mats or carving wooden implements.

The house-sites near the *lapang* are considered the most desirable, and change hands for relatively high prices. Hence most wealthy people live in the main streets and in piazzas not far from an assembly platform. Whatever their position all houses are constructed according to the same pattern. In the 1940s most houses stood on high poles, and ladders or notched logs led up to high open verandahs. From the verandah one enters a small lobby in which agricultural implements are kept and women pound rice in heavy wooden mortars. A door opening connects this narrow lobby with the main room of the house. Here the family and guests gather round the fire-places, cook, eat, sleep and perform various tasks for which little light is required. For the main room getting its light only from the two doors at both ends is usually very dark, and hence not suitable for such delicate tasks as weaving. In most houses there are two fireplaces and the one nearer to the entrance door is considered more prestigious and there guests are entertained while most of the cooking is done on the one at the back.

The long main room gives on to another smaller and lighter room sometimes used for setting up a loom, and from there one steps out on a second verandah, usually larger than that on the front of the house. Here Apa Tanis dry their grain and chillies and do various household chores. On one side of the house there is a narrow shelf protected by the eaves and accessible by a small door from the main room. It is part of the sanitary arrangements, for below it there is a fenced-in enclosure where pigs are kept, and these quickly dispose of human excrement and any kitchen refuse dropped from this shelf.

All houses of traditional type are of about the same width, for Apa Tani building technique does not permit a span of the gabled roof of more than about ten feet, and the size of a house can thus be only increased by adding to its length.

While most dwelling houses are concentrated in the centre of the village site, clusters of granaries, also built on piles, stand on the outskirts where they are relatively safe from the spread of fires. We shall see that in recent years their style has been modified much more than that of the houses.

Adjoining the houses and granaries there are groves of bamboo, carefully fenced-in kitchen gardens, groups of high pines and fruit trees. Narrow paths lead from the village through the groves and gardens to the irrigated rice-fields. There may be additional groups of granaries built on raised ground in between small terrace-fields kept flooded throughout the year and used as nurseries for rice-seedlings. In the winter they are covered with a layer of pale green slime, but in late spring they are luminous with a thick carpet of bright green seedlings. Beyond these nurseries, which are invariably close to the village, rice-fields follow each other in uninterrupted succession, extending into the centre of the valley as far as the boundary of the neighbouring village. Standing out from this large expanse of terraces are isolated hummocks of elevated land, and these are occupied by fenced-in gardens or bamboo-groves.

Paths connecting the villages run along the dams of terraces, and bridges made of stout planks span the Kele river and minor streams. Towards the hill-slopes surrounding the valley, the rice-fields extend right up to the rising ground, and wherever there is water, a small stream or even an oozing trickle, the Apa Tanis have constructed terrace fields in ravines and narrow valleys. On gentle slopes unsuitable for terracing and irrigation there are gardens, plots for millet-seedlings and tobacco, each strongly fenced in, and perhaps more groves of bamboo, fruit trees and pines. High-level ground is used for dry crops, and at the fringes of the valley there are bracken covered hillocks used as pasture land, and the curious fenced-in plots of luscious green which are kept for the cultivation of leafy plants from which a salty substance, the black "Apa Tani salt" is extracted.

The hill slopes surrounding the central valley are covered with forest, plantations of pine and other useful trees in carefully tended plots in which all trees are of the same size and kind. Only much higher up, at least 1,500 feet above the floor of the valley is the untended forest, with its rank growth of enormous rhododendrons, the many trees of the subtropical rain-forest and a multitude of climbers, tree ferns and orchids. Seen from any vantage point on these high ranges, the Apa Tani valley appears as an oasis of human order among the tangle of apparently uninhabited ranges stretching into the far distance.

The description of the environment and settlement pattern of the Apa Tanis reflects the situation as I observed it in the early 1940s. In many respects it applies also to present-day conditions but in others there has been considerable change.

The most immediately perceptible innovation, and one which has brought about changes in many spheres, is the construction of motorable roads. Entrance into the Apa Tani valley from the south is no longer along footpaths traversing long stretches of subtropical forest, but along a winding but very well constructed motor-road. In the vicinity of this road little forest has remained, though in recent years the forest department has initiated a programme of planting Khasi pines (*pinus patula*) which have the advantage of being more fire-resisting than *pinus excelsa*, the pine associated with the Apa Tanis.

The road descends in many hairpin bends to the district head-quarters Hapoli, and there bifurcates, one branch leading to the town centre, and the other cutting through the whole valley, and at its northern end leaving it in the direction of the Kamla river. Inevitably a sizeable acreage previously occupied by rice-fields, gardens and bamboo-groves had to be sacrificed at the time of the construction of this road, and more cultivated land had to be given up when feeder-roads to the individual Apa Tani villages were built. These have as yet no permanent surface, but except in very wet weather they are passable for jeeps and cars, with the result that such vehicles can now enter the villages at least as far as the main assembly platforms (*lapang*). In order to facilitate such traffic some of the main streets were widened, and this involved the demolition and rebuilding of many houses, and the reduction of the size of house-sites in the streets concerned. The rebuilding of houses of wood and bamboo was not a very onerous task, but the curtailment of sites, which meant that the new houses had to be much smaller than those pulled down, caused a certain amount of resentment among those affected.

Not only the motorable roads but also the narrow side-lanes have been much improved by the use of gravel. While in wet weather one would previously sink into the mud up to one's ankles, most streets and lanes have presently a fairly solid surface. As nowadays many Apa Tanis wear shoes or sandals this is of considerable advantage and while in the old days no one bothered about the state of the village-lanes the Apa Tanis have become conscious of the need to maintain the surface in a reasonable state.

The appearance of the villages has also been changed by a modification in the house style. While in 1944-45 most houses were built on wooden piles about 8-10 feet high, the piles are now seldom more than 4-5 feet high. As the reduction in the length of the posts on which the houses rest seems to have been a gradual one Apa Tanis are apparently not aware of the reason for this change, and most of the younger people do not even realize that the houses were ever different from what they are now. The most plausible explanation of the change is the shortage of timber caused by the prodiguous use of wood in the construction of the buildings of the district headquarter and the consequent deforestation of some parts of the valley. The stationing of many civil servants as well as some military units has also increased the demands for fire wood and so has the natural population growth of the Apa Tanis. Another innovation are crude steps of a cement-like mixture replacing the traditional ladders carved of one single piece of wood which were used for climbing up to the front verandahs. Such steps are not yet very common, but they are the first departure from pure bamboo and wood structures. In the construction of granaries this process has gone much further, and many Apa Tanis now build their granaries not on wooden piles but on square cement pillars. The superstructure of some granaries too is modified and instead of bamboo matting which gave little protection against rats, wooden planks are used in the making of the floor, walls and doors. The latter are almost invariably fitted with padlocks. Thus practical safeguards against grain-thieves have been added to the strong social sanctions against any kind of theft. The use of wooden planks has been made possible by the introduction of iron saws, for previously planks had to be fashioned with the help of an adze, and this was a laborious process militating against wide utilization of planks in house-building. Their relatively easy production by sawing has led also to a change in the type of roofs both of dwelling-houses and granaries. The roofs of traditional style were made of split and flattened bamboo covered with thatch of rice-straw. Nowadays rice-straw has been largely abandoned as facilitating the spread of fires, and most roofs are covered with thin planks.

A step further has been done by those Apa Tanis who use corrugated tin-sheets for the roofing of their granaries thereby protecting the stored grain both from fire and possible leaks. In houses of modern style, now found in places such as Hapoli, tin-roofs are common, but in the villages so far only ganaries and buildings such as schools are roofed with tin. There is little doubt, however, that sooner or later wealthy Apa Tanis will use tin-sheets also for the roofing of their village-houses.

A novel feature in most villages are small huts squeezed into any vacant corner or even standing in front of ordinary houses. Many of them are constructed of wooden planks, and they do not follow any recognized style. They have invariably been put up by young boys who seek more privacy than they enjoy in their parents' houses. Boys who have spent some years in boarding establishments, be it in school or university hostels, find the crowded and often noisy atmosphere in an Apa Tani house uncongenial and therefore build these separate quarters though continuing to eat in their parents' houses. No doubt, these small huts are used also for assignations with young girls, for the locking-up of granaries with padlocks has deprived lovers of the usual venues for adventures.

Even more recent than the opening of the villages to motor-traffic is the introduction of electricity. The initiative for this move came entirely from the administration, and Apa Tanis had no hand in deciding where the pilons and the street lights should be located. Aesthetically the high electric masts are certainly no asset to the village scene but the illumination of the village on dark nights is an undoubted advantage, and one which is provided free of cost by the government. So far few Apa Tanis have electric lights in their village houses, but those owning also a house in Hapoli almost invariably had it connected with the electric network. A very few men with strong commercial interests even have telephones in their houses, and it is now possible to speak from an Apa Tani village to Delhi.

After revisiting the Apa Tanis in 1962 I wrote: "Walking through the streets of an Apa Tani village or sitting round the open fire of one of the dark, cosy houses one notices hardly any change compared to the days when the valley had only the most tenuous contacts with the outside word" (*The Apa Tanis and their Neighbours*, p. 148). Thus it seems that very little outward change had occurred during the first 18 years after the opening up of the valley in 1944. Most of the change we are now observing took place in the years between 1962 and 1978.

We have so far considered the conditions in the seven traditional Apa Tani villages built on sites which appear to have remained inhabited for countless generations. The natural population growth and the fact that since the establishment of peace residence inside a compact settlement is no longer necessary for security, many Apa Tanis have moved out of their original villages and built houses in new settlements. This implies a mobility foreign to traditional Apa Tani society and has led to a considerable diversification of the settlement pattern. No longer do all Apa Tanis dwell in tightly packed villages but many now live in groups of scattered houses or in streets with only one row of houses on each side, and open fields behind those houses.

One of these new settlements is Limpia, a long drawn out village separated from Büla only by a small stream and a few rice-fields. The houses occupy raised ground formerly used for the cultivation of millet and a motor-road runs in between the two rows of houses which face the road. Limpia was founded by families of Tajang, one of the constituent parts of Büla. All of its 60 houses are still inhabited by members of Tajang clans, and there are separate village-officials, such as *panchayat* members, *gaonbura* and *buliang*. However, for ritual purposes Limpia still counts as part of Tajang and for the sacrificial rites at the time of the Mloko festival the individual families join their clan-members and worship at the traditional clan centre (*yugyang*). The settlers have built seven *lapang* and private rituals can be performed at these platforms, but not the communal rites for which the presence of a *nago*-shrine is required.

A similar new colony, known as Nenchangyang, was founded some ten years ago. It lies close to Old Ziro, the first administrative centre established in the early 1950s but given up in favour of Hapoli (New Ziro). Unlike Limpia Nenchangyang is a mixed settlement whose population consists of an overflow from Duta and Hija, and its inhabitants too retain their ritual links with their parent villages. The Duta people have moreover extended their cultivation in a place called Subu. In 1950-51 some poor families went there, made the land arable and built some houses. Later they sold most of the land to wealthier people, but the latter continue to live in Duta, though they cultivate in Subu.

In the southern part of the valley a number of settlements have sprung up in the area between Hang, Mudang-Tage and Hapoli. One of the earliest was Bri, which in the Census of 1971 was already listed as a separate village although the number of houses was only ten. Another settlement is Abuya, which lies on the motor-road between Hapoli and Michi-Bamin and is mainly inhabited by people from the latter village. It is a typical road-side settlement with several shops including a bakery. In Michi-Bamin I was told that some 160 families from these twin-villages have moved to the nearby Sebe, which is also listed in the Census, and other new settlements in the area. In these settlements referred to by the collective term Sebe there are nine *lapang* which are used for the performance of individual rites, while at the time of the annual festivals the inhabitants worship in Michi-Bamin.

Different from all these subsidiary settlements within the main valley are two new colonies, Süro and Dikopathar, situated in a valley watered by the Kele River some three miles south of Hang. The land there is Hang village-land and any Hang family had the right to settle there and take fallow land under cultivation. In the old days this valley was not considered safe enough for settlement or even cultivation, for Apa Tanis living and working there were exposed to raids by Nishis from such nearby villages as Mai or Pochu. But with the establishment of the administration in Hapoli this danger receded, and the people of Hang whose natural increase had led to pressure on the land closer to their village began to clear the land at Süro and Dikopathar. The first settlers came in 1966 and others followed between then and 1978. The number of families in the two settlements had by then grown to 73, and except for one man from Duta married to a Hang woman, all were originally from Hang. Those who came first occupied more land and those who arrived later had to be content with smaller holdings. The new settlers were by no means all down-and-outs who had no land in Hang, but some came from fairly well-to-do families and wanted to relieve the pressure on their inherited land for the benefit of sons or brothers.

Of the households whose names I was able to record 34 were of patrician (*guth*) class and 17 were commoners (*guchi*). Three of the clans represented in Süro have their own *lapang*, but despite the distance from the parent village Hang, the settlers have not yet taken the final step of establishing their ritual independence by building a *nago* shrine. This could be done only at the time of the Mloko festival and would have to be accompanied by the killing of a monkey and the sacrifice of dogs, pigs and fowls. The houses of Süro stand scattered along the rim of the expanse of irrigated land, and as timber is plentiful in the nearby forest, several of them are built entirely of wooden planks except for the bamboo floors. Some of the settlers have retained their houses in Hang and cultivate in both places, but most have passed on their original houses to sons or kinsmen, and have shifted all their possessions to Süro.

All the cultivable land near to Dikopathar and Süro has now been occupied, but more land, probably sufficient for about 50 families, would be available for clearing at an even more distant place known as Tarin. Not all settlers at Süro and Dikopathar are yet entirely self-sufficient in foodgrain, probably because part of the land was only recently brought under cultivation, and much effort has still to be expended on the construction of bunds and irrigation channels. They buy rice from other Apa Tanis or from government stores, and pay for these supplies with money earned by road-labour and other casual employment. Many worked on the road which leads now to the Tale valley, a prospective colonization area lying at an altitude of some 7,000 feet in the uninhabited forest-area southeast of the Apa Tani valley.

A few Apa Tani families have already been settled there and are assisted by government with money and supplies to weather the period while they experiment with crops suitable for the altitude of the Tale valley. If such crops can be introduced the Tale valley may be able to absorb the overflow from the Apa Tani valley for many years to come, for it is said that the potentially cultivable area is as large as that valley, and capable of accommodating a very substantial population. Within human memory the Tale area has not been cultivated or inhabited, and the climate may be too cold for the type of rice grown by Apa Tanis. Yet, at similar altitude rice is grown in the Jumla and Humla regions of Nepal, and further experiments may well lead to the development of a cropping pattern suitable for the Tale valley.

In the various new settlements Apa Tanis can still pursue their traditional life-style even though they no longer live in crowded villages rubbing shoulders with their neighbours all the time. An entirely new situation, however, has been created at Hapoli, the district headquarters also known as Ziro. There houses of Apa Tanis stand singly or in tight clusters between government buildings, quarters of minor officials and the modern shops of the bazaar streets.

Until 1960 the administrative headquarters of what was then the Subansiri Division (now District) were situated near an air-strip at no great distance from the villages of Hija and Duta. The site was called Ziro, allegedly so named after a tribal group of that name who had been settled there, but were driven out because of their aggressive conduct and their habit of capturing Apa Tani girls. Little is known of this legendary people except that after their dispersal some of the Ziro people fled to the west to an area now included in the Kameng District. Their dependants are believed to have mixed with the Akhas of that region. However this may be, the small administrative settlement was called Ziro, and when it was shifted to the southern part of the valley where space was less restricted, the name Ziro was retained although the new site was known as Hapoli. Ziro, however, remains the official name while Apa Tanis invariably speak of Hapoli.

The land on which the district headquarters were built is claimed by the village of Michi-Bamin, and there is some resentment among the Apa Tanis that the government did not purchase the land required for office-buildings and staff-quarters but apparently persuaded the village-headmen of Michi-Bamin to "donate" the land. They are all the more resentful because subsequently government allotted sites for shops to many Apa Tanis from villages other than Michi-Bamin. Formerly the area of Hapoli was used only as pasture, because like Süro it was too exposed to Nishi raiders to make cultivation involving work by women and girls a practical proposition, but since the pacification of the region many Michi-Bamin people have constructed irrigated rice-fields. Some of the land thus made arable has since been sold to Apa Tanis from other villages who have settled at Hapoli.

The total number of dwelling houses in Hapoli was 563 at the time of the 1971 Census, but for that year no break-down of the occupiers of these houses was available. According to a rough enumeration of the houses owned or occupied by Apa Tanis which my wife and I carried out in 1978, an approximate total of 230 houses were inhabited by Apa Tanis. Surprisingly the majority of those who had built houses in Hapoli were not men of Michi-Bamin who claimed the site as their own, but Apa Tanis of Hari village. In Chapter 10 we shall see that Hari is educationally the most progressive village, and there is no doubt that men of Hari have also been exceptionally successful in business and had therefore most incentive either to move entirely to the commercial centre of the valley or at least maintain there a secondary establishment. The majority of the Apa Tani houses at Hapoli are of the traditional type and there is one street, known as Para Road, which is very similar to one of the main streets in an ordinary village. Other houses stand in compact clusters behind the rows of modern shops, and there too the atmosphere is reminiscent of the narrow crowded lanes of a traditional Apa Tani village. Some of the wealthy business men, however, have built houses in modern "hill-style" modelled on the quarters provided by government for officials. Such houses have a famework of timber standing on stone or cement foundations, and walls made of plaster on a wattle background. They have wooden doors and usually windows with glass panes, and the roof is invariably covered with tin-sheets painted either red or green. Tables, chairs and bedsheets constitute the furniture, which varies according to the means of the owners, the wealthiest of whom have sofa-sets such as one might find in the bungalow of any official.

The houses in the main bazaar street are built for the purpose of providing on the ground floor a large space fitted with shelves, a counter and sometimes glass-fronted show-cases for the display of goods. Such shops have an open front but can be closed with wooden shutters. Some of these houses contain one or two rooms above the shop to be used as living quarters, but in others the owners stay in a room or shed at the back of the shop. In the same street, there are also a few tea-houses or so-called restaurants known as "rice-hotels" where customers sit on stools or benches and there may be a few wooden tables. In the largest and most modern of these eating and drinking houses there are coloured lights and loud-speakers spouting forth the music of radio programmes or taped cinema music. In Hapoli there are altogether 59 such business premises, and 11 of these are either entirely of the restaurant type or combine the sale of goods with the dispensing of tea and eatables.

Most of the Apa Tanis who built houses at Hapoli have retained also houses in their own villages, and as most own bicycles and a few even motor-scooters or jeeps, they can easily commute between their business establishments and their family homes.

In the locality known as "Old Ziro" where at the time of the use of the site as administrative centre the first tea stalls and small shops were established, there is now also a bazaar street. Houses and shops are on a more modest scale than those of Hapoli, but the lay-out is similar.

While even thirty years ago hardly any Apa Tani family had settled outside their home valley by 1978 hundreds of Apa Tanis were living in other places. Among the first of those who emigrated to establish permanent homes in the lower country is a group of settlers at Seajuli, a locality on the fringe of the Assamese plains some 10 miles from North Lakhimpur and only about an hour's walk from the Nishi village of Joyhing. Their houses at Seajuli are built in precisely the same style as those in the Apa Tani valley, with the one exception that there are no enclosures for pigs below the raised bamboo floor. Altogether ten families have settled at Seajuli. One came there as early as 1952, others in the late 1960s and the latest arrival only in 1975. Some of them are of patrician and others of commoner status. They all have been able to obtain land for cultivation, and all except one have plough-bullocks. Nearby, at Kakoi, there is a similar Apa Tani colony of seven houses, sharing a village site with seven Nishi families. They maintain contacts with their home villages, go there to attend seasonal festivals and are visited by kinsmen who can get by bus from Hapoli to North Lakhimpur in a single day.

The greatest concentration of expatriate Apa Tanis, however, is in Itanagar, the capital of Arunachal Pradesh. There exists no official census of their numbers, but the estimates knowledgeable Apa Tanis gave me was 400-500 individuals staying at any one time at Itanagar. Many of them are casual labourers employed by contractors for building work and road construction. Others have taken their wives and children with them and built houses either in traditional Apa Tani style or according to a pattern combining old and modern elements. Shop signs containing Apa Tani names prove that Apa Tanis are active in business and have even opened motor repair workshops. Some of such ventures are joint enterprises by Apa Tanis, who usually provided the capital, and non-tribal partners who possess mechanical or accounting skills.

Apa Tani entrepreneurs and government employees have followed the administration also to some of the circle headquarters north of the Apa Tani valley, such as Nyapin, Koloriang and Daporijo. They are not very numerous, however, and as other tribal groups are gradually catching up with the Apa Tanis' progress, local people are likely to replace them in business and possibly even in public service posts.

The numbers and distribution of Apa Tanis living outside the traditional seven villages, until the 1940s the only home of Apa Tani families, lead one inevitably to the conclusion that their old homeland is getting too small for a growing and dynamic population.

TWO

Farming and Land Tenure

EVER SINCE THE Apa Tanis established themselves in their present habitat rice-cultivation on irrigated terrace-fields has been the main base of their economy. We do not know whether they brought the techniques of terracing and of planting wet rice with them and sought out the valley as the most suitable place for the pursuance of this type of tillage or whether they were originally shifting-cultivators like most of the tribes of Arunachal Pradesh and their new environment imposed on them a novel type of agriculture. The legend of the draining of a lake inhabited by aquatic reptiles certainly suggests that the valley in its present aspect is the work of the early Apa Tani settlers. As they increased in numbers the most intensive utilization of the limited available land must certainly have become imperative, for by 1944 when the threat of potentially hostile neighbours impeded any dispersal the 20 square miles of arable land had to feed well over 10,000 people. Yet, the methods of tillage were—and still are—archaic, and indeed of a type usually associated with a neolithic economy rather than with a peasant civilization of the iron-age, in so far as they depended entirely on human labour and made no use of animal traction. In other aspects, however, they were highly specialized and reflected a far greater capacity for planning and concerted effort than the traditional methods of cultivation of many Indian populations long familiar with the plough and the use of animal traction.

The lay-out of the irrigated rice-land can best be visualized if we begin our description with the highest terraces at the top end of a side valley, where a stream is first tapped, and follow the course of water until it flows into the broad bowl of the main valley.

Every one of the streams rising on the wooded heights that ring the Apa Tani country is utilized for irrigation purposes soon after it emerges from the forest and reaches a gully wide enough to accommodate a series of narrow terraces. A short distance above the terraces the stream is tapped but here only a small amount of water is deflected and channelled to the highest fields. By opening or blocking the connecting ducts any field can be flooded or drained as required. At the head of the valley the terraces are on an average narrow: they are partly carved out of the hill-side and partly built up, with a difference in level of one to three feet between the individual terraces. As the valley broadens the terraces grow in size and the differences in level dwindle to as little as half a foot. Unlike such terrace-builders as the Angami Nagas, many tribes of Eastern Nepal or the Ifugaos of the Philippines, the Apa Tanis do not construct flights of terraces that cover a mountain side for 1,000 feet or more. Their skill as rice-growers has manifested itself rather in a meticulous care for every crop than in impressive engineering feats. Yet, the lay-out of terraces demonstrates a high degree of cooperation and considerable skill. In the side valleys the streams have often been tapped of most of their water, and when they fan out into the system of ducts in the main valley only a shallow flow may remain on each of the principal channels. The channels have been dug deep into the soil and their dams are secured against the onrush of flood water by rows of wooden stakes sometimes reinforced by strong bamboo matting. Along the embankments of the main channels run paths strewn with gravel and hence usable even in the wettest weather. Normally the water is not allowed to overflow the dams, and terraces are drained through wide wooden or bamboo pipes let into the dam.

The rainfall is so ample that the flooding of all the low-lying terraces is on the whole no problem. Water-rights are not bought or sold, and there are no fixed rules regulating the sequence in which the individual terraces receive water. Disputes over water seem to be rare. Fields in the central bowl of the valley served by perennial streams are kept under water or at least moist during the greater part of the year, but the terraces on higher ground are watered by rivulets flowing only during the monsoon. The two types of fields receive different treatment and are used for the growing of different types of rice.

The upkeep of the terrace-fields, dams and channels has always absorbed a major part of the Apa Tanis' time and energy, and traditionally men and women shared equally in the agricultural work.

We shall see presently that nowadays this is no longer so and young men tend to have different interests. The sequence of tasks, however, has remained more or less unchanged. During the winter, when the temperature sinks sometimes below freezing point, there is little work on the fields, but from February onwards men and women, particularly the latter, can be seen repairing dams and channels. By the middle of April, when the celebration of the Mloko festival has come to an end, this work is resumed with increased urgency. The Apa Tanis are not content with merely maintaining an established system of terraces and channels, but seek to carry out improvements whenever the yield of a field has not come up to expectations. They may divide a field perhaps not evenly watered into two terraces, or conversely turn two terraces into one, gaining thereby the space of the dividing dam. For the shifting of earth the Apa Tanis use large flat wooden trays of oval shape, on which they heap great lumps of mud. The trays with their load are then dragged over the slimy surface of the partially flooded ground. The only area where I have seen similar wooden trays used for the same purpose are the mountains of Northern Luzon where Ifugao rice-cultivators also transport earth in this way. When the work is done by men and women it is mainly the latter who hack up the soil and cut away the face of bunds, while the men load the earth on to the trays and drag them to the part of the field which requires building up. Flat wooden batons as well as iron hoes are used in the remodelling and repairing of dams and fields. The iron hoes are of the type used in the tea-gardens of Assam, and though even in 1944 they were in universal use, old men then still remembered a time when hoe-like wooden implements were employed for the purpose of building and repairing rice-terraces. The former use of such wooden implements in the absence of iron hoes is by no means unlikely, for even in 1945 I saw Hill Miris of the villages north of the Kamla using the shoulder-blades of cattle as hoes for the digging up of their hill-fields because they were short of iron.

We have seen that in the past three decades large expanses of land were newly taken under cultivation, but even before it was possible to open up relatively distant new areas such as the valley in which Süro is situated, there passed no year without some small plot being turned into terrace-fields. In the 1940s Michi-Bamin, Hang and Hari had still land suitable for the expansion of cultivation even in areas near enough to be relatively safe from Nishi

raiders, and in 1978 there was a plan to terrace some 80 acres of
Hari land with the technical and financial assistance of the Government.

There are two types of rice-fields: those permanently kept under
water or at least in a very moist condition, and those that dry out
and harden soon after the harvest. The former are considered the
more valuable, and it is said that the rotting stubble acts as fertili-
zer in addition to the manure which is scattered over the surface.
Such fields are used exclusively for late ripening varieties of rice,
known as *emo*. Close to them lie terraces which are allowed to
drain off, and these are cleaned and dug over with hoes before each
period of cultivation and then flooded. The water brought by
channels is allowed to filter slowly over the field and when the soil
is thoroughly impregnated it is puddled by men and more rarely
women who supporting themselves between two poles treadle the
mud underfoot so that to a depth of two feet the soil is churned to
a smooth paste. On these fields three varieties of early ripening rice
are grown: *pyare* which ripens first in August, *pyate* ripening in late
August, and *pyaping* ripening in September.

Distinct from low-lying terraces watered from channels fed by
perennial streams, are those on higher ground which depend almost
entirely on the monsoon rains. There the ground is dug over with
hoes and the clods are broken up by hand or with moon-shaped
hoes. There the water is scarcely enough to convert more than the
surface soil into mud at the time of transplanting, while during the
period of growth the rice is largely dependent on rainfall.

All rice is first sown in nurseries close to the village, which are
kept under water throughout the year and regularly manured. Before the sowing the soil is puddled into a thick paste in which the
workers sink in up to their knees. The seed is never pre-sprouted
before sowing but is broadcast dry as it comes from the granaries.
This work is largely done by women.

Transplanting begins in the middle of April. Women and girls
lift the seedlings of the early ripening *pyare* rice from the nurseries,
tie them into bundles and carry them in baskets to the fields.
Starting at the edge of the field they move forward as they work,
planting single seedlings at intervals of about eight inches.

Next *pyate* and *pyaping* rice are transplanted mainly on fields
thoroughly puddled. If any of the early ripening varieties are grown
on outlying terraces with scanty water supply, the transplanting

awaits the first heavy rain and may have to be deferred until the middle of May.

There are three late ripening varieties of rice; of these *empu* and *rade emo* are white and *elang* is red. They form the bulk of the Apa Tanis' rice crop and are often planted on fields which were kept under water throughout the winter and were not dug over but cleaned by hand. Most of the transplanting was always done by women, but in the old days young men and boys, by then largely free from the work of repairing dams, would join in the transplanting. By the middle of May it should be completed on all the fields in the central valley but work on distant, late flooded terraces in the side valleys might continue until the end of the month.

The weeding of the rice is done with great thoroughness. Permanently flooded fields are weeded two or three times and terraces less amply watered as much as five times.

The harvest of the *pyare* rice begins in early August, and the grains are stripped from the ears by hand. Some of the poorer people are by that time short of food, and the newly reaped rice is eaten almost at once. *Pyate* and *pyaping* are reaped in similar manner.

The main rice-harvest does not begin until October and may last until early November. It demands a great concerted effort, and men, women and children work without respite for two or three weeks. The method of reaping is quite different from that employed at the harvest of the early ripening varieties. Women cut the stalks with sickles imported from Assam, which have replaced the knives made earlier by local blacksmiths. Tied into sheaves the ears are thrashed out on the spot by being beaten against a slanting wooden board which stands in a large carrying basket. The rice slides into the basket which is carried to the owner's granary as soon as it is full. The straw, which used to be the Apa Tanis' principal thatching material, is stacked on the field.

Seed grain of all types of rice is separated from the rice to be stored for human consumption. Inside the granaries the rice is poured onto the floor and is never stored in baskets, a curious lack of foresight in a society so systematic in most economic activities. Heaped on the floor it is in no way protected against mice and rats, and the loss due to the inroads of rodents is considerable.

Apa Tanis do not express the size of fields in measurements comparable to acres or hectares, but in terms of the average yield of paddy. Thus it would be said that a certain field produced so and so many baskets of paddy or millet as the case may be. The baskets used for expressing the quantity of paddy normally reaped are known as *enti-yage* and contain approximately 35 kg of unhusked rice. Instead of quoting the number of *enti-yage* baskets which the produce of a field can fill, Apa Tanis often speak also in terms of granaries which can be filled with the yield of a field. A granary of the smaller type (*suchi-nesu*) can accommodate 120-200 *enti-yage* baskets, but there are also larger granaries (*suro-nesu*), and since modern building materials, such as cement pillars and walls made of sawn planks have come in the traditional standard sizes been exceeded. In the old days wealthy people used to build small granaries (*suchi-nesu*) for commercial purposes, selling the whole contents to a single purchaser, without measuring the paddy. The paddy and millet for their own consumption were stored in larger granaries. Trade with the merchants of Assam is gradually bringing in measures of weight, and it is probably only a matter of time until quantities of rice will be expressed in kilograms and hundredweights.

Dry crops such as millet and maize do not rival rice in importance, but the Apa Tanis nevertheless tend them with meticulous care. They are grown on slightly raised ground above the rice-fields and on the rolling land that leads up to the hillocks on the fringes of the valley. Besides the fenced-in plots for maize and vegetables that often adjoin groves of bamboo and pine, there are stretches of open fields, used almost exclusively for the cultivation of millet.

The principal dry crop is *Eleusine coracana* and of this two varieties are grown: an early millet (*mipa*), which is mainly planted along the bunds of rice-fields and in garden plots, and a later ripening millet (*sarse*) cultivated on open dry fields (*lapro*) but occasionally also planted on rice-field bunds. Both varieties are sown in seedbeds near the houses and later transplanted. This type of cultivation is a peculiarity of the Apa Tanis, for the neighbouring Nishis, who grow large quantities of millet, invariably broadcast the small millets on their *jhum*-fields.

Shortage of flat land has induced some Apa Tanis to experiment with slash-and-burn cultivation in Nishi style and a few slopes above Hapoli have been cleared in the process. Such *jhum*-fields are called *ribing*, and on these millet, maize and some dry rice are grown. Five men of Mundang-Tage started slash-and-burn cultivation in 1974, but two years later there was a decision of the local panchayat to ban all further *jhum*-cultivation. The area so far affected is small and it is not yet clear whether the opposition of the panchayat will be entirely effective.

Though valued for the brewing of beer, millet takes second place after rice, and the preparation of the dry fields has to wait until all the work on the irrigated terraces and most of the transplanting of the rice-seedlings has been completed. The dry fields are dug over with large iron hoes and this is traditionally man's work. Most dry fields are almost flat, but on the gentle slopes rough terraces are constructed to prevent erosion and too rapid a drainage. Women smooth the soil with small hoes (*palu*) made out of split bamboo looped so that the crossed ends form a handle. Finally the *sarte* seedlings are planted out one by one. Millet is weeded twice, and this too is done by women using bamboo hoes. The early *mipa* millet ripens in the first half of August. Women cut off the ears and take them home for immediate consumption. The harvest of *sarse*-millet follows the harvest of *emo*-rice early in November. The millet ears are cut off with sickles and carried to the granaries, where they are heaped on the floor.

Apart from being used for the brewing of beer, millet is also eaten in the form of a rough kind of bread. It is never sold to outsiders, and Apa Tanis sometimes even buy millet from neighbouring Nishis.

Apa Tanis cultivate three varieties of maize (*mire, nit* and *tani*) both in gardens inside the village, and in the more distant garden plots, but never on open dry fields. In view of the fact that maize, a crop indigenous in America, is believed to be a relatively late introduction in South Asia, it is remarkable that all three varieties are known by names which do not suggest a derivation from Indian or other foreign words. Maize is dibbled and not transplanted.

Other garden crops are beans, chillies, marrow, cucumbers, taro, ginger, potatoes, tomatoes and a coarse leafy vegetable, eaten in great quantities and available during about eight months. All these plants are sown in gardens in March, and chillies and tomatoes are transplanted a few weeks later. Potatoes and tomatoes are obviously a fairly recent introduction, and are not cultivated in large quantities.

Tobacco used to be of great importance. Both sexes, and even children smoked it in pipes, made either of bamboo or of metal, but in recent years pipe-smoking has become unfashionable, and men smoke mainly cigarettes, while women and children are seldom seen smoking. Such tobacco as is still grown is transplanted in the same way as chillies and tomatoes.

Since the establishment of the district headquarters at Hapoli several imported vegetables such as cauliflower, cabbage, peas and runner beans have been introduced and their cultivation is a significant source of income for the women, many of whom sell vegetables directly to the employees of the administration.

Cotton does not rank high among the crops of the Apa Tanis, even though their weaving is more developed than that of any of their neighbours. They used to buy nearly all their cotton from Nishis, often obtaining it by bartering rice, but of late they are also able to purchase imported yarn in the shops of Hapoli, and rarely cotton from Nishis.

Groves

One of the characteristic features of the Apa Tanis' land-use, and one which sets them apart from all their immediate neighbours, is their careful husbandry of bamboo and timber resources. Groves of bamboo and pine occupy an appreciable part of the land of every village and no man can be considered economically independent if he does not possess at least one small bamboo grove. The need for the systematic regeneration of bamboo and timber is obvious in a valley where thousands of houses have periodically to be rebuilt and there is hardly a year when fires do not take a heavy toll of the easily inflammable dwellings. In the hills surrounding the Apa Tani valley several varieties of bamboo occur, but not all are suitable for housebuildings and the transport from distant hill-sides presented great difficulties for a people lacking animals for traction and wheeled transport.

Hence the Apa Tanis came to cultivate bamboos sufficient for their needs in close proximity to their villages. The variety grown in their groves is a medium-sized straight-stemmed male bamboo which stands up well to the cold winters. According to tradition, the original Apa Tani immigrants brought this type of bamboo with them, and in fact it is not found in the surrounding countryside except where some nearby Nishis obtained it from Apa Tanis and initiated their method of cultivation. When Apa Tanis lay out a new grove they space the roots at two or three foot intervals and rigorously prune every shoot, allowing only one or two stems to grow from each root. Once established a grove retains its regenerative power indefinitely and can be exploited for many years. The roots for a new grove are lifted from overcrowded groves and planted in shallow holes. Being male these bamboos never flower or seed, and the planting of roots is the only way of propagation.

Pinus excelsa, the most characteristic tree of the Apa Tani country, is also grown in groves, sometimes interspersed with bamboos. Young saplings are brought from the forest or from other groves and planted in February or early March. The wood of *Pinus excelsa* is used for building purposes and also as firewood. The larger trees are often tapped and the resin serves for the manufacture of a medicament calculated to cure inflammations and swellings. Owing to its resinous content this pine makes very fine torches and before the introduction of electric torches and street lighting these were widely used.

Most groves contain besides bamboos and pines a number of fruit trees, such as a small variety of cherry, a kind of peach, a small pear and a greenish and rather bitter apple. Ritually the most significant is the *thakum* tree, a plum tree with white blossoms which plays an important role at the Mloko festival.

Apart from the trees standing in groves, all of which are private property, there are also individually owned pine trees growing in nearby forests which are clan property. Thus on a hill called Ganoputu near Hang village, which is jointly owned by the three clans of Takhe, Nara and Neha, individual members of these clans have planted pine trees and these are recognized as their property. Other trees on that hill may be felled by any clan members but any one felling a privately owned pine tree is fined one cow to be eaten by the men of the owner's *lapang*. This cow is ceremoniously slaughtered in the forest where the tree was cut and a priest (*nyibu*) invokes the gods of the locality.

While Apa Tanis had always some fruit trees in their groves and gardens, the fruit was of no commercial value, and added only marginally to their diet. With the help of government fruit farming on a systematic scale was begun in the 1960s and by 1978 there were already orchards with thousands of fruit trees, mainly apple but also some pear and plum trees. The saplings were supplied by government at a subsidized price and insecticides were also provided at low cost. The trees were planted on land which was individually owned and had previously been forest or pasture. In

Michi-Bamin, for instance, there were five families owning orchards; one man had planted 3,000 trees and another 2,000 trees. Bamin Kano planted in 1969 600 fruit trees, and in 1977 he sold 7 hundred weights of apples partly in Hapoli and partly in Itanagar for an average price of Rs 5-6 per kilogram. Though manuring with cow-dung and spraying involves some expenditure on labour, the profits of fruit farming are very satisfactory, and this new departure in horticulture promises to provide Apa Tanis with a substantial cash-income.

Ownership of Land

In traditional Apa Tani society a man's prestige and influence depended mainly on the size of his landholding, and it is only in recent years that other sources of wealth have come into being. In the value attached to land the Apa Tanis have always differed fundamentally from their Nishi and Miri neighbours who lacked the concept of privately owned land.

All land within the Apa Tanis' tribal territory can be divided into three categories: individually owned land, clan-land and common village-land. The first category comprises practically all cultivated land, i.e. irrigated rice-fields, dry fields, gardens, groves as well as house sites and sites for granaries. Clan-land consists of the sites for public assembly platforms (*lapang*) inside the village, meadow land used for pasture and burial grounds as well as tracts of forest, where members of the owner-clan have the right to hunt and trap. Common village-land, on the other hand, is confined to a few rather insignificant stretches of pasture inside the valley, and to forest tracts on the periphery of the Apa Tani country.

In 1944 and presumably for several generations before that time, the overwhelming majority of Apa Tanis of patrician (*guth*) class owned land of various kinds, but even then the disparity between rich and poor was very great, not so much in the standard of living as in the control over land. There were even then some poor patricians, a few of whom possessed only dry land, and among the commoners (*guchi*) and slaves—freed or only separated from their masters' households—there were many who had virtually no land except a house-site and perhaps one or two plots of dry land. As the population was then more or less static most men inherited a house-site, but men with many sons might have had difficulty in securing for each son a place to build his house on. The most valuable house-sites were those in the main streets, and poor people had to content themselves with houses in back-streets and narrow lanes.

At that time land including house-sites could be obtained only in exchange for mithan (*bos frontalis*). No other valuable was recognized as a medium of exchange suitable for transactions in real estate, and only very small plots or dry land might on occasion be exchanged for large pigs and such valuable articles as swords or textiles. For a desirable house-site in a main-street and near a *lapang* as much as ten small mithan might have had to be paid. The most valuable part of a man's property was always his irrigated rice-land. Near a village, where land was always most expensive, ten mithan or more were paid for a single terrace field about half an acre in size. Smaller plots in the same area used to change hands for two to five mithan, but it was only in the outlying side valleys where the water supply is unreliable that a terrace field of $\frac{1}{2}$ acre could be obtained for a small mithan or a large cow. An average family of five or six members could meet its consume of rice from the yield of approximately 1.5-2 acres of well irrigated land yielding about 300 *enti-yage* baskets of paddy. According to the distance of the land from the village, the price would not have been lower than 20 and not higher than 50 small mithan, and this corresponded at the time to a sum of between Rs 2,000 to 5,000 though Apa Tanis never thought in terms of money and all transactions were by barter.

Today Indian currency is widely accepted and most land-sales are effected by cash-transactions. In 1978 $\frac{1}{2}$ acre of irrigated paddy-land was worth about Rs 7,000-8,000, and for a large field near a village yielding approximately 130 *enti-yage* baskets Rs 30,000 to 40,000 were paid, and a similar field at some distance from the village would fetch Rs 20,000. As one *enti-yage* of paddy is worth about Rs 10, a return of Rs 1,300 on an investment of Rs 30,000-40,000 is only 4.3 per cent and hence much less than the 7 per cent offered by the bank at Hapoli. But the prestige of landownership and the security it provides, no doubt, must be balanced against the low return in money terms. A house-site in a main street is now worth about Rs 4,000 while in back-streets house-sites change hands for Rs 2,000-3,000.

As long as there was no great population pressure, poor men

possessing little or no wet land could sometimes acquire some irrigable land at no great cost. By investing their own labour in the transformation of some dry land near a trickle of water into terraces and then building a channel to irrigate them they could create small holdings of land suitable for rice-cultivation and grow at least part of their requirements of paddy on such marginal land. This possibility, however, hardly exists any more, for the population increase of the last twenty years has led to the occupation of all vacant land except in areas at the periphery of the Apa Tani country where colonists lack the support of their kinsmen and village-community. Thus landless men have to look for other sources of income, which fortunately for the Apa Tanis are at present not lacking.

To understand the crucial features of the system of land-tenure which still prevails among the Apa Tanis, it is necessary to consider the position as it existed before the integration of the valley into the wider economy of Arunachal Pradesh. The capitalistic trends which have been accentuated by the emergence of a wealthy merchant class have their roots in the traditional economy which favoured the accumulation of large holdings in relatively few hands. By 1944 the distribution of the cultivable land, and particularly of the valuable irrigated fields in the centre of the valley, was already very uneven. A few wealthy patrician families owned large numbers of rice-fields, whereas there were many poor families not only of *guchi* but also of *guth* class who held very little land, quite apart from the numerous domestic slaves who were excluded from landownership. As land could only be bought with cattle those who owned no or only very few mithan or cows could not even begin to compete for the ownership of rice-fields. Wealthy men, on the other hand, could easily add to their holdings without having to forgo the enjoyment of their existing wealth.

Two examples from the village of Hija will demonstrate the manner in which in traditional Apa Tani society holdings of wet land could be built up and enlarged.

Nada Tomu, a member of the most prominent patrician clan of Hija, and eldest son of Nada Tamin was given by his father 25 rice-fields, lying in groups of five, in different parts of the village land, as well as two bamboo groves and one garden. As the eldest of three sons he was entitled to his father's inherited land, but the latter's self-acquired land could and did go to Tomu's younger brothers. Tomu had from the outset far more land than he required to feed a family. He had 12 slaves to work for him and also employed hired labour to cultivate his land. Year after he sold rice to Nishis of such neighbouring villages as Jorum and Talo, and with the mithan he received in payment he bought more land. By 1944, when he was a man in his thirties, he had acquired altogether 62 fields in ten different places. At that time he annually bartered his surplus of grain for about three mithan, and these he used in turn for buying more land. In this case the purchase of land was in no way a necessity, but Tomu pursued the enlargement of his vast holding solely in order to increase his influence and prestige. His house and life-style were not different from that of less wealthy men and he had married only one wife. Unlike his contemporary Padi Lailang of Reru, who added martial expioits to his equally outstanding success in accumulating wealth, Nada Tomu was a man of peace and did not join a single raid. He had two sons who survived to adulthood and his large property was divided among them in equal shares. In 1978 I found his two sons continuing their father's concentration on landownership, and one of them seemed to have sufficient political ambition to get himself elected as member of the village-panchayat. Yet, he played no role in political activities outside the confines of his village.

Nendin Tagum, also of Hija, had acquired his land in a very different manner. He was the second of three brothers, and from his father he initially got only six rice-fields in two groups of three. Subsequently he bought three more fields for a total of 20 mithan. Three of these he had inherited, eight he had bartered for rice, and nine he had obtained as ransoms for Nishis, whom he had captured on various occasions. The capturing of men and women from other tribes was then an accepted way of acquiring mithan and valuables, and Nendin Tagum was a man of courage and enterprise who played the game of kidnapping with skill and success. But only a man of established social position who had reason to believe that his kinsmen would ransom him if he slipped up and was himself captured by Nishis could risk to engage in so hazardous an activity. Poor men lacking influential kinsmen had to resort to different means to obtain the cattle necessary for the purchase of land. By 1944 some of the landless Apa Tanis had begun to go occasionally to the plains of Assam, and earn some wages by working in tea-gardens or as seasonal agricultural labourers. With the money received they bought calves, drove them up to the Apa Tani valley and used them ultimately for purchasing some small plots of land.

The principle that all cultivated land is private property of which the individual owner can dispose of as he wishes is so deeply ingrained in Apa Tani mentality that village-boundaries are no real consideration in the transfer of land. For the sake of convenience everyone likes to have his fields as close to his village as possible, but nothing prevents a man from purchasing rice-terraces on the land of a neighbouring village. Indeed in the centre of the valley and particularly in the contact zones of the political units large holdings often cut across village boundaries with the result that the fields of the inhabitants of two adjacent settlement tend to dovetail.

We shall see presently that so far the Arunachal Pradesh administration has not taken cognizance of the rights of individual landowners by issuing documents confirming their ownership of the land they occupy and cultivate. In terms of the Indian revenue system no Apa Tani is a *pattadar* and all cultivation is *siwa-i-jama-bandi*. No cadastral survey has as yet been undertaken and the district authorities are hence unaware of the holdings of individuals and even of the precise village-boundaries.

Even in 1944 it appeared that there was no check on the accumulation of more and more land in the hands of a few very rich men. Yet there were always factors which counteracted such a development. The rules of inheritance laid down that a man's land should be divided among his sons, and many men used to partition their land when their sons married and set up their own households. The exact process of this division of assets will be discussed in the section on inheritance and here we need only mention that large holdings are seldom handed on undivided to the next generation. In the old days a wealthy man was expected moreover to provide some land for his dependants such as slaves who grew up in his house and were allowed to set up their own households. Any land given to them could not be reclaimed by their master unless they died without issue. Finally there were many vicissitudes of fate which might have compelled a rich man to dispose quickly, and hence at comparatively low rates, of some of his land. A long illness involving the need for innumerable sacrifices of mithan and cows might have forced him to sell land for cattle, or a member of his household, fallen into the hands of raiders, might have had to be ransomed with mithan and valuables obtainable most easily by the sale of land. Such an emergency does not occur any more, but people still fall ill and the availability of hospital treatment does not obviate the need to placate angry gods and spirits by the sacrifice of costly animals.

When I first got to know the Apa Tanis none of them ever gave land on lease or hire and the system of share-cropping so common in many parts of India including tribal areas was unknown. Hence a poor man had either to be content with the irregular income of daily wages, working alternatively for several rich men, or he had to join a wealthy landowner's household in a position hardly different from that of a domestic slave.

Today conditions have drastically changed. Not only are there many opportunities for landless men to earn good wages or engage in business ventures, but since 1976 the practice of leasing land has taken roots. The rent is either fixed in money, usually for one year at a time, or as a share in the crop. This innovation has been brought about by the absence of many landowners for long periods. Many Apa Tanis with business interests have moved to Itanagar, the capital of Arunachal Pradesh, and it is not always practicable to leave land in the care of close kinsmen. When no such possibilities exist, Apa Tanis let out their land rather than allowing it to remain fallow.

It is not surprising that the new flexibility in the usage of land is sometimes leading to disputes. Even in the old times there were occasionally quarrels about the inheritance of land particularly if there were no sons of the last owner and several kinsmen could claim about equal rights. But as no one ever abandoned his land to make his living and seek a fortune outside the valley, there was seldom any dispute over the rightful ownership of land. Middle-aged Apa Tanis who remember the days before the monetization of the economy also suggest that nowadays disputes over land-sales are more frequent than they used to be when land was bartered for mithan in long drawn-out negotiations and always with the co-operation of a go-between (*kiri-dun* or *kiri-in*) who saw to it that the parties left no ambiguities in their agreement on land-transfer. A *kiri-dun* is a kind of commission agent. People wanting to sell an article such as an ornament or valuable sword, a mithan or a piece of land, tell the minimum price they demand and let the *kiri-dun* find a purchaser. The commission (*dujo-mudu*) is paid by the latter and not by the seller. If a man sells land worth Rs 10,000 the middle-man (*kiri-dun*) gets from the buyer Rs 500 as (*dujo-mudu*). Middle-men are used even for small transactions. If, for instance, a man is ill, he will give some money to a *kiri-dun* and ask him to buy eggs and chickens for the healing-rites. The advantage of employing a *kiri-dun*, particularly in deals involving land or objects of great value is the prevention of subsequent disputes over the terms of the sale as the go-between can testify to the nature of the original contract.

In the absence of a cadastral survey and any kind of land-register it is impossible to trace changes in landownership with any accuracy. There are no village-maps of the type so common in most parts of India, nor is there any village-official comparable to the *patwari* of Peninsular India who keeps a record of land rights. Judging from the opinions voiced by educated Apa Tanis it would seem, however, that there is a trend to an intensified accumulation of land in the hands of wealthy men whereas the number of the landless is increasing. Men of modest means whose holdings do not yield sufficient rice to support the life-style present-day Apa Tanis aspire to tend to sell the little land they have and either seek their fortune in business activities or look for a salaried position in the public services or the defence forces. It is difficult to predict how far this development will go, but some young men argue that there will inevitably come about a polarization between the wealthy land-owners who cultivate their land largely with hired labour and the small holders who cannot make ends meet and have ultimately to sell out. The same young men foresee a time when Apa Tani men might not be prepared to engage solely in agricultural labour, and big landowners might bring in farm-labourers of other communities. Those who toyed with such ideas suggested that Apa Tanis would soon attain so high a level of education that they would look down upon work on the land. One student of political science even predicted that in future years Apa Tani "capitalists" would employ immigrant labour, such as Nepalis or Biharis, to cultivate their land. He thought that by that time the Inner Line policy would have been abandoned and discounted the possibility that the employment of outside labour may only be the first step to the alienation of Apa Tani land.

Such ideas held at present only by the members of a small educated élite may appear at first sight phantastic, but there are concrete indications that considerable numbers of Apa Tani boys and young men have in fact developed a distaste for agricultural work.

The traditional system of Apa Tani agriculture which I observed in the 1940s rested on the willing cooperation of all members of the community, barring the infirm and very aged, and though senior rich men would do less manual work than young men and slaves, no one considered work on the land as in any way demeaning. In families of average means most of the work in fields and gardens was done by husband and wife and their children as well as such relatives or slaves who were members of the household. On some days this working unit would engage in one and the same task, but at other times the members of the family would go about their different occupations, the husband looking mainly to the building and upkeep of dams, terraces, channels and fences, and engaging in the digging up of fields and the planting of trees, and the wife being mainly occupied with the care of nurseries and gardens, the transplanting of rice and millet and the weeding of crops. On many occasions, however, men and women worked side by side, be it in building a dam or in transplanting seedlings. Though a married couple was usually quite capable of coping with the normal work of cultivation, there were times when assistance was sought from other members of the village community.

The most important institution for the organization of reciprocal assistance in agricultural work was the labour-gang (*patang*) composed of members of several households. From childhood onwards every Apa Tani boy or girl belonged to a *patang* and this association continued until marriage and sometimes even longer. A *patang* consisted usually of young people of approximately similar age, and most of such gangs were composed of both boys and girls, although in exceptional cases *patang* were made up only of girls. There were *patang* of 20-30 members but many were smaller. Some were made up of boys and girls of the same clan, others of those of two clans of the same ward (*lapang*), and still others of members drawn from different *lapang*. The formation of *patang* occurred informally by agreement of neighbours with children of the same age. But once a *patang* was made up the members stayed together unless a serious quarrel induced a member to opt out. In *patang* made up of members of different clans it happened quite often that working companions became lovers and even married when they grew up. When a man married he could still work for some time with his *patang*, but a girl usually left her *patang* on marriage, her new domestic obligations interfering with her full-time cooperation with the other *patang* members. Yet, married women who once were members of the same *patang* often joined forces in the tedious work of transplanting rice-seedlings and in weeding, a group of four or five women working in turn on each other's fields, and the owner of the field providing a midday meal.

The members of most *patang* used to work together day after day throughout the cultivating season. They worked in rotation on the fields of their members' parents, and a man whose son or daughter had joined a *patang* had thus the right to the services of the entire gang when his turn came. These services were free except that the owner of the field had to feed the group on that day. Rich men with large holdings sometimes hired a *patang* out of turn for wages paid then in grain and divided equally among all its members. In 1978 I found that there were two types of *patang*, which either did not exist in the 1940s or had escaped my attention. One type is known as *konchi patang*, and the members of such a *patang* work only from 5A.M. till 7.30 A.M. and then go home and have a meal. No meal has to be provided by the owner of the field, and hire charges are relatively low. The other type is known as *alo patang*, and such a *patang* works from about 9A.M. until 5P.M., eating a midday meal on the fields. *Konchi patang* work only from March to July, whereas *alo patang* work at all times of the year.

The hiring of *patang* was only one of the means by which rich men obtained the labour necessary for the cultivation of their large holdings. Many poor men and women, mainly but not exclusively of *guchi* class, subsisted almost entirely on the grain received in wages for daily labour, and they had little difficulty in finding employment. For although most rich men had usually a number of slaves or dependants who worked for them throughout the year, they often needed additional labour to keep abreast with the agricultural calendar. The average daily wage was about 2 kg of husked rice which is just enough to feed two persons for a day.

Apa Tani agriculture depended thus both on the mutual help of the owners of small and medium holdings and on the labour hired by the rich. Cooperative and capitalistic trends existed side by side and in the 1940s neither trend showed any sign of eliminating the other. The man of modest means who cultivated his fields with the help of his family and the labour-gangs of his children, more than one *patang* being possibly available to a man with many children, was not in danger of being ousted by the owner of a large holding nor had the poor much chance of effecting a more equal distribution of the existing land.

By 1978 the position had considerably changed. The cultivation of land had ceased to be the only source of income and though land-ownership was still a symbol of wealth and prestige other goals had moved into the forefront of ambitions. Business deals and particularly work as government contractors offered profits equal to or even exceeding those attainable by farming, and young men were attracted by the earnings of cash which they could freely use whereas by working on their parents' land they earned only their maintenance without having any spending money. While in the 1940s farm-work was the normal activity for every Apa Tani whether unmarried or married, at present there are many choices and it seems that many boys and young men do not choose work on the fields as their first preference.

Another factor interfering with the traditional division of labour is the introduction of education both at the primary and secondary stage. There are now primary schools for children of both sexes in all Apa Tani villages, and it is obvious that regular attendance at school is incompatible with participation in the normal work of a *patang*. A few examples will demonstrate the numbers of children involved. In Hari, a village with a population of 1,759 (1971 Census figure) 327 children were enrolled in the local school; in the school of Hija, serving the villages of Hija (population 2,188) and Duta (population 605), there were 265 children, and in the school of Reru (population 1,435) there were 227 children, some of whom may have come from neighbouring settlements. Assuming that about half of the school children were old enough to be members of *patang* we can conclude that quite a substantial part of the potential labour-force is at least partially diverted from agricultural work. True, I was totd that school children also work in *patang* before and after school hours, as well as on Sunday, and that these special *patang* are organized by the school-going children themselves. During the long vacation some of the school children may also be re-integrated into the *patang* of those who do not go to school.

Even some of the high-school boys and girls are said to work occasionally in *patang*, but on the whole they do little work on the land and the divorce from farm-work is inevitable in the case of high-school students who live in hostels attached to the school at

Hapoli. Apart from the children who go to local schools there are also considerable numbers of Apa Tani children who study in boarding-schools outside the Subansiri District, and such young people have little chance of getting used to agricultural work.

My recent stay in the Apa Tani valley was not long enough to collect figures on the percentage of young people engaged in agriculture, but from observation and the statements of educated Apa Tanis I gained the impression that there has been a considerable change in the composition of the labour-force. In the 1940s one could see throughout March, April and early May fairly large labour-gangs, usually consisting of equal numbers of young boys and girls working on the fields, repairing dams and channels, levelling terrace fields, puddling the mud and finally transplanting rice-seedlings. The illustration No. 2 in my book *The Apa Tanis and their Neighbours* depicts such a *patang* and in this particular case the young men shown in the photograph even outnumbered the girls. In 1978 I did not see a single *patang* of such size and composition. Much of the work on the field was done by middle-aged women and a few middle-aged men. There were some groups of girls, usually not more than five or six, engaged in digging over fields, but the number of boys and young men working on the land seemed very small. On one occasion I saw what seemed like a *patang* of the old type levelling a field by shifting soil with the help of tray-like sledges, but a closer look showed that the men were much older than the girls, and were probably married householders who cooperated on a reciprocal basis.

At the time when work on the fields was done mainly by women and girls, and a few middle-aged men, one could see in the bazaar of Hapoli large numbers of able-bodied young men, often smartly dressed in western clothes, filling the tea stalls and gossiping with their friends. Numerous were also the boys riding on bicycles on the road between their villages and Hapoli. When I commented on the apparent imbalance of the sexes among the workers on the fields in conversation with some of my Apa Tani friends, they admitted that many of the young men were not pulling their weight, and that boys who had been to high-school rarely did much work on the fields although they expected to be fed by their parents.

An altogether novel element in the employment of agricultural labour is the payment of cash wages. A *patang* can now be hired on a cash basis according to the numbers and the time of the year.

The member of a *patang* who has a credit of a days' work by his or her co-workers but does not require their assistance because the work on the family's fields has been completed, can so to say sell the quota of work to which he is entitled. The person who engages such a *patang* (known as *patang ajo du*, i.e. "paid *patang*") pays the entire wage to the member whose turn it was to get the gang's assistance.

Cash wages vary according to the type of work and the degree of urgency to complete a phase in the process of cultivation. The average daily wage of agricultural labourers is Rs 5 for men and Rs 3 for women; in either case a midday meal and rice-beer are provided by the employer in addition to the cash wage. At harvest-time the daily wage for women is raised to Rs 5, and for the heavy work of levelling fields and rebuilding dams a daily wage is as much as Rs 8. During rush-times, when delay may cause losses, members of a *patang* of adults may get as much as Rs 10 to Rs 15 per head. These rates are considerably higher than government rates for unskilled work, but Apa Tanis pay them if the fate of the crops is at stake. In 1978 I was told that Padi Lailang, one of the wealthiest men of Reru, spent an annual average of Rs 3,000-4,000 on paying agricultural labourers. He had at that time three wives, all rather elderly, but his unmarried children were all at schools outside the Apa Tani country and hence not available to help with the field-work, either individually or as members of labour gangs.

The high cost of hired labour is one of the reasons why the letting out of land on rent has become customary in recent years. People who own land but are short of hands in their household and cannot afford to employ people to cultivate it, tend to hire it out for fixed cash payments. Even standing paddy crops are nowadays sold, and landless people who have earned cash by wage-labour, buy such paddy crops and do the harvesting themselves.

It is hardly surprising that these new types of transactions lead to numerous disputes the settlement of which is made difficult by the absence of any documentation of land rights. The new mobility of the Apa Tanis and the opening up of new areas for cultivation has done away with the old system where the older members of a stable village-community knew exactly the boundaries of plots and the history of any changes in ownership. Payments for land in mithan, the only medium of exchange acceptable in land-sales, were made in full public view and obvious for all to see, while cash-transactions can take place with no one except buyer and seller to know about it unless a middleman is employed. Ultimately the registration of land and the granting of title-deeds (*patta*) will have to be instituted if utter chaos in the sphere of land-rights is to be avoided.

At this stage in the development of the Apa Tani country, there is less urgency in the regularization of ownership-rights in clan-land. So far there has been no transfer of clan-land, and it seems that the traditional boundaries are generally known and hardly ever disputed. Clan-land comprises undulating pasture-land and bracken-covered hillocks, hunting-grounds in the forests surrounding the valley in addition to a few grassy stretches near the village. Generally clan-land is not held by a single clan, but is the joint property of two or three clans that inhabit a separate quarter of a village. The most important parts are the forest tracts used for the extraction of wood and cane, for trapping and for hunting. The tracts owned by a group of clans are usually not concentrated in one block, but are dispersed over the hills enclosing the Apa Tani country.

The two principal clans of Duta village, Koji and Chigi, for instance, claim traditionally 29 tracts of land outside the central valley as their joint possession. Each of them has a separate name, and they comprise a cluster of bare hills used for grazing, a piece of jungle with a salt-lick for mithans, and six tracts of forest at no great distance from the village used for cutting fire-wood and trapping jungle-rats and squirrels. The remaining tracts lie in widely dispersed areas, some near the Nishi cluster of settlements collectively known as Licha, others south of Hang, and yet others east of Hari village. Trapping on such clan-land is the prerogative of the members of the owner-clans, but hunting with bow and arrow, and more recently with guns is free to all Apa Tanis. It is clear that the setting of traps, and particularly of spear-traps, dangerous to men, must somehow be regulated, and in pursuance of this aim certain areas within such clan-land have been allocated to individual families within the clan. Such areas share several features with ordinary private property except that the owners' exclusive rights cover only the setting of traps and the extraction of cane. Such rights may be sold to other members of the clan or group of clans owning the whole tract of forest.

Individual villages also claim rights in certain forest tracts which are their traditional hunting grounds, and these rights may gain greater importance if the current project of opening up the Tale valley southeast of Hang for colonization should materialize. For this ambitious project which may extend Apa Tani habitation into regions lying some 2,000 feet higher than the main Apa Tani valley will involve the clearing of forest now claimed as clan property, and the allotment of plots to individual cultivators. If they succeed in turning such plots into cultivable farm land, the joint ownership of clans into large stretches of forest will have to be superseded by individual ownership-rights of the new occupants. Hence a registration of land-rights will ultimately become imperative, and this cannot be done without a cadastral survey.

Animal Husbandry

Despite changes in organization and division of labour Apa Tani agriculture has retained its main function of providing the people with the bulk of their food-supply and in addition produce a surplus to be used in barter. Animal husbandry, the other aspect of farming, on the other hand, has undergone very considerable changes, not so much in the methods employed, as in the role of domestic animals in the total economy.

In the traditional economic pattern the most important domestic bovine was the mithan (*bos frontalis*) which resembles in many aspects the wild gaur (*bos gaurus*) and occurs in the woodlands of an area extending from Arakan and Burma throughout Nagaland and Arunachal Pradesh as far as Bhutan.[1] Mithan have always been the supreme sacrificial animals required for slaughter at many ritual occasions and they served also as a source of meat if large numbers of people had to be fed. These functions the mithan have retained, but their role as a medium of exchange has been eroded by the introduction of money. We have seen that as late as the 1940s mithan were the recognized currency in all transactions to do with land. A man's economic status was judged by the number of his mithan almost as much as by the size of his land. Ownership of mithan was thus a matter of prestige, and it was not only at feasts of merit that mithan were slaughtered for the sake of prestige as

---

[1]For an exhaustive discussion of the zoological and ethnographic background of the mithan see F.J. Simoons, *A Ceremonial Ox of India. The Mithan in Nature, Culture and History*, Madison & London, 1968.

much as in order to propitiate the gods. Similarly in a contest for social pre-eminence both competitors would slaughter mithan rather than any other domestic animal. Bride-prices, ransoms and fines were usually paid in mithan and while pigs were, and indeed still are, the sacrificial animals par excellence at many communal rites, such as those of the Mloko, mithan were slaughtered at many feasts given by individuals.

In 1945 I estimated the number of mithan owned by Apa Tanis as being between 2,000 and 3,000, but in the absence of a cattle census it was—and still is—impossible to be sure about numbers. Only a very few of these animals were to be seen in the valley and Apa Tanis said that if they kept all their mithan near their villages and fields "there would not be a blade of rice or millet left." Mithan prefer the shade of forests to the open pastures, and roam singly or in small groups rather than in large herds. While Nishis frequently bring mithan to their homesteads and even tie them up below their houses for the night, Apa Tanis usually bring mithan to the villages only on the time of purchase, sometimes to treat some ailment and invariably, of course, at the time of slaughter. Usually they keep their mithan in some damp shady valley watered by a stream. In some of these valleys there are natural salt-licks and it seems that mithan let loose in such a haunt will not stray far afield. Some of these forest pastures are many hours' walk from the Apa Tani villages and theft of unguarded animals was one of the most frequent causes of trouble between Apa Tanis and their Nishi neighbours.

Many mithan-owners did not keep their animals in the Apa Tani country at all, but gave them into the care of Nishi and Miri friends. The reward for keeping another man's female mithan was one calf out of three or four according to an agreement. By dispersing his mithan over several localities an Apa Tani could also reduce the risk of losing his entire stock through an epidemic. Outbreaks of foot-and-mouth disease and rinderpest were fairly frequent occurrences, partly due no doubt to the practice of buying ordinary cattle in the plains of Assam, and such epidemics have been known to decimate the livestock of whole areas. Such disasters still occur even though a measure of veterinary aid is now available, and the danger of bringing disease into the hills may even have intensified by the improvement of communications and the resulting increase in the imports of plains cattle. In 1970 nearly all the mithan in the Apa

Tani country and in the Nishi region as far east as the Subansiri river died in an epidemic. Before the epidemic rich Apa Tani had owned as many as 100-200 mithan, and I remember my surprise when during a brief visit to Hapoli at that time I saw far larger numbers of mithan on the approach road to Hapoli than I had ever seen anywhere in the Apa Tani country.

When all the mithan and with them the disposable fortunes of quite a number of Apa Tanis and Nishis had been wiped out by the epidemic of foot-and-mouth disease, some people brought replacements from the Sagali region in the outer ranges and laboriously began to reconstitute their stock. By 1978 some rich men owned again 30-40 mithan, but it will take years before the previous position is restored. In the epidemic of 1970 only mithan but none of the Apa Tanis' and Nishis' ordinary cows and bullocks died, and this suggests that the epidemic was carried into the hills from the plains, and that plains cattle had sufficient immunity not to succumb to the infection.

Before the decimation of mithan by this epidemic the price of a full grown animal was about Rs 800, but it has now risen to between Rs 1,300 and 1,500. The use of mithan for the calculation of the value of land follows a complicated system which confused me for a long time. When an Apa Tani says that a piece of land is worth 20 mithan, this does not necessarily mean than 20 full grown mithan were paid for it. What the speaker means is that the land in question is worth twenty "mithan values" and a mithan value is only one-fourth of a big, full-grown mithan. The scale of evaluation of mithan is as follows:

sub-penge is a mithan calf without horns and this counts as one mithan value.

sub-sudohe is a young mithan with horns equal to the breadth of two fingers; this counts as two mithan values.

dorin-subu is a mithan with horns equal to the breadth of 3-4 fingers; this counts as three mithan values.

sub-ane is a mithan with horns equal to the span from thumb to middle-finger; this counts as four mithan values.

The general term for mithan is *subu*, but the above composite terms are used to indicate the size and value of individual animals. An ordinary large cow of the Assamese breed equals two mithan values, but nowadays the value of cattle is generally expressed in terms of rupees. Until 1977 the largest amount paid for a mithan was Rs 1,500, but in 1978 this was exceeded when an Apa Tani to whom a Nishi owed Rs 1,600 accepted one large mithan (*sub-ane*) in repayment of the loan.

Mithan are still being bought merely for investment. Thus in April 1978 Pumi, daughter of Padi Lailang and wife of Kuru Hasang, flying officer in the Indian Air Force, bought a female mithan from Nishis of Rakhe for 50 large baskets of paddy, which corresponds to about Rs 1,000. Pumi, who is educated and manages a pharmacy in Hapoli bazaar, did not see the mithan herself, but a kinsman had gone to see it and had reported favourably. She left the mithan with the farmer Nishi owner in Rakhe; the first four calves will go to Pumi and the fifth to the care-takers as fee for their trouble. In this particular case the sellers were probably badly in need of rice and therefore agreed to a care-taking arrangement slightly less favourable than the usual allotment of calves.

In the 1940s I was told that in addition to the many privately owned mithan there were also some animals which were the joint property of a clan or even a village, and had been bought by subscription to be used for sacrifices in the interest of the whole community. In 1978 I could not get information on any concrete examples of such communally owned mithan, and it may well be that the increasing individualization of Apa Tani society has led to the abandonment of the system of jointly owned mithan.

Mithan are by no means the only bovines reared by Apa Tanis. Already in 1944 there were a good many cows of plains origin (*bos indicus*) in the Apa Tani country, and since the opening of an all weather road from the plains to Hapoli many more have been driven from North Lakimpur to the Apa Tani valley. Some are used for breeding but all are ultimately meant for slaughter. Unlike mithan, cattle rarely leave the open parts of the valley, usually remaining on the grasslands near the villages. In the spring and summer there is ample grazing, but in the winter when the pastures are shrivelled, the cattle lives precariously on the rice and millet stubble of the previous harvest, for Apa Tanis make no attempt to feed their cattle. As soon as the rice and the millet are planted out the cattle is banished to the grazing grounds at the end of the valley and the fields in the vicinity are carefully fenced so that a cow would have to pass through a labyrinth of narrow passages before it could reach the centre of the valley where there are unprotected plots.

Very little care is given to this cattle, and there is no system of herd boys. Summer and winter the animals are in the open day and night. Crosses of mithan and plains cattle are known but not particularly encouraged; cattle and mithan are kept apart by their own habits and preferences for different grazing grounds. For ritual purposes hybrids count as mithan.

In recent years increasing numbers of cows and bullocks have been brought from the plains. In North Lakhimpur Apa Tani traders can buy ten cows of mixed quality for any sum between Rs 2,000 and 2,500, and in Hapoli or such places in the Miri and Nishi regions as Raga and Nyapin one cow can be sold for Rs 300-500. Hence profits are considerable and it seems that among the Apa Tanis there is an inexhaustible demand for beef. In 1978 daily six or seven cows were slaughtered in Old Ziro, and the meat was sold by piece and not by weight. In some Apa Tani villages there were butchers' stalls with joints of beef hanging up for sale. In Hapoli bazaar 1 kg of beef cost Rs 5-6, while pork which Apa Tanis prefer was sold for Rs 10-12 per kg. In the past Apa Tanis neither milked their cattle nor did they ever consume milk in any form. With the introduction of tea served in restaurants and tea-stalls with milk and sugar, the consumption of milk has become popular among all those frequenting the towns of Assam or even Hapoli bazaar. Tin milk is widely sold, and in the early 1970s four small private dairies were established by Apa Tanis with government aid. In each dairy there are about 15 cows, and the milk production is roughly 1.5 litres per animal. In Hapoli with its large population of non-tribal government employees there is a great demand for fresh milk which sells at Rs 2 per litre. The success of these dairies has stimulated the interest in milch cattle, and in 1978 twenty applications for government aid in the establishment of new dairies were pending.

Pigs are traditionally the favourite domestic animals, and here the word domestic applies in the narrowest sense. For Apa Tani pigs are kept below the pile-borne houses in boarded-up enclosures. Once a pig enters this enclosure it leaves it usually only on the day of slaughter. No pigs roam the village as they do in Nishi settlements, for if let loose they would endanger rice-nurseries, gardens and fields. This necessity of keeping pigs shut up sets a limit to their numbers, for unlike Nishi pigs which find a good deal of food rummaging about the village the pigs of the Apa Tanis must be regularly fed, and no household can afford to feed more than two or three full-grown pigs at a time. The food given to pigs consists of the husks of grain, the dregs remaining from the brewing of millet and rice-beer, kitchen refuse, and the sago-like pith of a certain forest tree which is collected for this purpose. The pigs feed also on human excrement falling into their enclosure when the inhabitants of the house relieve themselves on the narrow verandah running alongside the house. In villages of hundred of tightly packed houses the pig is a very necessary scavenger, and the absence of pigs from the houses of some poor men, is betrayed by the unpleasant smell emanating from such dwellings.

Despite the Apa Tanis' predilection for pork few pigs are bred. It is more profitable to buy young piglets and annually hundreds of pigs are imported into the Apa Tani country. In the old days most pigs were obtained from Nishis in exchange for Apa Tani rice, but although this barter-trade still continues to some extent, many piglets are now purchased in a special market at North Lakhimpur and brought to Hapoli by bus or truck. There they are sold to individuals Apa Tanis to be kept till they are full grown or the need for a sacrifice compels the owner to slaughter even a small pig. However, if a man decides to breed from one of his sows and has no boar of his own, he borrows a young boar and shuts it up for some time in his pigsty. For this service he either pays the boar's owner a small fee or promises him one of the piglets. Yet, Apa Tanis believe that reproduction spoils the flavour of the sow's meat and hence they prefer to fatten sows which have never littered. Boars are castrated when two or three months old, and as none are set aside for breeding purposes such sows as are allowed to reproduce are inseminated by very young boars. Castration is effected by the removal of the testicles and this is one of the few task which Apa Tanis consider defiling. A special person known as *kümar*, usually a woman, performs the operation. Her social status is low (see page 86) but she is never in want of food.

The pig is the sacrificial animal indispensable for many rites, and pork is more highly prized than any other meat. Sides of smoked bacon are not only the most acceptable gifts between friends and kinsmen, but are a recognized currency for ceremonial payments.

Apa Tanis are not interested in the keeping of goats, for goats are too destructive to be let loose in so carefully tended an area as their valley. A few men, however, own a few goats and keep them with Nishi friends in the latter's villages. Their meat is eaten and on occasion they are used for certain private sacrifices appropriate for the propitiation of disease-bringing spirits.

Fowls are kept by all Apa Tanis for the sake of their eggs as well as their flesh. They are frequently required for the taking of omens, which are based on the scrutiny of the livers as well as on the configuration of the yolk of hard boiled eggs. On the occasion of a single sacrificial rite one may count as many as a hundred egg shells broken in the course of the ritual and hung up on a bamboo structure. Required for so many vital purposes fowls and eggs have always been relatively expensive, and in the days before the introduction of money two eggs counted as a day's wage, and a hen cost as much as a knife, and a cook could be bartered for a small *dao* or a simple cloth.

Today many live chickens are brought from North Lakhimpur by truck or bus, and sold in Hapoli for Rs 10 per kg. As in North Lakhimpur the price per kg is only Rs 6-7 the profit of the traders is considerable. Eggs too are more expensive in Hapoli where three eggs are sold for Rs 2 while in North Lakhimpur the price of an egg is only Re 0.5.

Dogs are of mixed breed, and not very different from the pariah dogs common all over the plains of Assam. If the Apa Tanis ever had a special breed of dogs, such as some of the Naga tribes still possess, it has long been diluted by continual hybridization with mongrels imported from Assam. Many of the Apa Tanis visiting the plains return with several dogs which they picked up cheaply and can sell at a profit. Dogs are the sacrificial animals required for the worship of several of the fierce and dangerous gods causing disease and personal misfortune. In the days of raiding, a dog had also to be sacrificed before a party of raiders set out, and its head was taken along and thrown into the house to be attacked. Though Apa Tanis eat the flesh of dogs, few dogs are slaughtered merely for the sake of their flesh which is not rated very highly from a culinary point of view.

In the old days the Apa Tanis' surplus of rice enabled them to obtain substantial supplies of cattle and pigs from their Nishi and Miri neighbours, and thus they were used to a diet in which meat was an important component. There are not many parts of India where villagers eat as much meat, and one wonders whether the

Apa Tanis, who are by no means noted for their skill as breeders, will in future years be able to maintain their high protein diet. The present injection of money into their economy, which will be discussed in Chapter 3, enables them at present to supplement supplies of Nishi livestock by large scale purchases from North Lakhimpur, but their cash earnings are unlikely to remain at the current level, and the increase in population outstripping the possible expansion of the cultivated area has already cut down the surplus of grain available to be bartered for Nishi mithan, cows and pigs. Yet, the Apa Tanis are a resilient people and their craving for a diet superior to that of most Indian farming populations may well be an incentive to develop such new enterprises as the breeding of fish.

Fish-farming

An entirely new departure in the Apa Tanis' utilization of their environment is the breeding of fish in artificial pools. This innovation is entirely due to the efforts of the Department of Fisheries which introduced the practice of fish-culture to the Apa Tanis. In 1958 one consignment of the seed of scaled carp was brought from Shillong, and subsequently the government established a fish farm at Doimukh. From there the Apa Tanis have been supplied with seed and now there is also wild breeding. The Apa Tanis were encouraged to turn some of their rice-fields in the centre of the valley into fish ponds, and by 1978 there were 194 privately owned ponds. The fish are bred in these ponds and when they have grown to a length of 1.5 inches they are caught in small mesh nets, and transferred to flooded paddy fields. Within three and a half months the released fish grow to a weight of about 800 grams. Seed and nets have so far been provided free of cost by the government, but from 1978 onwards these are to be supplied on the basis of a 50 per cent subsidy, for the Apa Tanis' profits are so large that a 100 per cent subsidy is considered no longer necessary. Some of the pond-owners sell fingerlings to other Apa Tanis for release in paddy fields at a rate of Rs 10 per 100 fish. In the flooded fields the carps find ample food and when they have grown sufficiently large they are sold at the Hapoli market and also in the villages. In 1978 the price per kg was 12-14 which was twice as much as beef and even slightly more than the highly valued pork. From one single pond a profit of Rs 300-500 can be achieved, and this is far more than the yield of a rice-field of the same size. The Apa Tanis' decision to turn an appreciable number of fields close to irrigation channels into fish ponds is therefore economically sound and the loss of cultivable area is not large enough to affect the quantity of rice harvested more than marginally.

Until recently the Apa Tanis were the only tribe which had taken up fish farming, but in 1977 one Nishi of Talo village successfully started a fish pond, and his example encouraged others to seek government assistance in the development of the new venture.

THREE

The Development of Commerce

LONG BEFORE THE Government of India opened up the Subansiri region by the construction of roads, the Apa Tanis had acquired the reputation of skilful and enterprising traders. The exchange of goods was then a necessity for their complex economy, and the Apa Tanis evinced as much ingeniousness and persistence in pursuing every possible opportunity for a profitable trade as they had employed in developing the resources of their own country.

Though in 1944 a visitor to the Apa Tani valley may at first have gained the impression that the valley was a self-contained unit, distinct and largely isolated from the surrounding Nishi and Miri country, this initial impression would have been deceptive. In fact, at that time the Apa Tanis were self-sufficient only in regard to their requirements of foodgrain and vegetables. For the supply of animals for slaughter as well as for several raw materials needed by their craftsmen they depended on trade with neighbouring tribes and even with the population of the plains of Assam. Their main export was always rice, for whereas Nishis and Miris practised almost exclusively the archaic system of slash-and-burn cultivation which in bad years did not provide them with enough grain, the Apa Tanis' skill as wet rice cultivators usually enabled them to grow more rice than they needed for their own consumption. It was their surplus of rice which enabled them to dominate economically, though not necessarily politically, their neighbours often dependent on Apa Tani rice.

The relations between the highly specialized Apa Tani economy and the more primitive economy of Nishis and Miris are a remarkable example for the interdependence of basically different cultures. These relations, based principally on the exchange of grain for livestock, seemed to have remained fairly constant even though the Apa Tanis' trade-partners were by no means always the same. Tribal tradition tells us that Nishi clans which now stand in close trade relations with Apa Tanis dwelt as recently as four or five generations ago in distant valleys to the north-west. Trade with a people able to supply large quantities of grain must have been a novelty for their forefathers when they first settled in the vicinity of the Apa Tanis. But whatever their previous economy may have been, they apparently were not slow in availing themselves of the new opportunities. The position of the Apa Tanis was different. They seem to have been the one firm rock in a sea of shifting and warring tribes. More than once they must have seen their neighbours and trade-partners of yesterday defeated and scattered by more powerful newcomers. But such newcomers will soon have conformed to the same economic pattern as the populations whom they had displaced. They certainly were willing enough to step into a barter system by which they could obtain rice and the wares of expert Apa Tani craftsmen. Apa Tani economy has thus for long been tuned to the exchange of goods with the outside world and the establishment of trading contacts with the people of the Assamese plains was an extension of old trading patterns rather than a total innovation. A totally new situation arose only when in 1944 outsiders entered the Apa Tani valley, and a few months later the government gave effect to my proposal to establish a trading depot at Duta. There Apa Tanis could purchase salt, cloth and a few other commodities with the cash they were earning by working as porters for government.

The trade between Apa Tanis and their Nishi and Miri neighbours has always been based on the complementary nature of their economies. While the Apa Tanis are primarily agriculturists, the Nishis are indifferent cultivators, mostly without the knowledge of irrigation and terracing, but living in settlements loosely scattered over extensive areas of jungle-covered and grassy hill-slopes they have ample opportunity and considerable aptitude for the breeding of mithan, oxen, and pigs, animals which have always been greatly in demand among the Apa Tanis. At the time of the Mloko festival, hundreds of pigs are being sacrificed and until recently Nishis were the main suppliers of pigs. Similarly an Apa Tani intent on strengthening his social prestige could do no better than buying some mithan and slaughtering them at the Morom festival.

The need of the Nishis for the agricultural produce of their Apa Tani neighbours was less constant, and was not immediately linked with ritual observances. In years of good harvests, they may have been able to dispense with grain purchases altogether, while in times of scarcity they were prepared to pay double the normal price for supplies. Rice was usually paid for in mithan, and in normal years thirty carrying baskets of rice were the equivalent of one full-grown female mithan. But in years of scarcity among the Nishis, the same mithan would have fetched only fifteen baskets with a capacity of sixty pounds of unhusked rice each. A Nishi in need of grain usually came himself to the village of an Apa Tani friend, and if he succeeded in concluding a bargain he and members of his household, would carry the rice back to his village, perhaps making several trips. Often the price was paid at once, and many a prospective buyer would bring a mithan with him when he came to negotiate a deal. Yet, rice could also be obtained on credit, and many of the disputes between Apa Tanis and their Nishi or Miri neighbours resulted from trade deals which began with the sale of rice on credit. It would seem that some wealthy Apa Tanis even used advances of grain as a means of bringing a Nishi debtor gradually under their control, and according to Apa Tani custom it was perfectly legitimate that a man unable to repay a loan should work it off by becoming a bond-servant of his creditor. While among Apa Tanis such arrangements used to work fairly smoothly, and without hard feelings on the part of the bond-servant, similar relationships between Nishis and Apa Tanis frequently led to friction. Many were the cases of heavily indebted Nishi dependants giving their Apa Tanis masters the slip; they not only defaulted on the repayment of their debts but also led raids on Apa Tanis or their cattle to get their own back on their one-time creditors and masters.

Yet, despite such incidents, trade between Apa Tanis and Nishis rarely came to a complete standstill, and it was not unusual for one Apa Tani village being engaged in a violent feud with a neighbouring Nishi settlement, while the people of another Apa Tani village continued trading with the enemies of their fellow-tribesmen. The trade between the two tribes was never confined to the exchange of rice for live-stock. Besides buying Nishi pigs and mithan the Apa Tanis used to obtain from Nishis nearly all their cotton. Though they could have grown cotton themselves, they found it more profitable to use their skill for irrigation to produce rice, and then barter it for cotton which their Nishi neighbours could grow on dry fields. The Apa Tanis used to buy the raw cotton, gin it, spin and dye it, and then weave it into cloth, some of which was sold to the original suppliers of the cotton. Though some Nishi women also knew how to weave, Apa Tani women using the same type of stretch-loom produced cloths of particularly good quality and elaborate patterns. Some raw cotton was bartered for Apa Tani swords and knives, but there was also a system by which impecunious Apa Tani women could obtain supplies of raw cotton in exchange for their services as weavers. They went to nearby Nishi villages such as Talo, Jorum and Mai, and undertook to weave cloth of any desired type on the understanding that during their stay they would be fed and that at the end of their period of employment they would receive as wages a quantity of cotton equal to that which they utilized in weaving cloth for their clients.

Though not a cotton growing people Apa Tanis possessed more and better textiles than any of their tribal neighbours, and they used to weave not only to meet their own needs but also with the definite idea of using their products for barter transactions. The attractive Apa Tani cloths, and particularly those with broad borders in which yellow and blue were the predominant colours, fetched good prices among their neighbours, and even within Apa Tani society such cloths equalled in value one long sword (*dao*) or a small pig. Through itinerant Apa Tani traders, as well as through middlemen of other tribes Apa Tani textiles reached areas as distant as the Upper Panior valley, the Khru valley and Miri villages in the Upper Kamla valley.

Aesthetically Apa Tani cloths are far superior to the machine-cloth imported from Assam and their durability is at least four times as great as that of such bazaar cloth. Nevertheless weaving is declining among the Apa Tanis, for the availability of cheap imported textiles has led to a change of fashions and few of the young men wear nowadays the colourful flowing cloaks which used to be so characteristic of Apa Tanis. Only on ritual occasions are traditional clothes still generally worn.

Among the Nishis change of fashions has been less rapid, and Apa Tani weavers are welcome in such villages as Talo. After the rice-harvest Apa Tani women still go to Talo and weave cloth on the same terms as used to be customary in the days before both Apa Tanis and Nishis were in contact with the outside world.

In the old days *dao* and knives produced by Apa Tani blacksmiths were also articles of trade, and on their trading visits to villages of Nishis and Miris Apa Tanis usually carried with them *dao* and knives to be used as exchange goods. With these and cloths they used to purchase pigs, dogs, fowls, tobacco, cotton, gourd vessels, dried bamboo shoots, and also some articles of dress such as cane belts, cane hats and fibre rain-cloaks. Earthen pots too were items of trade. Among the Apa Tanis pots were made only in two villages, namely Michi-Bamin and Hang, whereas the women of several neighbouring Nishi villages were experienced potters, and often sold their wares to Apa Tanis in exchange for rice.

An unusal phenomenon in these barter deals was the Apa Tanis' practice of buying cheaply unburnt pots and carrying them across the country denuded of forest by the Nishis' shifting cultivation. As soon as they reached the high pine forests belonging to Apa Tanis they built fires and burnt the pots before carrying them home. Nowadays the use of earthen pots has greatly diminished because iron cooking pots imported from the plains of Assam are cheap and easily available. The Apa Tani women have largely given up making pots, and it is not unlikely that the craft will soon be extinct. Only for ritual purposes, such as the collecting of the blood of sacrificial pigs, are earthen pots still required and these can be purchased from Nishis. On the occasion of a recent visit to Talo village I still saw Nishi women preparing clay for the making of pots.

One commodity which Apa Tanis continue to sell to Nishis is a yeast-like substance (*ipo*) used for the fermentation of rice and millet beer. Considering that the Nishis' beer is rather better than that of Apa Tanis, it is strange that they consider the Apa Tanis' fermenting agent superior to the one they can make themselves. *Ipo* is produced from a mixture of old and new rice, and is made only in the month of August when new rice becomes available.

An item of trade which has lost all importance is the purchase by Nishis of the salty substance produced by Apa Tanis from the ash of leafy plants. With the availability of unlimited quantities of Indian sea-salt, there is no more market for such a salt substitute, although Apa Tanis still produce some for their own consumption as an appetizer at drinking parties.

When trading in distant villages Apa Tanis used to barter their wares not only for such commodities as pigs, fowls or cotton, which they required for immediate use, but accepted payment also in the shape of valuables such as beads, small bell-metal bells (*maji*) and bell-metal discs, which had then the character of a currency and were purchased with the idea of an advantageous resale. Almost all barter transactions between Apa Tanis and neighbouring tribes, even if involving *maji* which Nishis used for ritual exchanges, were simple business deals devoid of ceremonial associations.

Today money has taken the place of all other media of exchange, and objects such as *maji* have lost the character of a currency and are used only for ceremonial payments, mainly between Nishis and Nishis.

Apart from the barter of the products of Apa Tanis and Nishis, there has for a considerable time been a limited trade in Tibetan goods as well as trade between Apa Tanis and the people of the plains. The latter was the more important as far as volume was concerned. We do not know for how long the Apa Tanis have been in the habit of obtaining iron and salt from Assam, but by 1944 trade in these goods was well established and both were regarded as indispensable necessities. Apa Tanis bought them not only for their own use, but also for resale to tribesmen further in the interior who had no direct access to the plains. In those days Apa Tanis usually did not venture on journeys to the plains during the months April to September or even October. The rivers were then flooded and often unfordable, and a trek of five or six days through precipitous hill country involved considerable exertion. But in the cold season when communications were easier, numerous Apa Tanis visited the plains of North Lakhimpur. Their numbers varied from year to year but even before 1945, when the government began to employ Apa Tanis on a large scale as porters, many men and boys, and even a few women used to come to Assam every winter. They usually carried chillies of a particular large variety which they bartered for salt or for their requirements of food. Most of them found employment as agricultural and forest labourers, and worked for periods ranging from ten days to three months. Before the 1939-45 war they earned daily wages of four to five annas but by 1945 they could earn as much as Re 1 to Rs 1.50 a day.

Men of wealth and good status never went to the plains and when I first arrived in the Apa Tani country I found that none of the clan-headmen had ever left the hills. Only slaves and very poor men were in the habit of going to the plains, and the most enterprising among them succeeded in bettering their position by trade in goods only obtainable in Assam. Thus they bought salt cheaply and resold it to Nishis and Miris at inflated prices. They also brought back iron hoes, axes, bowls of bell-metal and more rarely brass-pots. Other goods purchased in the plains were Assamese silk cloth, Bhotia woollen cloth (which had reached Assam by way of Tawang or Bhutan), beads, bracelets, brass hair-pins and ear-rings, and safety pins. The trade in cows, dogs and pigs has already been mentioned.

Woollen Bhotia blankets were much prized, but they were rarely used in their original form. The Apa Tanis unravelled the woollen yarn, dyed it in various colours and used it for the manufacture of woollen ceremonial cloths and the embroidery of cotton cloth. Plain machine-made cotton cloth was bought mainly for resale to Nishis and Miris. Apa Tanis rightly considered it inferior and in those days only very poor men would wear it. Most beads worn by Apa Tani women were small, blue glass beads bought in the bazaars of the plains, but some larger beads had probably come from Tibet.

Assamese silk cloth and bell-metal vessels were clearly luxuries, but luxuries of a solid and useful type in keeping with the spirit of Apa Tani culture. Their introduction moreover served as a corrective to extreme differences between rich and poor. For trade in these commodities gave poor men a chance of bettering their position and even purchasing a little land, while the desire to possess such luxury goods induced rich men to part with some of their accumulated rice-stores and in certain cases even with land. We have mentioned already that work in the plains enabled some Apa Tanis to build up a small stock of cows, and in a country where cattle was practically currency and at the same time a symbol of wealth, the prospect of acquiring a few cows was for men of modest means a great incentive to brave the difficulty of journeys to Assam.

Though within human memory Apa Tanis never had any direct contact with Tibetans, they owned a good many articles of Tibetan origin which had reached them by devious routes through their Nishi and Miri neighbours. The employ of such Tibetan articles for ceremonial and ritual purposes points to an old association, and there are indeed indications that in the not too distant part most of the foreign articles needed by Apa Tanis came from or through Tibet rather than from Assam. Nearly every respectable Apa Tani possesses at least one Tibetan sword, and at the time of feasts thousands of Tibetan beads are worn. Large beads of conch-shell as well as sky-blue porcelain beads, though possibly of Chinese origin, seem to have reached the Subansiri area via Tibet.

Bronze plates of Tibetan make used to be one of standard valuables employed for larger payments. Tibetan prayer bells (*maji*) were never of the same importance as among Nishis, and few Apa Tani possessed famous specimens of high value. But the more ordinary types, such as might have cost two or three good cloths, served the Apa Tanis as useful barter objects.

While the Tibetan origin of such objects as swords or *maji* is unmistakable, we cannot say for certain whether the wool which the Apa Tanis require for the manufacture of their embroidered ceremonial cloths came of old from the same source. In the 1940s Apa Tani used to obtain strips of woollen cloth of either Tibetan or Bhutanese origin via Assam, and very similar woollen cloth reached the tribesmen on the Upper Kamla from villages standing in trade relations with Tibet, and it is more than probable that in olden times some such cloth filtered down as far as the Apa Tani valley.

Since the Indo-Chinese conflict of 1962 closed the border between the two countries the flow of trade across the Himalayas has largely come to a stand-still, though on the upper reaches of Khru and Kamla the one or other adventurous tribesman may still slip across the undemarcated international border to visit kinsmen or former trade partners. Thus no new Tibetan goods can reach the Subansiri tribes in significant quantities, and while very precious objects such as famous prayer-bells, considered the work of divine artificers, will undoubtedly be handed on from one generation of Nishis to the other, such practical items as Tibetan swords will get scarcer and scarcer. The rarity of such objects is reflected in the prices they now fetch. Thus Rs 300 have to be paid for a Tibetan sword while one of Apa Tani manufacture costs only Rs 20-30. Similarly a string of large white beads of Tibetan origin is now valued about Rs 1500-1600, while the factory made dark blue beads available in North Lakhimpur cost only Re 1 per string.

Quite apart from recent political impediments to contacts with Tibet, modern developments make a reorientation of the Apa Tani economy towards Assam inevitable, and apart from a few traditional trade links with Nishi neighbours, the Apa Tanis' commercial relations are exclusively with the business communities in Assam.

Moderns Trends in Trade

The most fundamental change in the commercial activities of the Apa Tanis is the specialization of individual men on shop-keeping or wholesale trade to the virtual exclusion of any other economic activity. Until the 1950s all Apa Tanis, barring a handful of such artisans as blacksmiths, were farmers, who only occasionally engaged in some business deals. But even these deals depended usually on agricultural produce which they were able to sell or lend. Today there are numerous Apa Tani businessmen who concentrate their energies almost entirely on the management of their shops or on the execution of government contracts. Most of them possess still some land, but this is either farmed by their wives and daughters or leased out on rent.

The expansion of commercial activities started in the late 1950s and early 1960s. The establishment of some government agencies first at Old Ziro and later at Hapoli led to the arrival of a number of non-Apa Tani officials and their families. To cater for their immediate needs a cooperative store was open and a few small shops owned by Apa Tanis sprang up in imitation of this store. By that time hundreds of Apa Tanis were earning wages by working in connection with road building projects and the construction of the new district headquarter at Hapoli. The very fact that they had cash at their disposal induced them to buy some of the consumer goods which had been brought to Old Ziro and Hapoli for sale to the employees of government. But at first the Apa Tanis though in possession of cash, showed considerable hesitation in spending it on anything one could describe as luxury.

After a visit to the valley in 1962, I commented on "the restraint of the Apa Tanis in acquiring novel consumer goods" (*op. cit.* p. 158). At that time I found that even in the houses of men who through trade or wage labour had earned considerable sums of money there were few articles of foreign manufacture. Apart from some iron cooking pots in place of earthen pots, metal buckets replacing gourd vessels, and some tin boxes with padlocks instead of store baskets, there were few innovations. Similarly the clothes worn by most men and women conformed still to the traditional styles, though a few young men in government employment had begun to wear shorts, shirts and shoes. By 1978 the scene had greatly changed. Among domestic utensils there was a variety of plastic and enamel mugs and vessels, electric torches were common possessions, and some wealthy men even had chairs and tables. The men's dress was a mixture of traditional and modern styles. While many old and middle-aged men still wore the red cane belts and tails as well as the characteristic hand-woven cotton cloaks with coloured borders, the majority of young men dressed in trousers or shorts, shirts, pullovers and occasionally even tailored jackets in western style. Women were more conservative and most wore skirts of local manufacture, but the quilted short-sleeved jakets previously worn by old and young were hardly to be seen, and had been replaced by blouses bought readymade or bodices of imported cotton material. Many young women had also bought square cloths in bright colours, mainly red or green, which they wore as shawls above their blouses. Canvas shoes or slippers were worn by many of the younger Apa Tanis of both sexes, and wealthier men also possessed leather shoes.

However, there were local variations in the degree of the modernization of dress and footwear. In the villages which had progressed most in education and business activities, such as Hari and Reru, the percentage of people wearing traditional dress was smallest whereas in Duta and Hija, which had lagged behind in these respects, the number of men and women who had made little change in their way of dressing was much larger.

The overall number of Apa Tanis who have become used to purchasing at least part of their clothes ready made is very large, and their needs are mainly met by the shops established in Hapoli and Old Ziro. The growth in the number of shops and the range of the commodities for sale is a remarkable phenomenon, and I know of no comparable development in any of the tribal regions of Peninsular India.

The first large shop in Old Ziro was started by a Bengali, who had come to the Apa Tani valley as a medical peon, and seeing the prospects for shop-keeping resigned from government service and devoted himself entirely to business. While other outsiders would not have obtained permission to settle in the valley, his past residence as government employee, had removed this hurdle, and his shop, then virtually without competition, prospered so much that he acquired considerable wealth and ultimately moved to a town in the plains of Assam, and opened there a much larger establishment.

The example of this pioneer was soon emulated and several prominent Apa Tanis including Havung Havung and Padi Lailang of Reru, Kago Bida of Hija, and Hage Hale of Hari, opened shops in Old Ziro. Havung Havung was the first notable businessman, but he died at a relatively early age, and his only son attained no prominence in the commercial field. Padi Lailang, on the other hand, is a remarkable example of a man outstanding in one sphere of activity being equally successful in quite a different and unfamiliar field.

When I first encountered Padi Lailang in 1944 he was one of the richest and most prominent men of Reru. He had several martial exploits to his credit and was particularly known for a raid against the Nishi village of Linia which he had led with much success. Unlike some other rich Apa Tanis he had not inherited great wealth. As he was the youngest of five sons he had received from his father only 2 acres of land, enough to live on but not sufficient to feed dependants and slaves. But Lailang was enterprising and ambitious. He reared mithan and cows, and shot many wild pigs. The sale of their meat enabled him to buy cows and with these he bought land. As his wealth increased he bought many slaves. There was a time when some Nishis were so poor that they would sell their own children—presumably after a series of bad harvests—and so he could obtain a number of slaves at relatively modest cost. In 1978 he told me that if slavery had not been abolished, his slaves and their off-spring would number about sixty. They still acknowledged their dependence by giving him the head of any animal they killed, and provided he paid them wages at the current rate they worked on his land. Padi Lailang had married four wives, and in 1978 twelve of his children were living.

When the coming of the Indian administration created opportunities for novel commercial ventures, Padi Lailang was one of the first to take advantage of the new economic climate. He built a house at Old Ziro, and opened shops at Old Ziro and at Hapoli, and helped one of his sons to establish a bakery. His business ventures were so successful that in 1970 he offered to invest Rs 200,000 if I could be persuaded to match the sum and go into partnership with him in establishing a large department store!

By 1978 he was gradually withdrawing from active business life, his elder sons being capable of looking after affairs. His triumph came in March 1978 when his son Yubbe won the only Apa Tani seat in the Legislative Assembly of Arunachal Pradesh and was subsequently elected Speaker of the Assembly. Yubbe's opponents maintained that Padi Lailang's wealth and his widespread kinship-ties and ceremonial friendships had helped his son's campaign, but however this may be Padi Yubbe's political success were the crowning of Padi Lailang's career as a prominent and apparently generally popular leader. In 1978 four of his sons, apart from Yubbe, were in Itanagar, two daughters attended mission schools in Assam and his daughter Pumi was married to the only Apa Tani flying officer in the Indian Air Force. Thus the family is clearly set on a course towards progress and modernization. His house in Old Ziro, to which he refers to as his "office", is built in modern style, furnished with cane chairs, and contains a telephone from which one can speak to Itanagar and Delhi. In his house in Reru, however, the lives in the same style in which he lived in 1944, spending much of the time sitting by the fire with a cat on his lap and consuming large quantities of rice beer. In another context, we shall see that he has rather grandiose ideas about his funeral monument (see page 216).

There are several other equally prominent businessmen among the Apa Tanis, and some are believed to surpass Padi Lailang in capital resources. It is clearly impossible to find out the volume of an individual's trading operations or assess his capital resources. Various indications demonstrate, however, the general level of the trading community's affluence. In the branch of the State Bank of India in Hapoli about 1200 tribesmen, most of whom Apa Tanis, have current accounts, a good many with balances of over Rs 100,000. When recently a wealthy middle-aged man wanted to marry a young girl as his second wife, her parents only agreed on the condition that he would open a joint account for himself and his new wife, with an initial deposit of Rs 30,000. He accepted this condition and his ability to do so indicates the affluence of some of the Apa Tani businessmen, an affluence which stands in stark contrast to the poverty of most tribal populations in other parts of India.

The major sources of the earning of Apa Tanis engaged in business deals are certainly government contracts. In the past twenty years there has been a great deal of construction work and road building both inside the Apa Tani valley and in the surrounding country, and Apa Tanis, who are disciplined and industrious, could easily compete with Nishis and Miris, neither of whom have a tradition of coordinated labour. No figures are publicly available for the total amounts spent by government on such undertakings, but the known cost of a single and relatively minor project can give us some idea of the magnitude of the sums involved. The fair weather road from Pangen to Tale was built by the Forest Department without calling for tenders, and the final cost was in the neighbourhood of Rs 500,000 most of which sum went to Apa Tanis in the form of wages. One can well imagine how many millions of rupees must have been shelled out for the construction of all the roads with permanent surface throughout Subansiri District, and Apa Tani contractors who could supply and control labour will certainly have earned a substantial share of the funds expended on the building of roads. The experience of wealthy patricians in directing the work of numerous slaves and hired labourers undoubtedly helped them in recruiting and controlling contract labour. Particularly in the first years of the administration's activities in the Valley, the leading men of the tribe most of whom were affluent landowners commanded still the loyalties of their former slaves and dependants, and hence could place disciplined labour gangs at the disposal of the government.

While without access to the official records of that time it is not possible to reconstruct the details of the cooperation between government and Apa Tani contractors and labour forces in detail, there can be no doubt that it was the influx of government funds through the channels of wage payments which gave the first impetus to the development of Hapoli as a commercial centre. The profits of contractors enabled them to establish shops at Hapoli and Old Ziro, and the wages earned by a broad stratum of Apa Tanis led to the emergence of an adequate clientele patronizing these shops.

In 1962 there were only a few shops and tea-stalls in Hapoli but Apa Tanis had already begun to supply the numerous employees of government with groceries and articles of daily use, and imported these provisions by truck from North Lakhimpur. One such trader was said to have made a profit of Rs 30,000 within the preceding three years, a considerable sum at a time before inflation had reduced the purchasing power of the Indian rupee. The explanation for the success of the relatively inexperienced Apa Tanis is the fact that the administration did not permit merchants from the plains to establish shops in the hills. While in other parts of India Marwaris and members of other trading castes have infiltrated into most tribal areas and prevented the emergence of any indigenous merchant class, the Apa Tanis were saved from such competition and could hence establish their own business enterprises, without being over-shadowed from the start by more skilled and more aggressive traders and moneylenders.

By 1978 the bazaar of Hapoli had grown to a very respectable size and the range of merchandize was comparable to that found in the shops of a minor Indian market town. There were 59 shops, tea-stalls and so-called "hotels" where meals and drinks were served. The majority of these shops stocked a variety of goods ranging from groceries and tin food to stationery and some textiles. But there were also specialized establishments, i.e. two radio shops, one of which was also selling watches, one photo studio, one bookshop, one bookseller and newsagent, one cycle shop, one carpentry shop, one dry cleaner. There were seven establishments described as "hotels" or "restaurants" one of which was combined with a bakery, and three tea-stalls. Of the numerous general stores some specialized more on hardware, some on tin food, biscuits, and sweets, and others on readymade clothes and shoes. With the exception of two Nishis, who kept minor general stores, all the shop owners were Apa Tanis, but the representation of the villages was very uneven: Hari 30, Michi-Bamin seven, Hang six, Hija five, Reru four, Mudang-Tage three, Kalung one, and Duta one. The prominence of Hari in education is matched by its outstanding performance in trade. More than half of the shops are owned by men of Hari. Mudang-Tage, Kalung and Duta, on the other hand, are very poorly represented within the trading community of Hapoli, and this seems to be due rather to the general attitude to change of these two villages than to an innate lack of commercial talent among their inhabitants.

Though all shops and establishments providing food and drink are owned by Apa Tanis, some are leased to outsiders or there are outsiders among those serving behind the counter. In 33 of the shops only the Apa Tani owner and members of his family are working, but the remaining 26 are either managed by outsiders or have non-Apa Tanis on the staff.

There are three ways in which outsiders can be involved in the running of a shop:

(*a*) The owner leases the shop to an outsider and receives from him a fixed rent.

(*b*) The owner purchases a stock of goods (e.g. Rs 5,000 worth of goods) and arranges with an outsider to run the shop and give him an agreed percentage of all takings; any profit above this percentage goes to the outsider.

(*c*) An outsider is employed on salary as salesman; he may or may not live in a room behind or above the shop.

Among the outsiders working in shops in Hapoli under the one or other of these arrangements there were two Nagas, one Sherpa, three Assamese, eight Bengalis, three Biharis, and one Madrasi. In exceptional cases the employment of an outside expert may be inevitable. Thus in the only pharmacy in Hapoli managed by the daughter of Padi Lailang and owned by her husband Flying Officer Kuru Hasang, a trained and licensed pharmacist from Assam is employed. Similarly a Bengali runs the photo studio because no Apa Tani has as yet the necessary qualifications. If it were not for the strict rules limiting the activities of outsiders, many shops in Hapoli would certainly have been taken over by people from outside Arunachal Pradesh, but such a development in unlikely, not only because of government rules, but also because of the watchfulness of the bazaar committees. In 1978 there were altogether three bazaar committees, one responsible for the main Hapoli bazaar, one dealing with the shops in Para Road and one known as the Ziro bazaar committee which is concerned with the shops in Old Ziro. The Hapoli bazaar committee was established in 1976 by a formal resolution of the Anchal Samithi, and in this it was laid down that this committee should manage the large covered market constructed with the help of government grants. In this market individual plots are allocated to traders who sell there such items as meat, vegetables and other perishable commodities, partly brought in trucks from North Lakhimpur. The traders rent the spaces on an annual basis and have to pay a deposit as well as a fee.

Apart from the current control of trading in the common market-shed, the bazaar committee has also enforced some political decisions. Thus it is said that the committee exerted pressure on the administration to prevent any Marwari from setting up a shop or moneylending business anywhere in the Apa Tani valley. The committee also insisted that no shop may be purchased or newly established by any outsider, a category which does not include Nishis from nearby villages. Facilities for obtaining money on credit exist even without the presence of Marwari moneylenders. Many of the traders and contractors engage also in moneylending and in 1978 the usual rate of interest was 5 per cent per month and 50 per cent per year. These rates seem high but we must take into account that most loans are given without security and are required only for short periods, mainly for the purchase of stock to be sold in shops. The interest paid by the State Bank of India on fixed deposits was 7 per cent.

In recent years the Apa Tanis of Hapoli have started a practice for which there was no precedence in traditional village life. Visitors from neighbouring Nishi or Miri villages who came to Apa Tani villages in pursuance of trade or on the occasion of such festivals as the Mloko were always put up and fed by friends or trade partners without the question of payment ever arising. Nowadays, however, numerous non-Apa Tanis come to Hapoli for the purposes of trade or because they have some business with one of the departments of the district administration or have to appear as parties or witnesses at the magistrate's court. A few may have close friends who give them free hospitality, but most of them have no such social contacts and must find accommodation elsewhere. The residents of Hapoli, in true Apa Tani style never slow to develop a new source of income, have begun to run lodging houses where visitors can stay for the night. They are not charged for accommodation but have to pay for food and drink. As a great deal of locally brewed beer is drunk in such houses the owners make good profits. Not only visitors from outside the valley but also local young people gather in such houses and spend long hours in singing, gossiping and flirting with the young women. Whereas in the old days Apa Tanis never charged for beer offered to visitors to their houses, the brewing and selling of beer has now turned into a profitable business. Rice and millet beer has for some time been sold in glass bottles of 70 decilitres, and a few years ago such *apong* was sold for 25 paisa a bottle. After some time the price was raised to 50 paisa per bottle. Then the sellers developed an allegedly superior beer which they called *hurpi* and charged Re 1 per bottle. Later they adopted the term "Number One" and charged Rs 2, and in 1978 they invented the term "Special" which they sold for Rs 3 though in fact the quality was the same as that of *hurpi*. It is said that a shop selling beer can make a monthly profit of Rs 500. Many Apa Tani girls use the brewing of beer to gain an independent income. They begin by doing some daily labour, such as for instance in the plantations of the Forest Department where they can earn Rs 5 per day. With their wages they buy rice from the government store. Rice worth Rs 2 will produce three bottles of beer, and these can be sold for Rs 3 each. Thus a modest investment of Rs 2 can quickly produce Rs 9. Such earnings enable girls and young women to buy cloth, ornaments and cosmetics, and there is no doubt that many women are now able to spend a good deal on their appearance. The Apa Tanis describe girls as well as boys who have modern tastes, are well-dressed and are somewhat allergic to hard work on the fields as *huha*. This term has a slightly derogatory flavour, but seems to be jocular rather than condemnatory. It is noteworthy that only a small minority—my Apa Tani friends suggested 1 per cent—of girls drink much themselves, even of those making beer professionally. Older women, on the other hand, who come to Hapoli to sell rice often buy some beer with the proceeds and drink it before returning home.

Distilled liquor is not freely available in Hapoli for the importation of commercially produced brands into the district is not permitted and there is not much illegal distillation. Nepali and Bihari road labourers have introduced some home-made liquor and some of the wealthier Apa Tani contractors occasionally obtain and consume rum. But on the whole Apa Tanis are content with their rice and millet beer, and distilled alcohol is neither of great social nor commercial importance.

Considering the trading pattern as it developed in the Apa Tani valley during the past 34 years one is impressed by the profound change which has taken place within the life-time of a single generation. During the same period there have been changes in the economy of other Indian tribal societies too but nowhere has to my knowledge the transformation been quite as drastic.

When I first knew the Apa Tanis their economy was in a state of almost complete equilibrium and trade relations operated within a system of well balanced interchange. The purchases of livestock, cotton and a few trade articles of Tibetan origin from Nishi and Miri neighbours were easily balanced by the regular and substantial sale of grain produced by Apa Tanis and surplus to their own requirements. Neither of the trade partners were likely ever to have to discontinue either their purchases or their deliveries, and had the region remained unaffected by outside events the traditional exchanges would probably be still continuing.

Today Apa Tani commerce can hardly be described as being in a state of equilibrium, even though the economy shows all outward signs of a boom with luxury goods such as radios and motor cars within reach of increasing numbers of tribesmen. The volume of exports of commodities produced by Apa Tanis, however, is small and one looks in vain for goods which could find a market outside the valley and of which sufficient quantities are available after the local people's needs have been satisfied. There is, as we have seen, still a limited barter trade with neighbouring Nishis, but this is rapidly diminishing. Indeed Nishis visiting the Apa Tani valley are more likely to patronize some of the shops of Hapoli and Old Ziro buying imported textiles and other consumer goods than to nego-tiate the purchase of Apa Tani rice in exchange for the mithan and pigs which they may have to offer.

As a matter of fact, the Apa Tani trade, hopelessly in deficit vis-à-vis the plains of Assam whence innumerable commodities now required by Apa Tanis are imported, is sustained mainly by the large earnings of cash dispensed by government in a variety of ways. In April 1978 no less than 342 Apa Tanis were in govern-ment employ and some of them, such as all gazetted officers, drew substantial salaries, a large proportion of which was spent locally though there were some government employees who served in other parts of the Subansiri District. Apart from all those who held per-manent posts there were many Apa Tanis who worked for daily wages in labour gangs. Together with the income of contractors all these earnings obviously balanced the large outgoings which were necessary to fill the shops of Hapoli and to enable numerous Apa Tanis to buy bicycles, motor cycles, jeeps and cars.

Educated Apa Tanis do not seem to be worried about the under-lying imbalance in the present economy of the valley—an imbalance veiled only by massive spending of government funds on the deve-lopment of the Subansiri District as one of the strategically sensi-tive areas near the Indo-Chinese border. They point to the alleged rich mineral deposits of Arunachal Pradesh, which are now the subject of intensive geological exploration, and argue that their ultimate exploitation will provide ample work for all those with a spirit of enterprise and enough flexibility to achieve a smooth transition from one economic system to another. They are strengthen-ed in their confidence in the future by their awareness that the Apa Tanis have already proved their skill as middlemen in the trade with Nishis and Miris who tend to shop in the Apa Tani valley rather than undertake the journey to North Lakhimpur and the plains of Assam.

Another example of the resourcefulness of the Apa Tanis in novel situations is the success of landless men from Hang who moved to Itanagar and there organized supplying the people of the new capital with such goods as fowls and eggs which they purchase in North Lakhimpur and sell at a handsome profit. In addition they brew beer for sale, and are so confident in their commercial prospects that some of them have sold their house sites in Hang and have moved permanently to Itanagar.

Better educated than any of their tribal neighbours the Apa Tanis can certainly expect to be for some considerable time in the forefront of the progress of the district and hence in a position to tap sources of income not so easily accessible to those lagging behind in education and commercial experience for at least one generation.

FOUR

Elements of Social Structure

COMPARED TO THE social structure of all neighbouring tribes traditional Apa Tani society was characterised by a high degree of stability, and the basic social framework has so far remained intact even in the face of great economic changes. The stability of the Apa Tanis was no doubt reinforced by a strong tribal sentiment such as exists neither among Nishis nor Miris, by the consciousness of their separateness, pride in their institutions and customs, and a passionate attachment to their small homeland turned by incessant labour into a veritable garden. Unlike his Nishi neighbour, who at any moment could sever his connection with the settlement in which he was born and seek his fortune in new surroundings without changing his life-style, the Apa Tani was tied to his valuable land and to the one valley where alone he could carry on the elaborate system of agriculture in which he was expert. Modern conditions and the availability of new sources of income have put an end to this spatial stability, and Apa Tanis have proved as mobile as any other tribesmen of Arunachal Pradesh. But in the old times even a move from one settlement to the other was rare and most Apa Tanis ended their life as members of the same village-community into which they were born.

The feeling of tribal solidarity, based on community of language and habitat, found expression in the unquestioning acceptance of certain forms of social conduct which distinguished the Apa Tanis from all their neighbours. All Apa Tanis agreed, for instance, that however strained relations between individuals or villages may be, quarrels within the tribe would have to be settled in a way altogether different from the course followed in disputes between Apa Tanis and members of other tribes, or even between two Nishi long-houses. The Apa Tanis realized that living in crowded villages of several hundred houses and concentrated in a small and densely populated area, they required the restraint of generally accepted social controls if their prosperity, based on an elaborately organized farming economy, was not to be jeopardized by the quarrels and feuds of individuals.

The cohesion of Apa Tani society was expressed in a system of ritual exchanges embracing all the seven villages of the valley. Thus the celebration of the two great seasonal festivals of Morom and Mloko involved the whole tribe even though different roles were allotted to the individual villages. Any comparable concerted activity among Nishis was unknown, even though many Nishis attended the Mloko celebrations as spectators and enjoyed the hospitality of their Apa Tani hosts.

The arrangement of the seven villages in three groups as outlined in Chapter 3 was—and still is—given expression by the alternating performances of the Mloko in a three-year cycle. Hang celebrates the feast alone, Reru, Kalung and Tajang (known under the collective name Büla) and Hari perform the rites simultaneously, and the group comprising the remaining four villages, Hija, Duta, Mudang-Tage and Michi-Bamin, also holds the Mloko in the same year. The two composite groups celebrating the Mloko simultaneously have distinctive names: Büla and Hari are called Hüte, and Hija, Duta, Mudang-Tage and Michi-Bamin are collectively known as Hüchi.

One puzzling feature of the wider structure of Apa Tani society is the fact that another alignment dividing the tribe into two groups cuts across the clusters associated with the performance of the Mloko. These two groups are referred to as *asso*, and one is known as Dübo *asso* and the other as Tin *asso*. In 1978 Dübo *asso* comprised the villages of Hari, Kalung, Duta, Mudang-Tage and Michi-Bamin, while Tin *asso* consisted of Reru, Tajang, Hija and Hang. This represented a divergence from the traditional pattern, and it was still well remembered that some 30 years earlier a dispute affecting a large section of the tribe had brought about a shift in the clustering and had thus produced the present pattern.

Normally the grouping of the villages according to *asso* has no political implications and serves only the regulation of certain ritual privileges and obligations, which in the description of the annual festival will be discussed in greater detail. Thus at the Mloko only certain ceremonial friends (*khübo ajing shedo*) from the villages of the same *asso* are invited and at the Morom celebrations members of the processions may rest only on platforms (*lapang*) of the villages of their own *asso*.

More important is the rule that disputes involving people of one *asso* may only be settled by the *buliang* of that *asso,* whereas disputes between members of two *asso* should be settled by *buliang* of both *asso*.

The story goes that until some 30 years ago part of the village of Reru, i.e. the clans Havung and Nani, belonged to the Dübo *asso,* and that two and a half clans of the village of Tajang also formed part of the Dübo *asso*. Yet, in a year when Hang village was celebrating the Mloko two men from Tajang, namely Rade Kane and Rade Talang were returning from a drinking party in Hang. On the way Rade Kane was ambushed and captured by Koj Nich of Duta who had some private grievance against him ; but he extricated himself and took shelter in the house of Tage Dolo in Mudang-Tage. Dolo protected him and sent him safely home to Tajang. Rade Kane, on the other hand, suspected his kinsman Rade Talang of having betrayed him to Koj Nich and charged him with disloyalty. Talang denied any involvement and as he was innocent he went to Duta, and damaged a bamboo-grove belonging to Koj Magang, a kinsman of Koj Nich. Koj Magang organized in protest a *dapo* demonstration (see Chapter 6) directed against Rade Talang, and the latter retaliated by organizing a similar procession against Koj Magang. When the two processions met in a third village they started a verbal battle, in the course of which Chigi Nime, a famous priest and leader of Duta, taunted the people of Tajang and Reru, saying that they were not "pure" and dependable because they were divided between two *asso*. Chanting in the manner of priests he likened the two villages to rice-ears bearing white and black grains, and thereby offended even those people of the two villages who were not involved in the quarrel. Padi Lailang, the leading *buliang* of Reru then persuaded Reru and Tajang to put an end to their internal divisions and join as united villages the Tin *asso*. This meant that the clans previously aligned with the Dübo *asso,* and hence with Duta, had to change their allegiance. Hence all parts of Reru and Tajang are now aligned with the Tin *asso*, and Chigi Nime's intemperate insult proved counterproductive as it led to the loss of some of Duta's ceremonial allies.

The above account is certainly not a complete explanation of the realignment of *asso*, and it is likely that animosity between Duta and Hija, which belong to different *asso* although they are neighbours and celebrate the Mloko simultaneously, dates from much earlier events. It flared up in 1947, as described by Ursula Graham-Bower in *The Hidden Land* (pp. 210-34), and there is a story, too long and involved to relate here, which refers to a dispute between Hija and Duta resulting in their alignment on opposite sides of the *asso*-division.

The Apa Tanis of the present generation are themselves confused about the origin of *asso*, but most of them think that the *asso* grouping does not go back to the immigration of the Apa Tanis into the Valley; they attribute it to later events of which they have no clear conception. In this respect their views contradict the tradition reported by Ursula Graham-Bower, according to which the villages of the Dübo group were founded by late-comers who had settled in the Apa Tani Valley after the main body of the tribe. Such contradictions are frequent in legendary history based on oral tradition, but whatever the true origin of the *asso* may have been today these groups are accepted at their face value as determinants of ritual relations.

The fact that in the recent and well-remembered past Reru and Tajang were divided between the two *asso* demonstrates that an Apa Tani village is not a monolithic unit, but consists of a number of elements each of which has a distinct identity. Each village (*lemba*) comprises a number of quarters inhabited by specific clans. The focal point and ritual centre of such a quarter is a small isolated hut known as *nago* which serves as a kind of shrine where important rites are performed and in past years trophies of war, such as the hands of slain foes, were kept until their disposal. The *nago* used by a group of clans lends these clans a certain unity, and the *nago* is usually named after the most prominent clan of the group.

While two or more clans share one *nago*, most clans have yet another focal point of social activities in the shape of a large open sitting platform (*lapang*). On this the men of the clan gather for gossip and work, as well as for the performance of rituals. Occasionally two or three closely allied clans may jointly own one *lapang*, while very populous clans may possess more than one such sitting platform. Many groups sharing one *nago* and possibly one *lapang* comprise both patrician (*guth*) and commoner (*guchi*) clans. Later in this chapter we will discuss the relations between patricians, commoners and the slaves of former years in greater detail. But in this context we have to consider the problem of the naming of *lapang* which are sometimes referred to by the name of a *guchi* clan although numerous patricians may be residing in the ward of which the *lapang* is the social centre. Such a situation has occurred in the village of Hija. One of the five *nago* of this village is known as Puna *nago*, and the three *lapang* associated with this *nago* are the Puna *lapang,* Haj *lapang* and Dani *lapang.* Haj and Dani are patrician clans, but the only members of the Puna clan are of *guchi* status, and these Puna *guchi* are the ritual dependants of the Haj clan. How can we explain that the *nago* is named after the only *guchi* clan though it is used also by the two patrician clans Haj and Dani? The only plausible explanation is the assumption that there was in the past a patrician Puna clan whose members owned slaves named, as it was then customary, after their masters. Some of these slaves may have been freed and the present Puna *guchi* must be their descendants. The patrician Puna families will have become extinct in the male line, with the result that the Puna *guchi* were the only representatives of the Puna clan left. After their Puna patrons' extinction the remaining Puna *guchi* may have attached themselves to the Haj patricians who had presumbly close kinship relations with the patrician Puna families. Similarly there was a patrician Nemp clan in Hija, and this became extinct without even leaving any *guchi* of the same name. There is still a Nemp *lapang* but this is no longer used for ritual purposes, but only serves the people of the nearby house as a convenient sitting-platform.

In traditional Apa Tani society every man had a strong feeling of solidarity with his village, and while women might have married into other villages, it was extremely rare for a patrician to leave the village of his birth and settle elsewhere. This attachment to the natal village has certainly diminished under the influence of recent economic developments, and there are now numerous Apa Tanis who left their homes and settled elsewhere, be it in colonies inside the valley or in distant areas. But even they usually maintain links with their original villages, and we have seen that colonists in the plains of Assam, such as in Seajuli and Kakoi, return to their home villages on the occasion of seasonal feasts.

In what respects does a village function as a social unit? The most obvious expression of its unity is the simultaneous celebration of the principal feasts and the observance of certain taboos (*anyodo*) compulsory for all inhabitants. Though some villages own communal forest and pastures, boundary disputes involving entire villages are rare. However, in the early 1940 Hang and Michi-Bamin quarrelled over a piece of land on which thatching grass grew. Michi-Bamin resisted the encroachment of the much larger Hang village, and was supported by several other villages. There were also cases when disputes between individuals were taken up by their respective village-communities and two or more villages formally opposed each other in a prearranged armed contest (*gambu*). In such an event the village clearly functioned as a political unit (see Chapter 6), but there were other occasions when only one ward of a village and the clans it contained were at variance with some or all of the clans of another village. Extreme examples of the lack of village-unity were provided by cases when one ward had a feud with a Nishi village involving killings and kidnappings on both sides while people in other wards continued their trade-relations with enemies of their co-villagers.

In modern days there are no more such war-like involvements testing the unity of a village, but we shall see that two neighbouring villages recently engaged in an armed contest over the name to be given to a new school (see Chapter 6).

Apa Tani villages never had chiefs or headmen wielding authority over the entire community, but the affairs of the community were run by an informal council of clan-representatives known as *buliang*. The role of these *buliang* will be discussed in Chapter 6, and here it is sufficient to state that although the *buliang* used to guide and formulate public opinion there was never any regular machinery to organize concerted action by all the inhabitants of a village except in ritual matters which were by definition uncontroversial. This was a source of weakness in the Apa Tanis' dealings with their warlike Nishi neighbours none of whom would have stood up to the forces a united Apa Tani village could have put in the field.

While an Apa Tani village pursued only seldom a common course of action, the clans associated with one and the same *nago* usually supported each other in dealings with outsiders, and the fact that all the households of Duta, with a population of 605 in 1971, looked upon one *nago* as their common ritual centre was mentioned to me as the reason for the high degree of solidarity evinced by the men of Duta on many recent occasions.

The one unit which could always be relied on to act in complete unison was the clan (*halu*), and in this respect the Apa Tani clan differs radically from the Nishi clans whose members were not bound by any sense of mutual loyalty and were not even debarred from raiding each other. Among the Apa Tanis, however, the clan has always been a very real social unit whose members were bound to each other by definite obligations of mutual help. Apa Tani clans are patrilineal and in principle they are exogamous. Many clans, and particularly those of modest size, have remained exogamous units and sexual relations between the members of such clans are strictly forbidden. Clans which have greatly increased in size, however, evince a tendency to fission, and emerging lineages no longer able to trace in detail their common ancestry may cease to regard unions between their members as incestuous. The splitting up of a clan into two or more lineages is symbolized by the establishment of separate ritual clan-centres (*yugyang*), and in order to understand this process we have to anticipate the description of the rites at the Mloko festival. On that occasion the members of a clan sacrifice pigs at a place inside their clan-ward where a plum-tree (*thakum*) has been planted. This place is called *yugyang*, and all those who share this cult-centre and may partake of the blood of the same sacrificial pigs are considered of the same close kingroup and may not intermarry. Many clans have only one *yugyang* and consequently remain exogamous.

If a clan increases in size and one *yugyang* cannot accommodate all the worshippers and sacrificial pigs, one branch will establish a new *yugyang*, and to do this a shoot from the plum-tree of the original *yugyang* will be planted there and a little earth from the old clan-centre taken to the new *yugyang*. As soon as this ritual separation has been affected the two branches of the clan are considered distinct units whose members can intermarry.

An example is provided by the Hage clan of Hari village. This clan is now divided into three sub-clans (*tulu*) and though all acknowledge descent from the same ancestor these *tulu* have separate names, i.e. Lako, Tai Gyati and Ekha, which are derived from the names of their respective forefathers. Until the Mloko in 1975 they shared one *yugyang*, but in 1978 two new *yugyang* were established, and the pig sacrifices took place in these three separate places. The members of the three *tulu* all still use the clan name Hage, but there is intermarriage between the three *tulu* and thus there are cases of Hage men marrying Hage girls. The members of a newly separated *tulu* may also build a *lapang* of their own, but this does not necessarily follow the fission of a clan. In the village of Hija, for instance, there are three *tulu* of the important Nada clan, but they do not intermarry and form one exogamous unit. Even more confusingly there are several pairs of "brother-clans" which have different names and separate *lapang* and *yugyang* but nevertheless do *not* intermarry. Padi and Havung and similarly Kuru and Nenkre, all of Reru village, are examples of such "brother-clans." Regarding Kuru and Nenkre, which share the blood of sacrificial pigs even though they have different *yugyang* and different *lapang*, I was told that in 1978 there were several known love-affairs between members of these two "brother-clans", and my informants foresaw that some of these affairs might mature into marriage. They thought that if such marital unions occurred the two groups Kuru and Nenkre would cease sharing the blood and hearts of pigs sacrificed during the Mloko, and that the fraternal ties between the two clans would be broken.

In Hang village the important Ponyo clan is also divided into several *tulu*. The richest and most influential man in the 1940s Ponyo Tamar, mentioned in various context in my *Himalayan Barbary* (pp. 70, 74-78), was a member of Layang *tulu* so called after its ancestor Layang. In 1978 it comprised 17 *guth* and 13 *guchi* households. Another *tulu* is called Kra *tulu* after Kra, son of Halyang the elder brother of Layang, and this consisted of eight *guth* and one *guchi* households. The members of this *tulu* were not healthy, but the *guth* families had enough land to subsist on the yield, while one *guchi* family had only sufficient crops of their own to last them for half the year. The third *tulu* known as Gyati *tulu* comprised ten *guth* and two *guchi* households. They were not rich but all except one *guth* family had enough land to meet their needs. Pali *tulu*, so called after Pali, a brother of Halyang and Layang, consisted of ten households, all *guth*; eight of them had sufficient land for their need, but the fields of two households yielded only enough rice to feed them for six months. One landless member of that *tulu* had moved to Itanagar where he worked in the employ of government as gang-leader. All *tulu* here listed shared one *yugyang* and formed one exogamous unit. Two other *tulu* of the Ponyo *halu*, named Ekhin *tulu* with 11 *guth* and nine *guchi* houses and Takhe *tulu* with nine *guth* and one *guchi* houses had a separate *yugyang*, and could intermarry with the other *tulu* but not with each other.

Apart from the subdivisions of a *halu* known as *tulu*, there are even smaller sections comprised within a *tulu* and these are known as *uru*. An *uru* is a sub-lineage traceable to one grandfather or greatgrandfather and referred to by the name of such a known ancestor. Within the Hage clan of Hari, for instance, there are not only the *tulu* Lako, Ekha and Tai Gyati, but within Lako *tulu* there are several *uru*, one of which is called Taman-Tarang after the ancestors of the sub-lineage.

There are in most villages also clans of very small size and these are without subdivisions into *tulu* and *uru*. The size of a clan in terms of membership does in no way effect its status. Thus the Mudo clan of Hari is believed to be the oldest in the village, and there is the tradition that from its *lapang* known as Dohang *lapang*, all others spread out. *Ropi* rites (see Chapter 7) which marked the killing of an enemy or of a tiger, are said to have always been performed at this oldest of all *lapang* of Hari.

The rank of clans and subclans has nowadays no real function. In the village of Hija, for instance, the Dimpa and Plagang *tulu* of the Nada clan claim to be of higher statuts than others but this reputation is not expressed in any concrete privileges. In 1944 I was told that two clans of Hang, Tenio and Tablin, neither of which comprised more than ten households, were considered senior to all other *halu*, because they were directly descended from the two eldest sons of the legendary forefathers of all the Hang people, known as Ato Tiling. Originally these two clans were "brother-clans", but they later decided to permit intermarriage, and they also agreed that in the event of either clan becoming extinct the other should inherit the other clan's land. At that time it was also said that because of the high status of these two clans their members would speak first in assemblies and their views would be accorded special weight. In 1978, however, my informants were unaware of such a custom, and denied the existence of any privileges enjoyed by the members of senior clans.

Apa Tani society has never been noted for extensive occupational specialization, and no clan has any monopoly on specific tasks. The nearest to a clan-based specialization is the manufacture of pots by the women of four *guchi* clans of Michi-Bamin. Women of other villages who married men of these potter clans could, if they liked learn pot-making. Today, pot-making has declined in importance, because of the prevalence of iron pots. It has moreover, never been an attractive occupation, for potters used to suffer from some social discrimination, not unlike that to which the *kümar*, the castrators of pigs are subject.

Another occupational specialization was that of a few families of professional iron-workers. In 1945 there were three blacksmiths in Reru village. One was of a *guchi* clan then described to me as a "proper" blacksmith clan whereas the other two were of *guth* status, and had learnt the craft from the same man, a patrician, who was the father of one of the two patrician blacksmiths. While anyone could learn and practice iron-working, the occupation lowered a man's status, even though he was not excluded from religious rites and other people could eat in his house. But his workshop, a simple shed, had to be some distance from the village, because the craft is fraught with magical dangers and there is the fear that certain deities would be offended if iron were to be worked close to the sites of religious performances.

In 1978 there was no blacksmith still actively engaged in his craft, but I was told of two men, one of Hari and one of Kalung, who had been engaged in metal-working but had given it up. Commercially produced implements and utensils available in the shops of Hapoli had undoubtedly replaced the wares of Apa Tani blacksmiths. Interesting features of the blacksmith's traditional equipment were bellows made not of skins but of wild-banana leaves, which lasted for about a month. The bellow-pots were of wood, and the tubes of bamboo.

While there was only a mild prejudice against blacksmiths, there is one occupation, still practised, which renderes the practitioners ritually impure. This occupation is the castrating of pigs, and the persons performing the operation are known as *kümar*. Only women act as *kümar*, and there used to be a *guchi* clan in Hija whose women traditionally engaged in this profession. When this clan became extinct women of the Tage *guchi* clan of Reru took up the work, and were still doing it in 1978. A *kümar* is debarred from participation in feasts and religious rites, and may not enter anyone's dwelling house. Her customers supply her with ample food, and though she may give some of it away to poor people, no one may eat cooked food in her house. It is not customary for a *kümar* to marry, but a poor man may go and live with such a woman though by doing so he becomes subject to the same disabilities. The children from such a union follow the mother's clan, and one of her daughters will take up her profession. The others can be purified and count then as ordinary *guchi*. A *kümar's* husband too can regain his normal ritual status after his wife's death.

Hierarchic Divisions: Patricians and Commoners

Besides the vertical division of Apa Tani society into villages (*lemba*), wards centred on a *nago*, clans (*halu*), sub-clans (*tulu*) and kin clusters (*uru*), there is the horizontal division into two endogamous classes known as *guth* and *guchi*, two terms which may be translated as patricians and plebeians or commoners, though neither of these designations is entirely apt. In previous publications I used the terms *mite*, which roughly equals *guth*, and *mura* as the equivalent of *guchi*. Educated Apa Tanis, who have learnt more sophisticated definitions than my informants of 1944 were capable of, have objected to the general use of the terms *mite* and *mura*. They pointed out that the term *mura* was being used only for a slave actually in the possession of a master, and not for all persons of slave-descent, and that *mite* meant strictly speaking owner or master of slaves. It is difficult to judge whether the present definition of these terms invalidates their use in regard to past conditions, but as then too the terms *guth* and *guchi* were current among Apa Tanis I have generally adopted the use of these two terms.

The division between *guth* and *guchi* is considered unalterable and so far neither wealth nor education and political success have enabled a *guchi* to rise to the status of *guth* except in rare cases of persons of mixed parentage. According to Apa Tani tradition, all *guchi* were originally the slaves of patricians, but even in the society such as I knew in the 1940s there was a large class of *guchi* who had been free for generations. Even then the distinction between patricians and commoners was not overtly noticeable for there were some wealthy *guchi*, who had gained prominence through the fairly newly established trade with the plains of Assam. Yet, the innate superiority of the patricians was never questioned, and every *guchi* stood in a relationship of dependence to a patrician family which involved certain obligations of a ceremonial nature.

The origin of the Apa Tanis' division into two classes of unequal status is obscure and conditions among the neighbouring Nishis and Miris do not provide any lead for the elucidation of the problem. Among these tribes we also find a grouping of clans into two classes known as *guth* and *guchi*, but free men as well as slaves can belong to either class. Moreover, Nishi and Miri slaves did not form a class of their own but becoming a slave was an incident of fate, and in no way an immutable condition. Any Nishi, of however prominent a family, could lose his freedom when captured by enemies and subsequently sold as a slave. Conversely a slave or a man born as the son of a slave could gradually improve his position and gain not only economic independence but also a social status equal to that of a free born man. This system is hence not comparable to the more static hierarchical division of Apa Tani society which excludes any mobility between the two classes.

We cannot rule out the possibility that the *guth* and *guchi* represent two different though largely assimilated ethnic elements, and there is no doubt that all foreign slaves ever acquired by Apa Tanis have been absorbed only into the *guchi* class. In 1944 I had gained the impression that there was a difference in physical type between the Apa Tanis of patrician class and the average *guchi*. This can probably be explained by the fact that the *guth* class had preserved the original Apa Tani type in much greater purity than the *guchi* did, for the latter were intermixed with many Nishis who as slaves were forcibly encompassed within Apa Tani society.

In the Apa Tani valley the institution of slavery, which used to be prevalent among many of the hill-tribes of Northeast India, had reached a higher degree of development than anywhere else. As I was able to observe this system in action before there was any interference on the part of the administration, it seems justified to describe in some detail its operation in the traditional society as well as the present position of the previous slaves and commoners.

In 1944 and 1945 there were a good many men and women, either of indigenous *guchi* class or aliens purchased or captured in war, who were the absolute property of their masters. A slave living in his master's house and dependent on him for every necessity of life, had in theory no rights whatsoever. He had to carry out his master's orders without questioning their reasonableness, he could be sold at any moment without being consulted, and if his unruliness or criminal tendencies made him a liability, his owner was free to kill him. Yet, the average slave's daily life did not reflect this insecure position. He was assured of food and shelter, shared his owner's house and meals, was provided with clothes only slightly inferior to those ordinarily worn by his master, and was addressed by the kinship terms appropriate to his age, such as *ato* (grandfather), *ate* (elder brother), or *anu* (younger brother). Nothing in his appearance or demeanour stamped him as a slave. The work he had to do was essentially the same as that of free men with the difference that even middle-aged slaves were supposed to do such strenuous physical work as wood cutting and the carrying of heavy loads of wood whereas free men used to do such tasks only when they were young. In 1978 when there were no more slaves some prominent elderly men of Hang, sons of the famous and extremely rich Ponyo Tamar, told me sadly that because of the freeing of their slaves, they had now to carry their firewood themselves, a task they clearly thought unsuited to men of their status.

In the old days a slave's position depended to some extent on the manner in which he or she was acquired, and there were various ways in which a man, woman or child could become the property of another person. Many wealthy Apa Tanis of patrician class inherited a number of slaves, some of whom might have been members of families associated with their masters for generations. Such slaves bore their masters' clan-name and were unaware of another clan-name by which their forefathers may have been known. They had either grown up in their master's house or might have started life in a separate nearby house allotted to their parents.

A young slave living in his owner's household used to work alongside the latter's own sons and daughters in the fields, and like all young Apa Tanis he was a member of a *patang* consisting of boys and girls of similar age, both *guth* and *guchi*. The slave's owner had the same right to the gang's labour as the parents of the other gang-members. When a young slave grew up he was at liberty to form amatory associations with girls of his own *patang* as well as with other unmarried girls of the village. In such love affairs the rules of clan-exogamy had to be observed, and this prevented flirtations between a young slave and his master's daughters whom he regarded and addressed as sisters. No offence was caused, however, if a slave won the favours of a patrician girl, even in the event of her becoming pregnant. But marriage across class divisions was inadmissable, and a slave had to find his wife among the daughters of other slaves or free girls of *guchi* class. If a marriage between two slaves was arranged with the consent of the owners of both groom and bride, the former's master was expected to pay to the girl's owner the full price for a young female slave, say one mithan, one cow and one *dao*, and such a payment would entitle him to all the children of the couple. If, on the other hand, there was no proper arrangement and the male slave's master paid but a small price, then only the sons resulting from the marriage belonged to him, and the daughters to the woman's former owner. If no price was paid all the children became the property of the wife's owner. Similarly the child of an unmarried slave girl living in her master's house belonged to him and took his clan-name. An exception to this rule was made only in the event of the girl's lover being a patrician claiming the offspring as his child.

No free man of *guchi* status was likely to arrange or favour the marriage of a daughter to a slave still living in his master's house. Such unions nevertheless occurred as the result of love affairs which the young people were not willing to break off. But a free *guchi* girl marrying a domestic slave became herself a slave and the property of her husband's owner. In theory she could even be sold together with her husband. A slave girl marrying a free *guchi*, on the other hand, gained her freedom, provided her husband paid her owner her full price. In 1944 when slavery was still a universal practice, I was told that the master of a slave girl could not prevent her from going to live with the man of her choice, even though he would thereby lose her labour. He could demand her price, but could not enforce payment. Yet, if no price was paid, he retained the right to any children resulting from the marriage.

It would seem that masters allowed their slaves some freedom in arranging their marriages, and that once married slave-couples enjoyed reasonable privacy. As soon as such a couple had one or two children, and sometimes even before the birth of a child, the husband's master usually gave him a house-site and helped him to establish a household of his own. Slaves living in houses of their own were known as *penam mura* ("separated slaves"), and there was a sliding scale in the degree of dependence between such slaves and their owners. Some *penam mura* were given only a house-site and a piece of garden, and continued to work almost every day for their master, who in turn provided them with their requirements of grain and clothes. But other separated slaves were given some rice-fields as well as dry land, and the yield of such land was theirs. Those who were industrious and enterprising could even acquire some additional property. Unless such a separated slave committed a grave offence or refused consistently to do any work for his master, public opinion would condemn any attempt of his master to take back the land the slave had been given. Nor could the master's heirs contest the *penam mura's* right to the land, which would be inherited by his sons. There can be little doubt that many free *guchi* families, if not the majority of *guchi*, are descended from separated slaves.

The children of slaves living in their own houses usually remained with the parents but had still an obligation to work for their parents' masters if called upon. In the event of their being orphaned, such slave-children were taken into their master's house and cared for like any other members of the household. They automatically resumed the status of ordinary slaves subject to the possibility of being sold irrespective of their late parents' status of "separated" slaves.

Not every slave was necessarily separated and provided with a house of his own. Men of little initiative who were not likely to make a success of an establishment of their own, often remained all their lives in their master's house. In 1944 I also met some sons of "separated" slaves who of their own free will had gone to live in the house of their master although they retained the ownership of the land given to their fathers.

Slaves inherited by their owners and hence regarded almost like family retainers formed only part of the slave population of the Apa Tani valley. In the 1940s there were many whom their owners had either captured in war or bought locally or from Nishis, and many of these were not of Apa Tani stock. I was then not in a position to compile a census of the slave population, but judging from the composition of a limited number of households I came to the conclusion that about half of the number of slaves living in their owners' houses had been purchased within their own life time. Many of such slaves had been bought from Nishis who had captured other Nishis in the course of raids and sold into slavery such prisoners as had not been ransomed by their kinsmen. Apa Tanis were less likely to sell slaves, but there were occasions when the sale of a slave was the quickest way of obtaining mithan required either for sacrifice in case of illness or for the payment of a ransom for a kinsman held captive by Nishis. In the 1940s a young slave of either sex fetched a price of up to three mithan, but a middle aged slave would change hands for as little as one mithan and one cow.

Relations between masters and slaves were usually cordial, but if a slave gave trouble or was excessively slack in his work, the owner would try to sell him or her. A slave could embarrass his master in various ways. Owners were held responsible for their slaves' conduct, and if a slave was repeatedly caught stealing, his master would do his best to rid himself of the nuisance. As no Apa Tani would buy a slave of whose criminal tendencies he was aware, there remained only the possibility of selling such a slave to a distant Nishi village unfamiliar with his anticedents. If this device did not succeed the owner had no other choice than to cut his losses and expel the unruly slave or even initiate punitive action which in extreme cases led to the culprit's execution.

While the selling and buying within the Apa Tani community was a common practice, public opinion did not approve of the selling of Apa Tanis to people of other communities. The right of an owner to dispose of a slave in any way he chose was not contested, but it was considered rather inconsiderate to sell a fellow tribesman, even if he was a slave, to Nishis or Miris. This prejudice against such sales did not apply to slaves of Nishi stock who had initially been acquired by capture or by purchases from a neigbouring tribe. In 1944 and 1945 I heard about a number of such sales of Nishi slaves, but of only one case of an Apa Tani being sold to Nishis. The slave concerned was an orphan boy whose thievish habits had caused his master a great deal of trouble, and who was finally sold to a Nishi of Mai, a village less than a day's walk south of the Apa Tani Valley.

The prejudice against selling slaves to persons outside the tribe was not shared by Nishis who lacked the community feeling of the Apa Tanis. Hence the latter were able to purchase numerous slaves from Nishis. Many of them were children who could be easily assimilated: they were dressed as Apa Tanis, spoke soon only Apa Tani, and usually married Apa Tanis of *guchi* class. As they bore their masters' clan-names they did not appear as strangers even to other villagers, and for this reason it was difficult to estimate their numbers. Some of them had come from distant villages on the upper course of the Khru river, and had been traded down by Nishis of villages nearer to the Apa Tani valley such as Licha. Apa Tani preferred to buy Nishi slaves from distant villages, for they were less likely to escape and there was little probability of their being traced by their kinsmen.

Slaves who had been acquired by inheritance, purchase or capture were not the only persons who might become available for purchase. Some Apa Tanis of *guchi* class, although born free, were sold by their own kinsmen. Thus there was in Hija a girl of Mudang-Tage whom her own brother had sold for four mithan when he was short of grain, and the status of such people was equal to that of other slaves. They lost their clan name and all rights to inherit from free members of their family. It was one of the differences between *guchi* and *guth* that patricians would never sell their own kinsmen however precarious their economic position.

An Apa Tani of *guchi* class could lose his freedom also on account of his inability to repay a debt. If a man borrowed rice or any other commodity, and failed to repay it within a reasonable time his creditor was entitled to attach his person and make him work as a bond-servant until the debt was repaid. During that period the debtor could earn wages by extra work for other men and was even allowed to go to work in the plains of Assam, and on his return clear his debt by selling the goods or the cattle bought there with his earnings. But if several years passed and the debt remained unpaid, his position turned gradually into that of a slave, and if he caused his creditor any trouble he even ran the risk of being sold.

This system of bond-service was the cause of a great deal of friction between Apa Tanis and Nishis. Normally Apa Tanis bartered rice for mithan which their Nishi customers brought with them or delivered as soon as they had carried the rice to their village. Occasionally, however, Apa Tanis sold their surplus rice to needy Nishis on credit, and possibly even in the expectation that their customers would be unable to pay for the rice, and would sooner or later be forced or persuaded to become their bond-servants. The mechanism of such transactions and their hazardous nature can be seen from the following examples:

(1) In the early 1940s Tajo Tanya of Licha borrowed rice from Dani Tana of Hija, saying that when he received the brideprice for his sister he would pay for the rice in mithan. But his elder brother disposed of the girl and withheld the share of the brideprice which should have gone to Tanya. The two brothers quar-

relled and Tanya left Licha and came to Hija saying he would pay his debt if and when he succeeded in recovering the part of the brideprice to which he was entitled. In the meantime he lived in the house of Dani Tana of Hija and worked for him as a servant.

(2) Lishi Tamo, a Nishi of Licha, came to Hija and stayed for one year in the house of an Apa Tani friend. During that time he purchased rice on credit from Haj Kacho. When he failed to pay for the rice, his creditor seized him and kept him tied up in his house. Haj Kojing mediated and released the Nishi by paying his creditor one bullock, one brass plate and one Tibetan sword on the understanding that Lishi Tamo would work for him as an unpaid servant until he had repaid the value of the ransom. But soon afterwards Lishi Tamo fled to Licha and Haj Kojing was left with an unenforceable claim against a Nishi beyond the reach of Apa Tani justice.

(3) Padi Lailang, one of the most prominent Apa Tanis of Reru, sold large quantities of rice to a Nishi of Pemir. When the latter died, leaving one son but no property, Padi Lailang took possession of the boy in compensation for his claim. The boy, however, did not take to life among Apa Tanis, and begged Padi Lailang to sell him to Nishis and take the price in clearance of his father's debt. Lailang agreed to this proposal and sold the boy to a Nishi of Licha for one female mithan with calf, one cloth and one pig. The buyer protracted the payment and when within a year the slave boy succumbed to an illness, he refused to honour his obligation.

The rule that a creditor may seize a defaulting debtor and make him work in his house applied in theory to Apa Tanis and Nishis, patricians and *guchi* alike. But in practice a patrician never served his creditor as a bond-servant. For all his kinsmen and even the members of his clan would subscribe to his ransom rather than suffer the disgrace of having their relative deprived of his freedom and kept like a slave.

Many of the Nishi slaves owned by Apa Tanis in the 1940s had been captured in raids either by Apa Tanis or by other Nishis who had then sold them to Apa Tanis. When Apa Tanis raided a village and took prisoners they usually held them to ransom. If no offers by kinsmen were forthcoming or the offered ransom was too small they sold the captives as slaves either among themselves or to neighbouring Nishis.

When in 1943 Apa Tanis of Hija and Duta raided the Nishi village of Linia they captured the two wives of a Nishi and his ten year old son. The two women were subsequently ransomed, but not the boy. The captor sold him for two mithan to an Apa Tani of Hija.

During a long drawn out feud between the Apa Tanis of Reru and the Nishi village of Dodum, the latter was raided twice in short succession. In the first raid ten Nishi women and ten children were captured and taken to Reru, but one of the Apa Tani attackers was hit by a poisoned arrow and later died. In revenge the two wives and the small son of the Dodum man who had shot the Apa Tani were killed in cold blood. Two boys and four adult women were released on receipt of ransom, but all the other captives were sold to various Nishi villages.

In the second raid ten women and ten small boys were captured. Three of the boys were ransomed, but all the other captives were sold, the women to the Nishi villages of Mai and Pochu, and the boys to Apa Tanis.

Apa Tanis never raided each other, and hence no Apa Tani prisoners were ever kept as slaves. Nor were in the years 1944 and 1945 any Apa Tani captives living in Nishi or Miri houses in the position of sales. Such Apa Tanis as at times had been captured by Nishis were usually kept in stocks and finally ransomed after protracted negotiations. The ransoms paid often exceeded the market price of a salve.

Thus a slave girl of Nishi origin brought up as an Apa Tani in the house of Padi Lailang of Reru, was captured by Nishis of Licha and kept in stocks for three months. Ultimately Padi Lailang ransomed her by paying: three female mithan, three mithan calves, four Tibetan bells, four bronze plates, four Tibetan swords, two Assamese silk cloths and 16 lbs of salt. This was far more than the market price of any slave and the payment of so extravagant a ransom is clear proof of the responsibility Apa Tanis felt towards their slaves.

The patron-client link between master and slave was by no means a relationship which one-sidedly benefited the patron. A patrician felt obliged to help his "separated" slaves and dependant *guchi* in times of need with loans of grain and to afford them protection for their persons and property. Such protection was of vital importance in a society where the individual can expect little protection from any institutional authority, particularly in the event of a free *guchi* or a slave falling into the hands of Nishi raiders.

Cases of Apa Tani slaves running away from their masters were rare, and this may have been due to the fact that the treatment of Apa Tani slaves was generally good and slaves were no less attached to their homeland than other Apa Tanis. The valley is so small that an escaped slave could not have hidden in another Apa Tani village and would have had to flee to a Nishi or Miri village to be sure of avoiding recapture. But to most Apa Tanis life among Nishis or Miris was not an attractive prospect. I heard of only one Apa Tani slave who escaped and successfully settled in a Nishi village, and this was a girl married to a Nishi slave. She and her husband absconded together and found refuge among the man's kinsmen.

The principle that a domestic slave would count as a member of his master's clan was not applied to Nishi captives. These were known by their own Nishi clan-name, and only their children, growing up in the Apa Tani owner's house were integrated into Apa Tani society and known by the master's clan-name. While slaves were not excluded from the general fairly promiscuous sex relations of the village youth, an Apa Tani slave owner was not supposed to have sexual intercourse with his own female slaves, who strictly speaking counted as members of his clan. Nevertheless, there were some cases of patricians keeping a slave girl as their mistress, and any child from such a union would inherit the father's clan-name though normally not his *guth* status. A son from a slave mother might have become the founder of a new *guchi* branch of his patrician father's clan.

In 1944 I met several Nishi slaves who expressed a strong sense of loyalty towards their Apa Tani masters, and indeed seemed proud to be the dependants of men of wealth and prestige to whose influence they owed various material benefits.

Even previous to the extension of Indian administrative control over the Tani valley dozens of slaves used to go year after year to the plains of Assam where they worked for wages and with the money earned bought trade goods. Almost without exception they returned to their masters even though they must have realized that the latter would not have been able to assert their right of ownership as long as a slave remained in a region under British administration.

In the hills slavery had prevailed because there the government of British India had not exerted any administrative control, and when India attained Independence this state of affairs continued for a number of years. The new administration, though determined to establish ultimately full control over the whole of the North East Frontier Agency, adopted a policy of gradual penetration and wisely avoided any abrupt changes which would have alienated the tribesmen and disrupted the social fabric. Though domestic slavery was disapproved of in principle, its abolition was not accorded high priority, and the gradual liberation of slaves was effected rather by persuasion than by compulsion. When the ground had been prepared by propaganda administrative action was taken in the middle 1960s. The government declared itself willing to compensate the owners of slaves for the loss of their workers, and the average compensation was Rs 500 for an adult slave, with proportionate sums paid to the owners of slave children to be set free.

Although I had no opportunity to observe the actual process of this liberation of the Apa Tanis' slaves, in conversation with former slave-owners I gained the impression that very little friction and ill-feeling were caused by the action of government. Some rich men such as Padi Lailang of Reru received very considerable sums in compensation, and invested them successfully in various business ventures. The position of the freed slaves was very similar to that of the "separated slaves" of former times, and many of them continued to work voluntarily for their former masters though now for wages. The liberation of slaves came at a time when there were many opportunities to earn wages by work in government construction projects, and hence those slaves who wanted to sever their economic ties with their masters experienced no difficulty in maintaining themselves and their families by wage labour. The only obligation towards their former owners which remained and indeed is still being honoured is the ceremonial gift of the head of every animal slaughtered or killed in the chase to the previous master or to a member of his family. But this obligation is observed also by free *guchi* who are traditionally used to present their patrician patrons with the heads of the animals they kill, and ex-slaves do not find it demeaning to follow the same practice.

Whereas those of the former slaves who were members of old

established *guchi* clans and considered themselves entirely as Apa
Tanis remained in the villages in which they had been living, most of
the Nishi slaves seem to have left the Apa Tani valley, and returned to their original home villages. However, in 1978 I did hear of
one Nishi ex-slave married to an Apa Tani woman who had settled
in Hang, and there may be other cases of Nishis who sought integration into Apa Tani society.

The relations between patricians (*guth*) and commoners (*guchi*)
have undergone a considerable change. There is as yet no blurring
of the class distinctions and patricians are conscious of their superior
status while *guchi* do not deny that there remains a difference
between the two classes. Yet, not all *guth* evince the same attitude
towards *guchi*. I have met young educated patricians who spoke
about the unsurmountable barrier between them and *guchi*, and said
that they could not imagine marrying *guchi* girls. One of them explained that *guchi* had an innate sense of inferiority and did not
feel completely relaxed in the presence of patricians. He had studied
in Delhi and there he had met African students who felt uncomfort-
able among Indians, and he compared the uneasiness of *guchi* in
the company of *guth* with the inferiority complex of such African
students. Such views were by no means universal among educated
patricians, and others played down the difference between the social
classes. They argued that Apa Tanis should strengthen tribal solidarity by encouraging social contacts across class lines, and should
give up their prejudice against marriages between patricians and
commoners. By 1978 there were about ten to twelve such marital
unions. This is not a large number in a population of over 15,000,
but is nevertheless indicative of a gradual lowering of class barriers.
So far such marriages cannot be concluded with full rites involving
the participation of the kinsmen of both sides, and the couples face
some difficulties in the conduct of social relations. The *guth* partners
in such unions, who are usually the men, suffer under some discrimination, because at the great festivals and particularly the Mloko
they cannot sacrifice their pigs at the *yugyang* of their *guth* kinsmen,
but must join the rites of the *guchi* members of their clan. As mixed
marriages are a new phenomenon, there is as yet no definite rule
about the status of the children, though conservative Apa Tanis
maintain that they will be considered as *guchi*.

Unlike the permanent loss of caste status suffered by a Hindu who
enters an irregular union with a low caste partner, the diminishment

of a patrician's status by a marital alliance with a *guchi* lasts only as long as that union persists. Thus a patrician girl who lives with a *guchi* husband is only a "temporary" *guchi*; if she divorces him or is widowed and returns to her parents' home, she regains her *guth* status. She can then conclude a regular marriage with a *guth* man, and her children from that second husband will be fully privileged *guth*.

In recent years new problems have been created by marriages of patrician men with girls of other tribes whom they met, often in educational institutions, outside the Apa Tani country. In the old days inter-tribal unions occurred only between *guchi* and Nishi slaves living in Apa Tani villages, but now the Apa Tani spouses are usually patrician young men of modern education and professional status and their non-Apa Tani wives, be they Nishi, Adi or Khasi may also have educational qualifications. The number of such marriages is as yet exceedingly small, but opportunities for meetings of young people of different tribes are increasing, and some Apa Tani reformers even speak in favour of such inter-tribal unions as a means of creating a sense of unity among the ethnic groups of Arunachal Pradesh. Despite such progressive ideas of a small educated élite, those who have concluded mixed marriages find it difficult to live in an Apa Tani village, and they are likely to stay either at Hapoli or outside the Apa Tani country altogether wherever the husband and sometimes also the wife may have found employment in government service. In 1978 a *guth* of Hage clan of Hari village was living in Hapoli with his Nishi wife who came from Jorum village. I was told that he was not permitted to participate in any rite of his clansmen, but that a priest (*nyibu*) would serve him if he wanted to perform a sacrifice in his own house; his children would be accepted among the Hage *guchi*, but even if his own brothers wanted to give him *guth* status and include him in their ritual activities others "would insult him and call him a *guchi*." No doubt in this case too the dissolution of the marriage would restore the husband to patrician status, and he might then marry a *guth* wife whose children would be regarded as patricians even if they had *guchi* half-brothers or sisters.

The introduction of a democratic system of government with village and district councils (*gram panchayat* and *zila parishad*) whose members were elected by adult franchise enabled members of the *guchi* class to attain positions of responsibility in a sphere where inherited status was not of decisive importance. In 1978 *guchi* occupied a large percentage of the seats on such elected bodies. Of the 13 seats on the village *panchayat* of Michi-Bamin for instance, eight were held by *guchi* and only five by men of *guth* statu. Admittedly Michi-Bamin is a village with an uncommonly large *guchi* population, and in villages such a Reru the percentage of *guchi* members of elected bodies is much smaller. It is significant, however, that the important position of vice-president of the *zila parishad*, the elected district council, was held by a *guchi*. While the Deputy Commissioner is ex-officio the president of this body which represents all the tribal people of the district, the vice-president is the highest elected office-bearer. In this particular case the *guchi* incumbent, a man of enterprise and sufficient education to give him fluency in English, owed his election partly to the fact that the candidature of two influential men of *guth* class had split the patrician vote. Yet, I did not notice any resentment on the part of patrician Apa Tanis, and there was no suggestion that the vice-president's class-status would detract from his ability to assert himself in the execution of his duties. As vice-president of the *zila parishad* he automatically chaired the meeting of the *anchal samithi*, which covered the entire Apa Tani valley, and among the 27 members of that body there were including the chairman only two *guchi*, all the other members belonging to prominent *guth* families. In addition to this duty the vice-president also acted as chairman of the important finance committee of the *anchal samithi*. Thus we see that a democratic process had elevated a *guchi* to one of the key positions in the new political system, and his performance certainly did not bear out the suggestions made by some educated *guth* that *guchi* were labouring under a feeling of inferiority.

In 1978 the majority of the political leaders as well as most of the prominent businessmen and contractors were patricians, and their preeminence was probably due to the family fortunes which facilitated their start both in commerce and in politics. But the rise of some *guchi* suggests that the dominance of the patricians is gradually diminishing, and that within a generation or two class-distinctions may lose their relevance, perhaps not in ritual but very probably in political affairs. Such a development is one of the avowed aims of the Youth Organization, and we shall see in Chapter 10 that several other aims have already been achieved to a surprising extent.

A modification of traditional views on the position of *guchi* found expression in a recent dispute which merits discussion in some detail. A rich man of Tajang village, Milo Havung had one son, Tama, and five daughters. While Tama was still alive Havung gave some of his land to two of his daughters, who by that time were already married. As his father had a great deal of land, Tama agreed to this transfer of land to his sisters, and there is the general belief that had Tama lived the two women would have remained in undisputed possession of the land in question. But Tama died without issue soon after his father's death. It was then remembered that Havung had had also another son, whose mother was a *guchi* girl of Hija who had been a maid-servant in the house of Havung. She had been his mistress, and as it was not considered right for a man to have sexual relations with his slaves or dependants, Havung had sent her back to her family in Hija as soon as he learnt of her pregnancy. She subsequently bore a son, whom she called Chatung, but this son was not recognized by Havung, though it is probable that Havung provided for mother and child. When both Havung and Tama had died and there was no close kinsman of Milo clan to claim the large property, one of the maternal uncles of Tama, in whose interest it was to maintain the affinal relations with so wealthy a family, agitated for the recognition of Havung's illegitimate son who was living among *guchi* in Hija. As this maternal kinsman was an influential and persuasive man his proposal was approved and Chatung was installed in Havung's house as a son entitled to the father's property. The supporters of this action then arranged for Chatung a marriage with a patrician girl of Nani clan of Reru, thereby strengthening his claim to *guth* status.

Chatung then claimed the land which Havung had given to his daughters, but as their husbands were men of influence and substance they contested the claim, arguing that Chatung was a *guchi* and could not inherit a *guth's* land. The dispute dragged on and finally led to a *lisudu* (see Chapter 6) between Chatung and the husbands of Havung's daughters. As the Apa Tani *buliang* were unable to settle the dispute it was finally referred to the administration, and the Deputy Commissioner decided in favour of Chatung, presumably because it is the policy of government not to perpetuate the distinction between *guth* and *guchi*. However, a compromise was made by compensating the daughters of Havung. They were to give the land in dispute to Chatung, but he in turn would pay for it in mithan. As mobile property can be passed on to daughters even if there are male heirs, the transfer of mithan was within the rules of Apa Tani custom. Chatung emerged from the dispute as a rich man whose patrician status was publicly recognized and whose children would have all the privileges of a *guth*. He subsequently performed an *un-pedo* (see Chapter 7), a feast of merit, thereby manifesting his claim to social prominence.

In the 1940s I had not heard of any *guchi* performing feasts of merit, and was then under the impression that only patricians engaged in any of the ceremonial activities aiming at raising a man's status. This impression may have been due to a misunderstanding, for in 1978 my informants denied the one-time monopoly of *guth* to the performance of feasts of merit. Nowadays *guchi* are certainly free to hold such rites. In Michi-Bamin two *guchi* performed *un-pedo* rites in 1978, and in Hang a freed slave of Nishi extraction who had worked for the Public Works Department, and with his earnings had purchased some land, subsequently performed a *rung-che* rite.

All this demonstrates a social mobility hardly imaginable in the old days when status was closely linked with the possession of land and men of *guchi* class had few opportunities to gain wealth and with it the possibility of engaging in activities apt to increase their prestige.

FIVE

The Pattern of Family Life

APA TANI SOCIETY is characterized by a high degree of
tolerance in the conduct of interpersonal relations. There are no
cumbersome rules and taboos which interfere with the behaviour of
individuals in the course of daily life, no spatial segregation according
to sex, age or social status, no restrictions on the contact between
persons standing in specific kinship relations to each other, and none
of the dread of pollution so inhibitive in Hindu society. Men,
women and children go about their business without having to be
concerned about the possible critical comments of relatives or
neighbours. The lack of inhibitions in women and children even in
the presence of strangers must strike anyone used to the shyness of
women, except the very old, in many Hindu or Muslim villages.
The usual atmosphere in an Apa Tani household is remarkably
relaxed and cheerful, and even as long as there were slaves they
freely joined in the general conversation and gaiety.

Children are disciplined when it comes to household or agricultural tasks in which their cooperation is required, but otherwise
they have a great deal of freedom. From an early age they are
aware of the sexual relations between the older boys and girls, and
this encourages them to indulge in sexual play often long before
they reach maturity. Their parents do not object to such activities,
and it is generally expected that adolescents have sexual experiences
which are often of a fairly promiscuous nature. Thanks to the tolerance of adult society, little secrecy is involved in such love affairs.
Although young people may joke in a very unambiguous manner,
there is never any public display of affectionate gestures.

In the old days lovers used to spend many nights in the safety of
granaries, but since these are nowadays usually locked such havens
are no longer easily available. In dry weather bamboo groves
were also favoured places for amatory assignments, and boys

and girls would take blankets and sometimes also some snacks to make their nocturnal meetings more comfortable and enjoyable. As girls avoided flaunting their adventures in the face of their parents, they often pretended to spend the night in a girl-friend's house, and though such pretexts deceived no one the alibis were used to maintain a certain decorum. Premarital pregnancies were not frequent—the relatively infertile period immediately after maturity probably saving most girls from early conception—but even if a girl became pregnant there was little embarrassment or social disapproval. Usually the couple would marry, but if class diffences prevented such a course because the lover of a patrician girl was of *guchi* status the illegitimate child could be brought up in the house of the girl's parents, and her chances of a subsequent marriage with a man or her own class were not seriously prejudiced.

Despite the sexual freedom enjoyed by the young, relations between boys and girls do not lack a romantic element and this is given expression in songs. There are numerous occasions when young people amuse themselves by singing in small groups, either in the evenings or even when working in the fields, and boys and girls often sing alternatingly answering each others verses. Such songs refer sometimes to fictional situations. Thus one song recalls the time of the immigration of the Apa Tanis when some groups got separated from the other. With such a situation in mind the young people sing: "There are so many mountains and rivers between us and so we cannot meet any more, but when the plum tree flowers we think of the Mloko festival, and how we used to enjoy ourselves together." In another song separated lovers sing: "When we see the primulae flower we think of our lovers and how we collected them together, and when we see the wild-growing vegetables, we think of our lovers and how we went together to the forest to collect vegetables and herbs."

A collection and translation of such songs is still outstanding but even the few examples I was given indicate that romantic sentiments are not foreign to young Apa Tanis. It would seem, however, that sexual attachments seldom give rise to very deep and traumatic emotional involvement, and that jealousy is not a force liable to lead to violence of serious disputes between rivals. This sober attitude to sex is probably the result of the very uninhibited sexual behaviour of Apa Tani youth. In this respect the Apa Tanis differ markedly from their Nishi neighbours. Among the latter a much higher standard of sexual morality is expected of young girls as well as married women, and any indiscretion on the part of a wife may rouse her husband to uncontrolled rage, resulting in fights and often murder, a behaviour not in keeping with Apa Tani temperament.

The matter-of-fact attitude to sex is reflected also in the paucity of prohibitions and taboos relating to the reproductive process. Women are not subject to any taboos during their period and the Apa Tanis do not share the common Indian view on the polluting nature of menstrual blood. Nor do they mark girl's first menstruation by any observances or celebrations. The only time when there is a strict taboo on sexual intercourse is during the first thirteen days after a woman's confinement. For the first ten days both the woman and her husband are considered impure, and may neither cook nor draw water from a well or stream. After this period mother and child are bathed, and for the next three days husband and wife may sleep on one mat but must abstain from sexual intercourse. On the fourteenth day all restrictions come to an end, but many men desist from marital relations for a very much longer time.

Marriage

The great freedom enjoyed by young Apa Tanis of both sexes colours also their attitude to marriage. Boys and girls, who were able to choose their partners for per-marital love affairs without experiencing any interference on the part of their parents, tend to exercise a similar independence in the choice of those they wish to marry. In the case of wealthy families parents undoubtedly try to dissuade their sons and daughters from entering unions with partners of different economic status and to arrange instead alliances within their own social stratum, but it is unusual to insist on a match against the express wishes of either of the potential spouses. In many case the initiative is taken by the young couple whose wishes their elders respect provided there is no serious objection to a union between the two families.

Unlike their Nishi neighbours who use marriages for the forging of political alliances and derive economic advantages from the large bride-prices paid for their daughters, the Apa Tanis look upon marriage primarily as a means to provide for a life-long partnership of two congenial individuals. While polygamous marriages are by no means rare, the nuclear family consisting of a couple and their unmarried children is one of the basic elements of Apa Tani society. Houses are not large enough to accommodate joint families consisting of more than one married couple, and there is hence the unalterable principle that if at all possible every married couple should be housed in a separate duelling, even if this means the construction or purchase of a new house as soon as a son takes a wife and establishes his own household.

Many couples have been lovers for some considerable time before they decide to live together on a permanent basis. There is no need for a formal engagement or even a wedding ceremony. Once a man and a girl have agreed to live as husband and wife, they move together and for an initial period stay either in the man's parental house or in that of the girl's family. Such accommodation is considered purely provisional, and all concerned, and particularly the man's parents, will seek to establish the couple in a house of their own however modest. Yet, in the case of a young man taking a wife without obtaining his parents' consent and dispensing with formal negotiations and wedding ceremonies, the parents are not bound by the normal obligation to provide a married son with a house-site and some cultivable land. There is no concise Apa Tani term for "love marriage" but such a union has been described to me as *nyimu mia salaka mi milo lasune*, which means literally "female and male fall in love and become husband and wife."

Apart from the usual love-matches concluded without the co-operation of the kinsfolk of both partners, there is an even more unorthodox and consequently rare practice known as *milo-chi-adu* which involves the uninvited entry of a woman into a man's house on the plea that he promised her marriage. Such a forcible entry of an "unwanted" woman (*adu*) is not easily resisted without creating something of a scandal, particularly if the girl can prove the giving of "presents of engagement" (*larsudu*). There are even rare cases of girls entering in this way the house of a man who has already one wife, and if the latter does not object all three may stay in the house together although such arrangements usually do not last very long.

We have discussed already the prejudice against marriages between particians and commoners, and there is no doubt that the families of the patrician partner, if alerted of the young people's intention, will try to dissuade him or her against entering so unorthodox a union. Particularly a man's mother's brother should try to counsel his nephew to abstain from such a marriage, but if the nephew is adamant and ignores his uncle's advice, the latter should still stand by him when his action gets him into trouble.

More usual than marriages entered in an informal way are negotiated alliances which involve wedding ceremonies of extreme complexity in which the kinsfolk of both partners cooperate in a variety of ways. Such marriages are known as *mida*, and Apa Tanis distinguish between the *dachi mida* of ordinary people and the more elaborate *datu mida* of rich families. In a marriage of this type bride and groom may know each other well and may even have taken the initiative, or they may be very young and the marriage may be the idea of the parents of either or both of the parties. The consent of the mother's brother of each partner is sought in all negotiated marriages.

The preliminaries of an arranged marriage begin with the taking of omens by a priest (*nyibu*) acting for the groom's parents. If the omens are bad the project will be abandoned, but if they are good a kinsman of the groom approaches the girl's parents and tells them of the good omens. If the girl's parents are considerably wealthier than the boy's family, they will not reject the proposal openly, but make excuses saying that the omens their priest took were bad. If both families are of equal status and in principle agreeable to the match, the omens of both sides are allowed to decide. In the event of favourable omens the next step is that the groom's go-between (*gutang*) and the groom will be invited to the house of the girl's parents. They are accompained by the groom's parents, his best friend, and two of the groom's elderly clansmen (*subu-bonu*), so called because later they will take the groom's mithan (*subu*) to the bride's father. When the party arrives at the bride's house, specially prepared beer is offered to them and the bride's relatives gathered in the house. The bride's mother then give the groom a white cloth with yellow border known as *magbo-pulye* ("son-in-law's cloth"). This ceremony is performed early in the morning, and a meal, usually of rice and beef, is offered to all those present. It is mandatory that the groom and the members of his party are presented with pieces of smoked pork.

Next the groom's parents perform the rite of *subu-tado* at their own *lapang*. A mithan and a cow are sacrificed while a priest prays for the welfare of the bridal couple. Both groom and bride must be present and put rice-powder on the mithan's forehead. During this rite which may extend over more than one day, the bride should stay in the house of the groom, though if she is still immature she may stay in her parents' house, but must observe all the taboos imposed on the participants of the rite.

The next stage in the marriage ceremonies known as *aripadu* involves the exchange of gifts. The groom's parents present one mithan to the bride's parents or if they are no longer alive to her eldest brother. If no mithan is available cash can now be given instead. If the marriage ranks as *datu mida* Rs 2,000 are given in place of a mithan, but at a *dachi mida* Rs 800 suffice. Whoever receives these large gifts must accept some responsibility for the welfare of the couple. In return he presents the groom with paddy, the value of which should be more or less equal to that of the mithan or cash gift. If the bride's parents are very rich they give paddy of a value superior to that of the groom's gifts.

Another gift is given by the groom to a brother or father's brother's son of the bride. It should be of the value of a medium-sized mithan, i.e. of circa Rs 500-600 according to present prices. This gift too is reciprocated in the shape of paddy of equal value.

The third presentation used to consist of two small mithan, but is now invariably replaced by two gifts of Rs 200-250 each because cheap mithan are no longer available. These sums go to two brothers or cousins of the bride who have to give rice in exchange, and who resume the responsibility of assisting the married couple in the event of any difficulties. If the bride's father is no longer alive and she has no real brother, the recipients of those gifts, who must be close kinsmen of the bride's *tulu*, will be responsible for her welfare.

The final move of the bride to her husband's house is the occasion for another ceremony. The groom is accompanied by his parents, his go-between (*gutang*) and the latter's wife, two friends (*ari-boni*), two brothers-in-law, i.e. sisters' husbands (*liyi*) and one priest (*nyibu*). All these arrive at the bride's house in the morning and are expected to stay till evening. When they enter the house the groom cannot go beyond the first hearth, should sit in a corner near the door of the main room and not move about, while the bride sits at the far end of the house behind the second hearth; she may move about the house. The bride's father is expected to dole out gifts of money to the members of the groom's party, and these have taken the place of gifts in kind which used to be distributed in past days. A wealthy man may give Rs 140 to the groom's parents, Rs 100 to the *gutang*, Rs 80 to each of the two *ari-boni*, Rs 80 to each of the two *liyi*, and anything between Rs 50 and 80 to the groom's priest. There is a certain amount of bargaining about these payments, and it is the accepted practice that *ari-boni* and *liyi* bargain on behalf of the groom's party, while the bride's father will denigrate the value of the mithan which had been given by the groom's party and argue that they were not big enough. This bargaining has a ceremonial character and does not create any ill-feeling.

It is part of the obligations of the bride's family to entertain the guests lavishly and never to allow a plate to remain empty. The guests have brought baskets and go on filling these with the meat placed on their plates. Thus a large amount of cooked meat is transferred from the bride's to the groom's party.

At the end of the feasting, the bride heads a procession of the groom's party, which moves to his parental house or his own house if a new home for the couple has already been completed. The bride carries a side of bacon which should be unblemished, and tied to this is a dried squirrel whose tail must be intact. She also carries one big hen and some small chicks. While leading the procession she may on no account look back to her parent's house. Her girl friends and female relatives follow the procession, carrying with them paddy and millet from their own granaries as last gifts to help her in the setting up of a new household.

When the bride and her friends enter the groom's house, they are offered food and beer. While her friends and kinswomen soon leave, the bride from now on stays in her husband's house, whether it is his own or that of his parents. The latter have kept one cock for the groom and one hen for the bride, and a priest sacrifices both, sees the omens, and prays to Chantung, the earth deity, for the couple's prosperity. But the chickens which the bride brought with her are kept for rearing. For five days after the sacrificial rite for Chantung the bride should not leave the village.

There is some flexibility in the arrangements of the ceremonies surrounding a marriage, and depending on the season and the means of the families concerned there may be modifications of the sequence of events. Many weddings are held towards the end of the agricultural season, and the paddy to be given to the bridal couple

in exchange for the mithan or cash which the groom's party gave
to the parents and kinsmen of the bride is that of the new harvest.
Thus the father or brother of the bride, whose role at the wedding
is known as *dirang*, and who has received the largest mithan or sum
of money, gives the greatest amount of paddy, such as 50-150 *yagi*
baskets, while the brother or cousin of the bride who received a
medium-sized mithan, will contribute 30-80 baskets, and the other
brothers or cousins who had received Rs 200-250 provide smaller
quantities. All the paddy promised to the couple by the bride's kinsmen in exchange for the various gifts of cattle or cash must be
collected at harvest time from the donors' fields by the kinsmen and
friends of the groom. The couple should be present at the harvest
on each of the fields from which the contributions of paddy are to
be taken. The harvesters work in pairs, the girls cut the rice-ears,
and the boys beat them out in big baskets, which they then carry
to the groom's granary.

On the new husband's fields which he is likely to have received
from his father, his bride must cut the first ears and the husband
has to thrash them. When all the paddy has been brought to the
couple's granary the bride takes some paddy, pounds it and shapes
without cooking the rice some balls consisting of rice-flour mixed
with dried meat, and these balls are placed into two baskests containing the rice first brought in by the newly wed couple, which will
be kept apart and may be eaten only by the husband and wife, and
their parents.

The next morning a priest performs a sacrificial rite in the
couple's granary, and this is called *nesum payanu*. He is given five
or six small chicks, one big hen, and five or six eggs. Before he kills
the chickens the young wife sprinkles them with rice-flour and beer.
The priest then cuts off their heads and smears the blood on
the paddy and the door of the granary. This rite is intended to
prevent the wasteful use of the grain stored in the couple's granary.
It has, however, still another purpose. The omens taken from the
intestines of two of the chicks decide whether the management of
the granary and indeed the whole household should be in the hands
of the wife or the husband. In the case of the marriage of Kuru
Hasan, who was a flying-officer in the Indian Air Force, the omens
indicated that his wife, the daughter of Padi Lailang, should
manage their domestic affairs and ever since she has been in charge

of their business activities which include the management of a pharmacy at Hapoli.

Nowadays a newly married couple may not be present at the first harvest after their wedding, because one or both may be serving or studying outside the Apa Tani valley. In such an event the groom's kinsfolk collect the paddy given as wedding presents on his behalf, and store it separately from other grain in the groom's or his father's granary.

The last of the ceremonies connected with a wedding, known as *elibadu*, is held usually 15-30 days after the ceremonial harvest. On that occasion the bride's mother calls all her kinswomen, and each of them brings some paddy or millet. The bride then goes for the *last time* to her parents' granary, and fills a specially prepared basket with *emo* rice, and puts a ginger plant from her mother's garden in such a way into the unhusked rice that the leaves protrude from the grain. She then leads a procession of women, carrying the basket with rice and ginger, while her mother carries rice of another variety, and the bride's younger sisters carry all the chickens which she had reared in her natal home.

As the procession reaches the husband's granary the bride places her basket with *emo* rice and ginger next to the two baskets which contain the newly harvested paddy and the balls made by the bride of rice flour and dried meat. Each of the women in the procession places her rice or millet into the granary and receives in return a gift of Rs 2. The whole party of women then proceeds to the husband's house, where they are entertained with cooked meat and rice, and not only eat as much as they can, but also put some of the meat into their baskets.

This is considered the women's day, and all the women of the husband's clan, living in the neighbourhood, come with contributions of beer and various edibles. After the women of the bride's family have had their fill, the women of the groom's clan sit down and enjoy the feast. When these ceremonies are over the young husband and his bride must remain in the house for three days, and after this period of confinement is over they may leave the house, but may not go to the house of the bride's parents until on the fifth day the bride has planted the ginger from her mother's garden plot.

The elaborate exchanges of gifts at a wedding have the purpose of creating permanent ties between the two families which involve obligations of mutual help. We have seen already that those of the bride's kinsmen who receive gifts of mithan or nowadays cash from the groom's family are under an obligation to assist the couple in any emergency. Similarly a man can expect help from the husbands of his sisters, as during his sister's weddings he exchanged gifts with these men. Apa Tanis say that any man who has no sisters is at a serious disadvantage in all disputes.

In view of a man's dependence on his affinal kinsmen in times of need, the choice of a wife is obviously a serious matter and one in which factors other than sexual attraction must also be taken into consideration. Unlike many other Indian tribesmen Apa Tanis have no system of preferred marriages which favours alliances within a narrow circle of related families linked generation after generation through marriages of cross-cousins. An Apa Tani may not marry either his mother's brother's daughter nor his father's sister's daughter or mother's sister's daughter, but he may marry a girl of his mother's clan provided no consanguineous link can be traced within the past four generations. Marriage within the sub-clan (*tulu*) and in the case of clans (*halu*) not divided into intermarrying *tulu,* even within the clan is not permissible but otherwise there are few restrictions on the choice of spouses except the over-riding prejudice against unions between patricians (*guth*) and commoners (*guchi*). A man is permitted to marry his wife's elder or younger sister, and even his brother's widow irrespective of the relative age of his late brother.

Sexual congress and implicitly marriage with any wife or widow of one's father, however young she may be is forbidden, and in this respect the Apa Tanis differ radically from the Nishis among whom it is normal practice for a man to inherit his father's wives, except of course his own mother. An Apa Tani should also abstain from any sexual relations with the wives of his father's brothers as well as his mother's brother. Even if such a women becomes widowed this prohibition normally remains valid. An exception is made, however, if a young and childless widow of the mother's brother has returned to her parents' house. In that case she may have sexual relations with her late husband's nephew and even become his wife.

There is also a rule against marriage with the father's brother's son's daughter, and it is explained that such marriages are avoided not because of the closeness of consanguineous ties, but because such marriages within the circle of kin lessen the chances of widening the web of kin ties by alliances with unrelated families.

Polygamy is permitted, but far less frequent than among Nishis and Miris. In 1944 I found only three polygamous marriages among the 433 households of Hija, but though I have no statistical data for the situation in 1978 I came across a number of cases of polygamy and the practice may be on the increase. At that time several prominent men lived in polygamous marriages. Padi Lailang, the richest man of Reru, had married four wives; three of them were still living and staying in his house. His son Yubbe, then speaker of the legislative assembly of Arunachal Pradesh, had two wives. But another prominent man Kago Bida, who in 1945 had planned to marry three wives in addition to the one he was already married to (see my *The Apa Tanis*, p. 94), had added only one more to his household before he died at the hand of his own brother in 1977. Judging from the histories of the few prominent families I was acquainted with, great wealth was undoubtedly an incentive to the enlargement of a household by marrying additional wives, and the present tendency to establish secondary households in business centres may have increased the motivation for marrying more than one wife.

While the women in polygamous households seem to maintain as a rule amicable relations, the children of third or fourth wives—unusual as such large families are—are often disadvantaged because most of their father's property may already have been handed over to the sons of the older wives before they are old enough to marry and raise a claim to a share in the land. In 1944 I was given the impression that the taking of a second wife may be regarded as an insult by the first wife's kinsmen who might seize the husband and cut off his hair in retaliation for the disgrace brought upon their kinswomen. I then also knew a young man whose marriage was childless, but who did not dare to marry the girl with whom he had a long-standing love-affair because he feared the wrath of his wife's brothers. In 1978 I heard of no such case and my Apa Tani friends, many of whom had been educated on western lines, did not seem to have any prejudice against multiple marriages. This may well be due to the fact that tolerance of a number of different life-styles, traditional as well as modern, engendered the attitude that the kind of marriage a man wants to have is his own affair, and that the kinsmen of a jealous wife cannot be expected to intervene on her behalf, provided of course her husband's second marriage does not affect her and her children's material security.

The last serious dispute, involving kinsmen on both sides that arose from a wife's and her brothers' objection to her husband marrying a second wife, occurred in Duta and Hija in the late 1960s. Koj Nibo, the richest man of Duta, was married to Yamin, the sister of Kago Bida, one of the leading men of Hija, who himself had then two wives. When Koj Nibo wanted to marry a second wife, namely Haj Yanya of Hija, his first wife and her kinsmen objected. Nibo argued that he was rich enough to provide comfortably for two wives, but Kago Bida was adamant in demanding redress of the alleged loss of face suffered by his sister. He claimed one of Nibo's fields as compensation for the disgrace inflicted on him and his whole family by Nibo's second marriage, though in fact Nibo's action ran by no means counter to accepted Apa Tani practice. Kago Bida's arrogance infuriated Koj Nibo, and he sought to put his interfering brother-in-law in his place by selling the piece of land in question to his own kinsman Koj Goru. Kago Bida reacted to this by starting a *lisudu* against Koj Nibo, and Nada Bakhang, another rich man of Hija, who was the mother's brother of both Kago Bida and Nibo's first wife, undertook a parallel demonstration against Koj Goru, because the latter had bought the field which Kago Bida had been claiming. The quarrel between these four prominent men of the neighbouring villages of Duta and Hija, intensified as each party tried to humiliate their opponents. They tried to outdo each other by slaughtering more and more mithan in the traditional style of *lisudu* competitions, and in addition destroyed some of their own valuables as a demonstration. In the end each of them had killed 20 mithan and broken some elephant tusks and bronze plates. To pay for this futile expenditure the contestants had to sell some land, but Nibo said: "I shall not sell any of the land which I allotted to my new wife, but I shall sell all the land which my first wife used to cultivate." He did so, and when in the end the quarrel was settled by a compromise, the main sufferer was Nibo's first wife who after his death became very poor. Had she tolerated her husband's second marriage, she would have been very comfortably off, but by instigating her brother and mother's brother to violent opposition, she harmed her own cause, without deflecting her husband from his determination to marry a second wife. By the time I recorded the case only Koj Goru and Koj Nibo's second wife were alive.

Any breakdown of a marriage is considered more damaging to

the prestige of the wife and her kinsmen than to that of the husband, unless it is caused by the wife's unfaithfulness, for this reflects on the honour of the husband whose social status suffers if he is known to tolerate a prolonged adulterous association. A married woman caught in adultery will not necessarily be punished or divorced, but the aggrieved husband may seize her lover and redeem his prestige by extracting a substantial fine as compensation. Once this has been paid the matter is settled, and it does not seem that husbands of fickle wives are given to outbursts of jealousy.

After some years of premarital adventures, most Apa Tani women appear to settle down to a stable and on the whole harmonious married life. The fact that each married couple soon acquires a house of its own precludes tensions arising from incompatibility between a young wife and her mother-in-law, and most Apa Tani wives work so hard that little energy is left for interests outside the home. Apa Tanis frequently quarrel over land, trade transactions or matters affecting their influences in the community, but unlike their Nishi neighbours—and indeed many other Indian tribesmen—they seldom fall out as a result of rivalry over the favour of women. When marital disputes lead to quarrels between the respective families, the issue is usually not so much competition for the possession of a woman as the loss of prestige suffered by the kinsmen of a woman neglected or discarded by her husband. For prestige is gauged by the protection a man or a kin-group can afford to relatives, dependants and guests, and the desertion or expulsion of a wife by her husband reflects more adversely on her natal family than a wife's adultery reflects on that of her husband. In Chapter 6 we shall see that a husband expelling a wife without grave provocation runs the risk of retaliatory action of her kinsmen, and in the old days of kidnapping and holding to ransom might even have lost his freedom for substantial periods.

A tolerant view had always been taken of casual sexual relations of married men with unmarried girls, and it is well known that during the later stages of their wives' pregnancies and often also in the months after the birth of a child, many man do not sleep with their wives but seek the company of unattached young women. It seems that on the whole sexual relations do not cause great emotional crises, and this sober attitude to sex is probably the result of the very uninhibited sexual behaviour of Apa Tani youth.

Whether a marriage is concluded with full wedding rites or the spouses entered their union in a more casual way, husband and wife are considered equal partners, each of whom has separate responsibilities and rights. We have mentioned that during the wedding ceremonies there is provision for determining by omens which of the spouses should have control over the household affairs and grain-supplies, and as in this decision the odds must be even, there is every probability that in 50 per cent of the marriages the wife plays an important role in economic matters. Even in relations with outsiders women have never been overshadowed by their husbands, for it used to be normal for the less affluent Apa Tani women to go and work as weavers in Nishi villages, and to bring back cotton which they obtained as wages for their services. Women could also engage in other trade deals and nowadays they are active in supplying the market of Hapoli with vegetable produce, eggs and home-brewed rice-beer. The income derived from such activities enables them to purchase clothes and various consumer goods, without having to depend on their husbands for the necessary cash. In monogamous households the allocation of land does not arise, as husband and wife jointly cultivate the land and dispose of the produce. But in the event of a man having two or three wives, each of them is allocated cultivable land, and a granary for storing the grain she reaps. This gives her a considerable measure of independence, and diminishes the likelihood of bickerings between co-wives.

The dependence of a man on his wife in all agricultural operations is far greater than that of the Indian plough-cultivator who does the strenuous work of ploughing, harrowing and usually also thrashing, because all these processes require the aid of bullocks who are the responsibility of men. Among the Apa Tanis, on the other hand, the greater part of the agricultural work is done by women, and it seems that in recent years their share of this work has even increased, while men tend to engage more in outside activities bringing in cash earnings.

When discussing the position of women with Apa Tanis in 1978, one of my informants was emphatic in his statement that "nowadays men and women have equal rights; men can divorce wives and women can divorce men." However, some inequality between men and women exists still in the rules of inheritance, which have wisely not been tampered with by the present administration.

Inheritance

The character of Apa Tani families and their development from generation to generation can be understood only if we consider the system of inheritance which involves in many cases frequent moves of middle-aged couples from house to house, as they make room for their grown up sons when the latter marry and establish families of their own. Traditionally all inherited land should be passed on to the eldest son, but fathers are free to give their self-acquired property to any of their sons, and as land often changes hands, rich men have ample scope for providing also younger sons with as much land as they require.

Koj Bokr of Duta was such a rich man, of whom it was said that at one time he owned 200-300 mithan, most of which he entrusted to Nishis of neighbouring villages as well as to other Apa Tanis. He had two wives, who bore him four sons and one daughter. When his eldest son Kamin married, Bokr gave him his own house as well as land, and bought for himself and his remaining family a new house-site and built a house on it. He also bought a great deal of new land for which he paid 80 mithan. When his second son Chiliyang married Bokr gave him the house in which they had lived and a large holding of land. For himself and his two younger sons Tajang and Yabo he again built a new house, but this he also gave away when Tajang married and needed a house. Bokr then built once more a house of normal size and lived in it with Yabo and his only, surviving wife. When finally Yabo also got married, Bokr left him in this house, and built for himself a small house. To each of his younger sons he gave as much land—all self-acquired—as he had given to his second son Chiliyang. By the time of Yabo's marriage, Bokr's second wife had also died, and so he married an old widow, of Kalung village who had been living alone. The old couple did not cultivate any more, and the wives of Bokr's four sons took turns in providing their father-in-law and his wife with as much food as they needed.

The process of moving from one house to the other was repeated in the next generation. Chiliyang married three wives and had from each one son. The oldest Takur, who is trained as a pharmacist, got his father's house and all the land which Bokr had given to Chiliyang. The latter built a new house for himself, and in 1978 he lived in this with his only surviving third wife and his two younger sons. He had bought land worth Rs 5000 ; one field at Kalung, one field at Tajang and one field at Hija. Land closer to Duta was not available, a fact which reflects the growing pressure on land.

While the division of Koj Bokr's property was straight forward and all his descendants were fairly provided for, the disposal of the property of the one time richest man of Hang, Ponyo Tamar, was much more complicated. Ponyo Tamar had married four wives and his youngest son from his fourth wife was still a child when he died. The following tabulation shows the division of his property.

Tamar's eldest son, Dole, received on his marriage:

One house, originally that of his father.
Land corresponding to three granaries, each holding 100-150 maunds.
One bamboo grove.
One male slave (Apa Tani) with six children.
One female slave (Nishi).
Ten mithan.
Eight Tibetan bells worth ten mithan.
Two bronze plates each worth eight mithan.
One string of beads worth ten mithan.

Dole had one arranged marriage, and when his first wife died, he took another without formalities. From the first wife he had one son, Tanyo, and one daughter, from the second wife four sons and three daughters. When Dole died the property which he got from his father was divided: the biggest plot corresponding to two granaries and the biggest bronze plate went to Tanyo, and the rest of the property went to the eldest son of the second wife. The remaining three sons got no ancestral property; they had to earn their livelihood by working, and each bought with his earnings land corresponding to half a granary. Most of Dole's mithan had died in an epidemic, and as he had been sickly he also had sacrificed many mithan to achieve a cure. Dole's one-time slave had three sons; two of them purchased some land, the third was in 1978 still landless.

Tamar's second son: Taka received on his marriage:

One house site, vacated by Tamar.
Land corresponding to one and a half granaries.
One bamboo grove.

One male slave (Nishi).
One Tibetan bell.
One bronze plate.

Taka had one son, who got all his fathers's property; two daughters died unmarried.
Tamar's third son; Rambo, received on his marriage:

One house site vacated by Tamar.
Land corresponding to one granary.
One bamboo grove.
One male slave (Nishi) called Tatang.
One bronze plate.

Rambo married two wives; the first had one, and the second two sons. The first son received land corresponding to one granary, and one bamboo grove. The other sons received no ancestral land. For his slave Tatang Rambo built a house and arranged for his marriage to an Apa Tani *guchi* girl of Hang. Tatang worked for the Public Works Department, and with his earnings bought land. In 1978 he performed a feast of merit (*rung-sere*) and to do this he sold most of his land. Tatang is now accepted as an Apa Tani *guchi*.
Tamar's fourth son; Lampung, alive in 1978, received on his marriage:

One house site vacated by Tamar.
Land corresponding to one granary.
One bamboo grove.
One male slave (Apa Tani).
Three mithan.
One bronze plate.

Lapung married two wives, both living in 1978; Tida, only son of the elder wife, was married; the two sons of the younger wife were still unmarried. Lapung gave Tida his own house and built another for himself, as well as land corresponding to one granary, one bamboo grove, one female slave, whom he bought, and one bronze plate.

Tamar's fifth son, Dolyang, alive in 1978, received on marriage:

One house site vacated by Tamar.
Land corresponding to one granary.
One bamboo grove.
One male slave (Apa Tani)
Three mithan.
One Tibetan bell.
One bronze plate.

Dolyang married two wives, both alive in 1978, and had one son from each wife. The elder wife's son Dukhung, also married two wives. Dolyang gave him his house and all the land he had received from his father Ponyo Tamar.

Tamar's sixth son, Yaku, was the only child of Tamar's fourth wife Yerin (see *Himalayan Barbary,* Fig. 9) and he was a small boy when Tamar died. By that time Ponyo Tamar, once the richest man of Hang, had no land left, and he had built his last house on land belonging to one of his grandsons; his sons provided him with food. Hence Yaku did not inherit any house or land from Tamar. His mother Yerin remarried and died in 1977.

This account of the manner in which the property of one wealthy Apa Tani family was passed on from generation to generation illustrates several features of the rules of inheritance. The principle that as a man's sons get married, they should take over the father's house site, was adhered to, and Ponyo Tamar built a new house for himself every time one of his sons married and established a separate household. There was also general adherence to the rule that the eldest son is entitled to most of the ancestral landed property although it is not clear how much of the large acreage given by Tamar to his many sons was ancestral land and how much was self-acquired and hence available for distribution to younger sons. The old system may have been workable at a time when the population was more or less stationary owing to the limitations to growth set by epidemics and also the casualties in feuds with neighbouring tribes. In a family in which six sons survive to maturity and again produce sons the pressure on inherited and acquired land must obviously be great. Moreover the abolishment of slavery must have made it difficult for Apa Tani landowners to maintain their production of grain at a level enabling them to sell surplusses and purchase additional land when parts of the ancestral land had to be passed on to their eldest sons. Another factor interfering with the maintenance of wealth in prolific families is the decline in the number of mithan as the result of epidemics caused by increased contacts with the plains. As long as rich men owned hundreds of mithan their wealth was virtually self-perpetuating, and mithan could be passed on to sons as they got married as well as be used as currency for the purchase of land for younger sons.

The shift from landownership and agricultural production to commercial enterprises and wage-earning has affected the pattern of family relations in various ways. Previously all members of a household concentrated the greater part of their efforts on the cultivation of their land and the tending of their livestock while occasional trading trips and the work of some women as weavers for wages were only minor diversions from these tasks. Now many men derive their main income from business activities conducted outside their villages and some hold government posts which necessitate their presence at Hapoli or even outside the Apa Tani valley. Commuting between the various villages and Hapoli has become a widespread practice, and numerous men have established secondary domiciles at Hapoli where their shops are located. Usually this means that wives live in the village looking after house and land, whereas the husbands spend such time in Hapoli, partly in the company of men friends and partly with unmarried, widowed or divorced women also engaged in commercial activities. The inevitable result has been that some men took second wives and established them in their houses in Hapoli. Hence a new incentive for polygamous unions has developed.

Commercial enterprises are still so recent a phenomenon that there exists not enough information on the way in which business premises or bank deposits are passed on from one generation to another. As skill in business is not necessarily a prerogative of eldest sons, and commercial assets can hardly count as "ancestral" property, there would seem to be no reason why such assets should be inherited by the eldest son in preference to younger sons who have perhaps been more active in the development of a shop or a contractor's business.

One principle, however, continues to prevail so far and this is the rule that immobile property is normally not inherited by women. Rich men are at liberty to give their daughters cattle, ornaments and grain, but in the case of Milo Havung we have seen that the gift of land to his daughters could be challenged even by an illegitimate son from a *guchi* mother (see Chapter 4). In 1944 I was told that a man may help a poor son-in-law in establishing himself, and may even give him land and cattle as presents, but in 1978 I did not hear of any concrete cases of such a practice, perhaps because nowadays any man of modest means can improve his economic position by wage-labour and even buy land with cash earned in this way. However, as wealthy men were always allowed to help separated slaves to establish themselves by free gifts of house sites and land, there can hardly have been an absolute ban on gifts of land to a son-in-law in need of material help.

Whereas there is a strong emphasis on the male line in descent and succession to property, it seems that the transmission of status and privileges through the female line is not totally excluded. Thus an orphan living with his mother's kinsmen as well as an illegitimate child can be integrated within his mother's clan, provided he or she is not claimed by his father's clansmen. If no such claim is made such a child can adopt the mother's clan-name and his class status will be that of the mother irrespective of that of the father. Such treatment of fatherless children is clearly a compromise resorted to for practical purposes. An illegimate child is known as *hipro* and normally such a child suffers the discrimination of not being allowed to partake of the blood of the pigs sacrificed by the mother's kinsmen at the Mloko. But if her clansmen want to admit such a child to full membership of their clan they symbolize such acceptance by admitting the *hipro* to their ritual meals. Exceptionally integration into the mother's clan can occur also in different circumstances. In 1944 I knew of a man who was the legitimate son of a patrician of Hibu clan, but who had adopted the clan-name of his mother's brother in whose house he had lived for some time after his father's death. He joined in the rituals of his adopted clan, and had severed all connections with his paternal clan. All such arrangements are exceptional, however, for Apa Tanis believe that "a child is deposited in the mother's womb, but is from the beginning of the father's blood." Succession in the female line is the rule, however, in the case of *kümar*, castrators of pigs, one of whose daughters usually succeeds her mother in this despised but profitable occupation.

Kinship and Ceremonial Friendship

A sphere of social life so far only marginally affected by recent changes is the kinship system. In this context it will suffice therefore to sketch the ordering of kinship relations in rough outline, and to concentrate mainly on the obligations and responsibilities various categories of kin have towards each other.

The most characteristic feature of the Apa Tanis' kinship terminology is the extreme paucity of kinship terms and the use of the same terms for persons of different generations, and in some cases even for both consanguineous and affinal kinsmen.

Thus the term *ato* is used for father's father, mother's father, husband's father's father, wife's father's father, as well as for husband's father and wife's father, and the term *ayo* for father's mother's is extended in a similar manner.

The term's *aba*—father and *ama* (or *ane*)—mother are used only for ego's own parents.

The term *ate*, on the other hand, covers a wide range of kinsmen, i.e. elder brother, father's brother's son (if older than speaker), father's brother and father's father's brother. Similarly the term *ata* is used to address the elder sister, mother's sister, mother's sister's daughter (if older) and all kinswomen on both the mother's and father's side older than the speaker.

The term *aku* is used to address the mother's brother, the father's mother's brother, the mother's brother's son, and the husband's elder brother; usually the personal name is added, such as *aku* Bida.

The term *au* is used to address the sister's husband, as well as the father's sister's husband.

The term *barme* is used for younger sister, sister's daughter, brother's daughter, father's sisters, father's sister's daughter, father's father's sister, father's father's sister's daughter.

The term *achi* is used for elder brother's wife as well as for father's brother's wife, mother's brother's wife and mother's brother's son's wife.

Magbo (also pronounced *mabo*) applies to sister's husband, daughter's husband, brother's daughter's husband, father's sister's husband, and father's father's sister's husband. The corresponding term for son's wife is *am*.

An unusual phenomenon is the absence of distinctive terms for son and daughter; son is *oho* and daughter *nyim oho* (literally "female *oho*").

Sister's son and father's sister's son is *ohobo*, and the suffix-*bo* is also used in the term *atobo* used to address the wife's brother (both elder and younger) and the wife's brother's son.

Milo: husband and *mihi*: wife are descriptive terms not used for any other relationship except as parts of collective compunds such as *miloho nyam* father's mother's brothers.

The use of many terms for a large number of relations of different generations indicates that the Apa Tanis think of groups of kinsmen who stand to them in a relationship involving the same obligation. There are moreover several compound terms which designate such relationships. Thus the term *nyim nyan* is used for all the mother's affinal relatives, who are individually addressed as *aku*. Similarly *milobo nyan* is the collective term for the father's mother's brothers. These two groups of kinsmen are under an obligation to render a man assistance in emergencies. In the old days of feuds with neighbouring Nishis they were responsible to assist in ransoming a man fallen into enemy hands or to avenge his death. On the occasion of a *lisudu* compensation betweed opposing Apa Tanis they were also under the obligation to give moral support to their kinsmen. Today, when there is no more kindnapping and even *lisudu* have become obsolent, such support is given to candidates contesting elections. Thus when in the elections of 1978 Padi Yubbe of Reru won a seat in the Legislative Assembly against the competition of other prominent Apa Tanis it was said that although the Padi clan is not very large, the Padi men had had many sisters in the last two generations and got the support of the latter's husbands.

Another group known by a collective term are the *barm atang*, i.e. the sisters and their families. While *nyim nyam* gave moral support in a dispute leading to a *lisudu*, the *barm atang* and their husbands, i.e. the contestants' brothers-in-law and sons-in-law gave material help in the shape of mithan. Such help was partly given in repayment of all the meat which on the occassion of the Mloko and Morom festivals sisters receive from their brothers.

Similarly in the event of a fire the affinal kinsmen of the victims are under a compelling obligation to render assistance to the victims whose houses were gutted. This custom is eminently reasonable because in an extensive village fire all the houses of a clan or sub-clan clustered together in one ward may have been consumed by the flames, and members of the same patri-kin group are hence likely to be fellow-sufferers and in no position to render help. Affinal relations, on the other hand, are almost certainly distributed over other wards and other villages, and being unaffected by the fire are able to provide assistance in the shape of materials and labour. The speed and efficiency with which such help is forthcoming is one of the most impressive demonstrations of the solidarity between Apa Tani kingroups.

In April 1978 ten houses of the Pura ward of Hija village got accidentally burnt down. At once the emergency service of the concerned kinsmen and friends moved into action. Charred posts and rafters were removed and the house sites cleared for rebuilding. Men of the affected families as well as numerous affinal kinsmen went to their respective bamboo and pine groves to cut and bring building materials. Women of the affinal families meanwhile brought rice, meat and beer to feed the workers. Two days later the rebuilding of several of the destroyed houses was already far advanced, with the piles and the bamboo frame of the roof standing. All the time men carrying heavy bundles of newly cut bamboos were arriving, while others were cutting and splitting such bamboos. Yet others were plaiting wattle walls, and groups of men were putting all these materials together in the construction of the houses. Everybody seemed to know exactly what to do. There was no confusion, but only uninterrupted activity, with old and young working incessantly except for an occasional break to eat a snack brought by kinswomen and other women friends. The other parts of the village were virtually deserted. On the eighth day after the fire all the houses had been reconstituted, and a priest sacrificed a cow and several fowls to appease the deities who cause fires (see Chapter 8).

Obligations between relatives are expressed also in the giving of food, mainly meat, on the occasion of many rites and ceremonies. Thus when a man whom we may call X performs the *subu-tado*, the sacrifice of a mithan at the Morom festival he gives a particular piece of meat known as *ali* to all the descendants of his mother's father whom we may call Z. If X has a daughter (Y) she and her husband inherit this obligation but the portion of the mithan to be given is called *gyasi*, and this term also expresses the relationship. If the woman Y has a daughter, and that daughter marries, she and her husband have still an obligation towards the decendants of Z, and this is now called *liyo-pani* and involves no longer the gift of mithan meat but can be discharged by presents of pieces of pork. Z's decendants are her *nyan*, and the relationship called *kutin* in the next generation still necessitates gifts of small pieces of pork.

Another obligation inherited from generation to generation is that which compels a man performing a mithan sacrifice at the Morom festival to present one leg of the animal to the oldest kins- woman of his wife, e.g. to his wife's father's father's sister or if the latter is no longer alive to his wife's father's sister.

At the Mloko festival too, there is occasion for the presentation of ceremonial gifts of meat to a large number of affinal kinsmen. A man who wants to raise his prestige may perform a Mloko *mudu* and this involves the giving of shares of meat to all his affinal rela- tions up to the ninth generation which in practice means all the members of the clans with which the donor's forefathers inter- married. Some of these shares are specified. The wife's parents get parts of a pig's chest and liver, the wife's brothers or brother's son get also parts of chest and liver, the wife's mother's brother and the donor's own mother's brother get either a side of bacon or a piece from a mithan's shoulder. Minor pieces go to the wife's grand- parents' descendants and other further removed kinsmen in the wife's village or ward. The expenditure of such a Mloko *mudu* is great and it is therefore rarely performed. However in 1978 Tasso Gryayo of Hari, one of the defeated candidates in the elections for the Legisla- tive Assembly of Arunachal Pradesh, performed such a rite, presum- ably in order to bolster up his prestige and consolidate the support of his kinsmen for future contests.

In addition to their links with consanguineous and affinal kins- men, Apa Tanis establish relations of ceremonial friendship which in their effect are very similar to kinship ties. Ceremonial friends are known as *buning-ajing* and a man chooses such friends from clans with which he does not have any affinal relations and normally from villages of another Mloko group. The *buning-ajing* relationship thus has the purpose of closing gaps in the social network, and such a friendship can be concluded even between *guth* and *guchi* though normally *buning-ajing* are of the same class. People have on an average three to six *buning-ajing* relationships, and such bonds are passed from father to son with the result that many carry on with inherited friendships and forge only one or two new *buning-ajing* pacts. The relationship begins with a ceremonial exchange of gifts and involves further gifts on the occasion of rites and festivals. Thus at the Mloko there is a special day when the inhabitants of the village celebrating the festival invite their *buning-ajing*. There is a pig sacrifice, called *ajing-gyedu*, when the ceremonial friends are given presents of pieces of pork, usually large sides of bacon. When the *buning-ajing* perform the Mloko in their village they in turn give their friends similar pieces of pork.

At the time of Morom *buning-ajing* entertain their friends with beer when they come to their village in the course of a procession, and if there is any quarrel or disturbance in connection with the ceremonial progress of the procession it is the responsibility of *buning-ajing* to mediate. The *buning-ajing* assist also by organizing the distribution of the meat of mithan sacrificed at the Morom (see Chapter 7).

While *buning-ajing* normally function at ceremonial occasions they also assist in the rebuilding of their friends' houses after a fire, and in the days of raiding they helped to ransom friends captured by Nishis. Nowadays political leaders try to establish as many *buning-ajing* relationships as possible in order to assure themselves of support at the time of elections.

A different kind of ceremonial friendship known as *gyatu-ajing* is usually concluded between Apa Tanis and Nishis, but there is no bar to the conclusion of such a relationship between two Apa Tanis of different villages. *Gyatu-ajing* relationships involve the exchange of mithan and valuables, and thus resemble the ceremonial friendship pacts which used to be so important in the Nishis' political and social system (see *Himalayan Barbary*, pp. 198-199).

A third type of friendship called *punyang-ajing* involves the exchange of the heads of animals sacrificed at religious rites but has no specific link with either the Morom or Mloko festival. Every Apa Tani can have only one *punyang ajing*, who may be of the same or of another village.

In a society in which such village dignitaries as *buliang* exercised their authority only within narrow limits, and allowed individuals to settle their affairs and disputes with a minimum of public interference, personal ties of kinship and friendship with all the moral and material support they involved were obviously of great importance in providing security and aid in emergencies. Such relationships are still kept alive by the frequent exchanges of small gifts of food, which though often of symbolic rather than practical value create an atmosphere of mutual interdependence and of confidence in a social fabric providing every individual with some protection against adversities or accidents. For the time being the system of safeguards based on kinship and ceremonial friendships is still intact, but it will be interesting to see whether the introduction of regular administration and legal controls will gradually render some of these safeguards obsolete and erode the confidence in the power of kinsmen and friends to guarantee the well-being of the individual members of Apa Tani society.

A section of Bŭla village (1978)

A labour gang repairing the bund of a rice-field (1944)

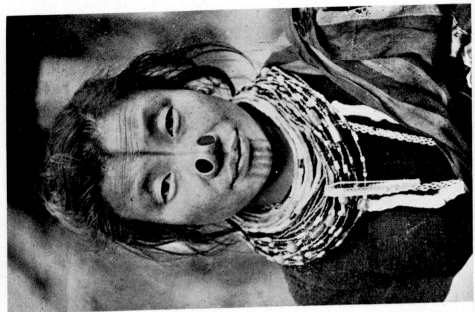

Kago Dining
daughter of
Kago Bida
of Hija
(1978) →

Padi Lailang
of Reru (1944)
←

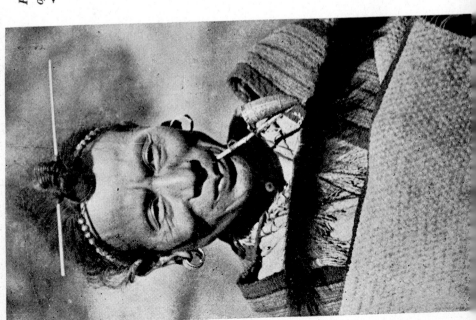

*Kuru Hasang
and his wife
Pume (1978)*
←

*Young men of
Michi Bamin
(1962)*
↑

The bazaar quarter of Hapoli (1978)

A street in Reru village (1978)

Fish pond near Hang (1978)

Men and women planting rice (1944)

Acrobatic during the Mloko festival (1962) →

Funerary monument at Michi-Bamin (1978) ↓

Padi Lailang and his son Yubbe (1978)

Lod Kojee with his wife and son (1978)

SIX

Traditional Social Controls and Values

THE APA TANI valley has for long been an island of order and peace in a sea of stormy conflicts and upheavals. Though attacks of militant Nishis inhabiting the surrounding highlands occasionally eroded some of the defences Apa Tani society had erected against external aggression, on the whole life in the valley was peaceful and Apa Tani men and women enjoyed a high degree of safety as long as they remained within the confines of their villages and cultivated land, and did not expose themselves to Nishi raiders by venturing alone or in small bands too far into the forest. We shall see in Chapter 9 that when provoked they did not hesitate to retaliate and raid the villages of hostile Nishis. Within Apa Tani society, however, unrestricted violence was hardly ever resorted to in the course of disputes, and there were other means of dealing with conflicts between individuals or the rivalry of villages.

The Apa Tanis knew well that their complex economy and their whole pattern of living, so different from that of the much more volatile Nishis, could be maintained only if peace reigned in the valley. Peace was assured by formal treaties of friendship, known as *dapo*, between the individual villages. These pacts were fundamental parts of the political system, and their conclusion lies in so distant a past that no one remembers the events which led to their formulation. Apa Tanis repeatedly told me that without the *dapo* treaties they "could not live even for a month," and they were no doubt quite sincere in their belief in the indispensability of the assurance of peace within the valley.

Yet, there never existed a centralized authority exercising control over the entire tribe, and even the affairs of a single village used to be managed in an informal and often even haphazard manner by clan-representatives who in their plurality constituted a kind of village council. These representatives of individual clans known as *buliang* were men of character and ability, who had attained their position either because they were members of a family which owing to its wealth and status always furnished one or two *buliang* or on account of their personal standing and popularity in the community. The older men among these *buliang* were known as *akha buliang* and these had to be consulted on all important matters, even if their age limited their participation in current affairs. Those junior to the *akha buliang* were called *yapa buliang* and they were active in the settling of disputes and other more demanding duties. There were also men known as *miha* (or sometimes *ajang buliang*) who assisted the older *buliang* in their work by such tasks as carrying messages. Though the *buliang* were collectively the upholders of tribal custom, they acted primarily as the spokesmen of their own clans and not as village-headmen with clearly defined functions. Their duties were those of arbiters rather than of judges, and they usually did not take action unless a dispute had become a public issue which had to be dealt with by the community as a whole, be it by mediation or the use of force.

For their services to the community the *buliang* were rewarded by ceremonial gifts of beer and meat on the occasion of village festivals. Moreover, during the Mloko, celebrated by the three groups of villages in rotation, every *buliang* received—and indeed still receives—gifts of meat from his opposite number in the village which stands to his own village in a relationship of reciprocity.

In Chapter 10 we shall see that in recent years the importance of the *buliang* has greatly declined, because they now share their influence with *gaonbura* appointed by government and the elected members of the village panchayats.

The manner in which Apa Tani justice was being applied before the establishment of the Indian administration can best be demonstrated by the concrete case of the imposition and execution of a death sentence, which occurred in 1945 during my presence in the Valley.

Chigi Duyu, a member of a patrician family of Duta, had been involved in various dubious cattle deals and was known as a thief for years. He had stolen cows and mithan from Apa Tanis, slaughtered them in the forest and sold the meat to Nishis, and conversely had stolen Nishi mithan and sold the meat in Apa Tani villages, thereby causing friction between Apa Tanis and Nishis, as well as dissension among the Apa Tanis themselves. When once he was found selling a cow stolen from a man of Hang, the prominent men of Hang village held council and decided to enlist the support of other villages. They went from village to village and the case was debated on the assembly platforms of all villages except the offender's own village Duta and the neighbouring Mudang-Tage. The majority of prominent men were thus familiar with the case, and they all agreed that Chigi Duyu should be apprehended and killed, but it seems that no hint of the impending danger reached the prospective victim.

Shortly before the Morom festival several prominent men of Hang and Reru surprised Chigi Duyu on a *lapang* of Mudang-Tage and dragged him off to Hang in full view of the people of Mudang-Tage. No one intervened when he was taken to Hang and tied up at one of the public platforms. Two days later the men of Duta, led by Chigi Nimi, Duyu's clansman and an influential *akha buliang* and famous priest, went in solemn procession on their annual visit of goodwill to Hang. There they found, much to their embarrassment, Chigi Duyu, his leg fastened in a log, tied to a *lapang*. Chigi Nimi offered a ransom of four mithan for Duyu's release, and the man whose cow Duyu had stolen was inclined to agree to the deal. But the other captors did not consent to the acceptance of a ransom. Although they were not affected by his last misdeed, they were adamant in their insistence that a stop must be put to the nuisance of Chigi Duyu's depredations, and that he had to die.

Without waiting for further offers from Duyu's kinsmen several prominent men of Hang and Reru assembled at the *lapang* where the prisoner was tied up, and told him that he had to pay with his life for his many misdeeds; it was his own fault and he should not bear them any grudge for carrying out the punishment. Then they cut off his right hand "with which he had stolen," slashed him over the eyes "with which he had spied on other men's cattle," and over the mouth "with which he had eaten stolen goods." In a few minutes he was dead. The men of Reru took one of his hands to their village and kept it in their *nago* as it is customary in the case of captured enemy hands, and the rest of the body was burnt in Hang.

The reaction of Chigi Duyu's kinsmen to his execution demonstrates the acceptance by the community of what can only be described as a judicial decision. After an initial show of indignation interspersed with threats of ultimate retaliation, they soon calmed down, unable to deny that the executioners had acted as the representatives of public opinion and within the principles of tribal custom. Had Chigi Duyu been killed by Nishis, possibly in revenge for exactly the same type of cattle lifting, his kinsmen would have felt obliged to avenge his death or at least demand heavy compensation.

The execution of a thief of patrician class was nevertheless a rare occurrence, and most of the thieves who paid for their offences with their lives were of *guchi* class. A first offender, no doubt, was not dealt with so severely, the punishment consisting only of his or her being tied up for some days beside a *lapang* with one leg fastened in a heavy log of wood. Subsequent offences could perhaps be expiated by the payment of heavy fines, but the punishment of habitual theft was normally death. In the case of slaves it was often their own masters who acted as their chief prosecutors.

One case may suffice to demonstrate the way in which Apa Tanis dealt with slaves who had ceased to be an asset and became a liability to their masters. An unmarried slave girl of Hang had the reputation of being completely irresponsible. She often strayed from her master's house and had casual sex relations with numerous young men. While her promiscuous habits were a matter of indifference to the other villagers, her habit of stealing rice, fowls and beads caused general annoyance and frequently embarrassed her owner. When one day she was caught red-handed in an act of theft, her master decided to inflict on her the customary punishment for habitual stealing. He had her seized and tied up at his own *lapang*. The leading men of the clan gathered and agreed that she should die. Her master's other slaves dragged her to the execution place outside the village, and the *buliang* and clan-elders followed. Then she was killed by all those present. They hacked her to pieces and threw the pieces of the body into the Kele river together with her clothes and ornaments. Subsequently a simplified *ropi* ceremony was held at the *nago*, the explanation being that this was done because like a captive enemy she had been tied up at a *lapang*. In fact, the *ropi* rite is intended to prevent the spirit of the slain from harming the killer.

Though executions of criminals were not frequent I heard in 1944 of several similar cases of the killing of habitual thieves. It seems that Apa Tanis took a far more serious view of offences against property than of almost any other breach of custom.

There was, however, a fundamental distinction in their attitude to what appeared to them as common crimes and to acts of violence and high-handedness occurring in the course of a dispute between equals. The Apa Tani, for all his social sense, is a great individualist and if he was wronged by a fellow tribesman his first reaction was not to appeal to the *buliang* to mediate in the dispute, but to retrieve his loss or vindicate his honour by taking the law into his own hands. As a rule it was only when a quarrel had dragged on or when it began to undermine the peace of the whole community that the *buliang* entered the field of action.

Surprising as it may seem, the Apa Tanis were in no way perturbed if two villagers fought out a quarrel over the ownership of land or an injury done to a member of their household or to a guest by attacking each other's property or even capturing each other's children or relatives. More than once did I see houses fenced in with high bamboo palisades within which the owner held a co-villager imprisoned and it was no unusual thing to kidnap a defaulting debtor or a troublesome relative and guard against his escape by putting his foot into a heavy log. A few examples will demonstrate this system of private enforcement of the law.

In 1944 I found in the main street of Reru a house surrounded by a firm bamboo palisade and was told that the owner Nani Jile was there living in what amounted to self-inflicted confinement. He had quarrelled with his father's brother over the possession of certain rice fields, and in the course of the dispute had captured his cousin's wife and had kept her for a month with a log on her foot in his house. To effect her release her husband had paid a ransom of five mithan cows and five mithan calves, but Jile had still not set her free and in the end the husband with some friends forced their way into Jile's house and rescued the woman. Fearing that his cousin would take revenge and capture him or a member of his family, Nani Jile fortified his house and for five months neither he nor his wife and his children had left the narrow space enclosed by the palisade. From their verandah they could see out through the fence on to the village street and chat with passers-by, and their friends and relatives were free to climb over the carefully guarded fence and keep them company inside the house. But only Jile's two slaves ever went out, and it was they who fetched water and brought in foodstuff provided by Jile's relations-in-law. The latter helped the slaves also in the cultivation of Jile's fields, but he and his wife and children were debarred from any productive work.

After some months, however, Jile relaxed his precautions, and when about half a year later I came to Reru, the fence round Jile's house had been removed and another across the street was fenced-in. It was his cousin's house and Jile himself was kept in it as a prisoner. Soon after he had ventured out of his house his cousin, still smarting under the insult heaped on him and his wife, had captured Jile and had refused to set him free unless Jile's affinal relatives paid him full compensation for the loss of prestige he had suffered through Jile's capture of his wife and for the ransom extracted from him under duress. The dispute dragged on until I left the Valley, but subsequently I heard that ultimately the cousins reached some kinds of agreement which freed them from the fear of capture.

The *buliang* had taken no action and the general attitude of the people of Reru was that the quarrel of the two cousins did not concern anybody but themselves and their nearest kinsmen and relatives-in-law.

An even more bizarre case of capture and imprisonment had occurred at about the same time in Kach, a small hamlet just outside Hang. There I saw a house belonging to Ponyo Tamo surrounded by a bamboo fence, higher than its roof, with only one opening and that so high up that to enter one had to climb up a ladder outside and down a ladder inside. A platform, higher than the gable of the house, served as a kind of sentry-box. The reason for these fortifications was the presence of a prisoner in the house, and this prisoner was no other than Tapi Pusang, the son-in-law of Ponyo Tamo. Tapi Pusang had been married to Tamo's daughter Sante for some ten years but the couple had remained childless. Ultimately Pusang had grown tired of his wife and had told her to leave his house. Sante, however, was not willing to leave him, and though he drove her out again and again, she kept on coming back. When Pusang came to Tamo's house and told him to take back his daughter, the enraged father seized him and tied him up with a heavy log on his foot. To prevent his flight or rescue he surrounded the house with a palisade and erected a platfrom where he or another man of his household kept watch every night.

Tamo said that he would release Pusang only if he either took back his wife or paid a heavy ransom to atone for the insult to Sante and her whole family. For seven months Tamo and his whole family, including his daughter Sante and her imprisoned husband, had been living in the fenced-in house, and Pusang was adamantly refusing either to take back Sante or to pay damages.

When I revisited Kach a year later the fence had been removed, and I heard that Pusang's clansmen had ransomed him by paying Tamo forty mithan-values. The parties were reconciled, but Pusang and Sante had finally separated. In this case too the *buliang* had taken no action to prevent the imprisonment of one villager by the other though at the final settlement they acted as mediators at the request of the parties.

While claims between Apa Tanis often led to the capture of one of the opponents followed by the payment of a ransom there were still other means of fighting out a dispute. If an Apa Tani of wealth and good social status thought his honour at stake, he resorted to a very different procedure to vindicate himself, and humiliate his opponent. This procedure, known as *lisudu*, involved the ritual destruction of wealth and recalled in that respect the *potlatch* rites of the North-West American Indians. A man who challenged a co-villager to a *lisudu* competition started by killing one or several of his mithan in front of his opponent's house and leaving the meat to be distributed to the relatives of his opponent. Sometimes he added to the holocaust certain valuables such as Tibetan bells, bronze plates, elephant tusks and swords. All these were smashed and thus made useless. If his opponent accepted the challenge he had to slaughter at least the same number of mithan and destroy property of equal value in front of the challenger's house. The next move was that the latter killed an even greater number of mithan and this number had again to be matched by his rival. The competition might go on until both parties were nearly ruined, and in theory the man who could continue longest with this destruction of wealth won thereby his opponent's entire remaining property in land and movable possessions. But I have not heard of any concrete case of a *lisudu* carried as far as the utter defeat of one of the competitors. Usually the *buliang* intervened and negotiated a settlement which spared both parties the humiliation of defeat.

A few examples will demonstrate the types of disputes which may result in *lisudu* competitions.

In 1944 Ponyo Tamar of Hang told me of a quarrel he had with Belo Lampung, a man of his own village and also very wealthy.

There had been no dispute over any material possession and the *lisudu* arose only because Belo Lampung offended against Ponyo Tamar's dignity. Some years previously Licha Seke, a Nishi living in Talo village, had taken part in the capture of a mithan belonging to Belo Lampung. Subsequently Licha Seke who had quarrelled with the people of Talo had sought refuge in Hang and went to live there in the house of Taj Tako, a freed slave of Ponyo Tamar. The incident of the stolen mithan seemed forgotten and for a full year Licha Seke stayed unmolested in Hang. Then one day while he went to cut firewood Belo Lampung had him captured and taken to his house. Ponyo Tamar, hearing of the fate of his freed slave's guest, approached Belo Lampung with the offer to ransom Licha Seke promising a payment of five mithan. Lampung rejected the offer and had Licha Seke killed.

Ponyo Tamar reacted to this insult by capturing two cows of Belo Lampung and slaughtering them near his house. As Lampung did not rise to this provocation, Ponyo Tamar challenged him to a *lisudu* and began the destruction of property by killing three of his own mithan in front of Lampung's house and breaking one Tibetan bell, one bronze plate and one sword. Lampung retaliated by killing four big mithan in front of Ponyo Tamar's house but did not destroy any valuables. The next day Tamar killed ten big mithan and a day later Lampung topped this by killing 20 mithan. The competition escalated by the slaughter of 30 mithan by Tamar and Belo Lampung killing 60 mithan on one day. Thereupon Tamar collected 80 mithan and was ready to slaughter 70. At that point several prominent men of Hang and other villages intervened and persuaded Ponyo Tamar not to go any further but be content with matching Belo Lampung's last holocaust by slaughtering also 60 mithan. Ponyo Tamar agreed to this solution, and when he had killed 60 mithan the competition was declared to have ended in a draw. Belo Lampung agreed moreover to pay Ponyo Tamar one mithan cow as compensation for the initial injury to his pride caused by the killing of Licha Seke, whom Tamar regarded as having been a guest of one of his dependants. Ponyo Tamar had killed 60 of his own mithan and 20 mithan which his sisters had contributed though he had not specifically asked for them.

All these events had occurred twenty-five years before Ponyo Tamar, then a very old man, told me about them but it was clear that he remembered every mithan and valuable destroyed in the *lisudu.* He also told me that had the *lisudu* gone on he would have won and would have been entitled to seize Lampung and hold him until by selling his land Lampung would have compensated Tamar for every mithan killed.

It is usual for a man's affinal kinsmen, i.e. his sisters' husbands and his father's sisters' husbands and their descendants, to help him by providing mithan for slaughter, and though such mithan are sometimes repaid there is no compelling obligation to do so.

One of the last *lisudu* was performed in 1966 in the course of the dispute between Koj Nibo and Koj Goru on the one side and Kago Bida and Nada Bakhang on the other, mentioned already in Chapter 5 as having arisen because of Kago Bida's violent opposition to Koj Nibo's marriage to a second wife. Kago Bida challenged Koj Nibo and Nada Bakhang challenged Koj Goru. Each of the four competitors killed 20 mithan and Kago Bida and Koj Nibo also destroyed valuables. The meet of the animals slaughtered at a *lisudu* was always distributed by the competitor in front of whose house they had been slaughtered. Thus in this case the animals killed by Kago Bida in front of Koj Nibo's house were cut up by Koj Nibo and his kinsmen, and distributed to his relatives, the largest shares going to the husbands and the children of his sisters, i.e. his *barme magbo.* Kago Bida had no hand in the disposal of the meat. As soon as he and his men had killed a mithan they left the scene, and it was for Koj Nibo's party to dismember the animal and distribute the meat as they saw fit.

This *lisudu* ended by the mediation not of *buliang* but of the students of the Hapoli High School. They proposed an *ari ten kasudu*, i.e. a comparison of the horns of all the mithan slaughtered. This was done and when all the mithan horns were laid out it was found that those of Koj Nibo and Koj Goru were larger than those of their competitors. The students then proposed that Kago Bida and Nada Bakhang should not match this by killing more mithan but that each of them should give to his opponent three live mithan which were not to be slaughtered. In this way the *lisudu* could be regarded as having ended in a draw though in fact the challengers Kago Bida and Nada Bakhang had lost face. Not all of the mithan slaughtered had been owned by the competitors; some had been bought for the purpose and others obtained on credit.

Another relatively recent *lisudu* occurred in Tajang village and was also triggered off by a quarrel about status and prestige. Rubu

Pilia, a *guchi* whose father had grown rich by trade and bought land, refused to comply with the traditional obligation to present the head of all animals he slaughtered to his patrician patron Nyilang Yapa. Hence the latter challenged him to a *lisudu*, and each of the contestants killed 30 mithan. This meant that a great deal of meat was available for distribution. That of the mithan killed in front of Nyilang Yapa's house was distributed to all his relatives and supporters, many of whom stood to him in the classificatory relationship of sister's husband. Even relatives living in other villages as well as some Nishis who had helped Yapa got shares of meat. Similarly the meat of Nyilang Yapa's mithan slaughtered in front of Rubu Pilia's house was spread over all villages in which supporters of Pilia were found. As the *buliang* failed in the attempt to settle the dispute an official of the administration intervened and proposed a compromise acceptable to both parties. In future Rubu Pilia was to give the heads of his animals to another member of the Nyilang clan though not to Nyilang Yapa. Apa Tanis of patrician class told me that before the coming of the Government no *guchi* had ever engaged in a *lisudu*; had he done so "the *guth* men would have cut off his head."

Another *lisudu* which also arose from a dispute between men of different status occurred in the case of the land of Milo Havung claimed both by his daughters and his illegitimate son Chatung from a *guchi* mother as recounted in Chapter 5. When the husband of Milo Havung's daughters refused to relinquish the land given to their wives by their father Chatung challenged both to a *lisudu* and in its course killed 40 mithan. The two husbands, Lod Rekha and Nyilang Tabin, each killed 20 mithan, but the dispute had ultimately to be settled by the Deputy Commissioner.

While normally such contests were between men of different clans, though more often than not of the same village, there were also cases of *lisudu* in which the opponents were brothers quarrelling over property.

Thus in 1934 Kimle Tara and Kimle Dübo of Hija village quarrelled about the land they had inherited from a *guchi* of Budi clan who had died without heirs. The Budi clan which had stood to the patrician Kimle clan in a client relationship had become extinct and the two Kimle brothers were entitled to all the land and a house site left ownerless. The quarrel arose over the house site of the *guchi* which Tara claimed because it was close to his house. Dübo then challenged his brother to a *lisudu* and began by killing four mithan whereupon Tara slaughtered five. Altogether 65 mithan were slaughtered, and strangely enough all these mithan were provided by affinal kinsmen and relations-in-law though the brothers must have had largely identical kinship ties. Some, but by no means all these mithan were later repaid, particularly those provided by more distant affinal relatives. The dispute was finally settled by dividing all the land as well as the house site to equal parts.

An even odder dispute between two brothers was about the possession of a slave girl and in this case mithan of a value many times that of the slave in question were slaughtered by each of the two contestants. The two brothers were Hibu Riku and Hibu Goji of Hang, and the girl was the daughter of Tiling Tayo, a *guchi* who had been a slave of Michi Tamo of Michi-Bamin village, and had quarrelled with his master and had found refuge in the house of Hibu Goji. For reasons not remembered his master had made no effort to recover him and his wife and daughter. As Tiling Tayo was short of food he sold his daughter Mado for rice of the value of one mithan to Hibu Riku without informing Hibu Goji in whose house he was living. But Goji intervened saying that he would not let the girl be taken away by Riku. As the latter insisted on his right to the girl whom he had purchased, Goji challenged him to a *lisudu* and began by slaughtering two mithan. When Goji had slaughtered 22 mithan and Riku 25 the *buliang* of Hang intervened and the girl was given to Riku while her parents remained with Goji and became his slaves. Later Riku sold Mado for six mithan to Hibu Rade, but when she had worked for Rade for ten years he allowed her to marry a freed slave and move to his house without demanding any compensation.

Lisudu between near kinsmen were quite frequent and their rivalry seems to have usually arisen over matters of prestige. Thus in 1940 Talyang Bida and Talyang Pila of Kalung village, who were the sons of two brothers, quarrelled over an accusation of theft. Pila's wife had lost some valuable beads and Bida was accused of stealing them. Bida denied any guilt and began the *lisudu* by slaughtering one mithan at the *lapang*. The next day Pila killed a mithan at the same *lapang*, and this went on for twenty days, each slaughtering one mithan on alternating days. The mithan were not their own but were provided by their near kinsmen. Later they paid back some of the mithan but not those contributed by their own brothers and their sisters' husbands. Finally, Talyang Bokar, an influential *buliang* of Kalung, stopped the slaughter, but no compensation was paid by either of the hostile cousins.

When personal honour is at stake Apa Tanis have always been extremely sensitive, and many long drawn out disputes arose from relatively minor slights. The memory of an unavenged insult is sometimes nursed for decades and the obligation to redress a grievance is passed on from generation to generation. This happened in the case of Sano Rali, a *guchi* woman, whom in March 1944, I had found tied up with a leg in a heavy log at a *lapang* in Hija (see *Himalayan Barbary*, Fig. 12 and pp. 72-73) accused—as it later turned out quite wrongly—of the theft of a bronze plate. She had been used as a scapegoat in a dispute between some influential patricians and had been dragged from the house of Hage Tatum of Hari, in which she had been living. As the result of a face-saving deal between the patricians concerned she was handed over to Nada Chobin, then the richest and most powerful man of Hija, and lived in his house in the position of a domestic slave for more than twenty years. Hage Tatum often told his four sons of the injustice done to Sano Rali and asked them to avenge the insult to his family and bring Rali back to Hari. But as long as Nada Chobin was alive there seemed to be no chance of implementing such a plan. In 1966, however, when both Hage Tatum and Nada Chobin were dead, Tatum's son Hage Hanyan who was then a Village Level Worker in the employ of government decided to organize the return of Sano Rali to Hari. He sent a woman to Rali with the message that Rali should secretly leave Hija and come to the house of Hage Rambo, the oldest of the four sons of Hage Tatum. Unnoticed Rali slipped away from Hija and came to Rambo's house, but when her absence was noticed by Chobin's son Nada Tadu he and many of his kinsmen came to Hari and demanded the return of Rali. Though this elderly woman was no great asset, Nada Tadu felt his honour at stake and was determined not to let the Hage brothers get away with the rescue of Rali. However, supported by all the Hage men of Hari the brothers stood firm and refused to give in to Nada Tadu's demand. A bitter dispute ensued and Nada Tadu challenged Hage Rambo to a *lisudu*. Several mithan and cows were killed by both men, but in the end the dispute which dragged on over months was referred to the Deputy Commissioner for judgement. He decided in favour of Sano Rali and the Hage men and Nada Tadu attributed their success to the fact that there were several educated men among the Hage men while he and his kinsmen did not know any language other than Apa Tani and had to argue their case through interpreters. It is said that thereafter Nada Tadu sent his children to school, so that they should not suffer from similar disadvantages.

In 1978 I met Sano Rali in the house of Hage Hanyan in Hari. As he was living mainly in a new house in Hapoli Sano Rali was caretaking for him in his old house. She was very well dressed and wore several strings of valuable beads which must have been worth several thousand rupees. The Hage brothers were clearly anxious to show how well they treated their recovered dependant, and Sano Rali herself told me how happy she was in Hari, where she was reunited with her children who had remained in Hari looked after by Hage Tatum. She remembered all the details of our first encounter almost to the day 34 years earlier and my plea for her release from her bonds. Her present freedom among her old patrons is regarded as a triumph for the Hage brothers and implicitly a loss of face for the previously so powerful Nada clan of Hija.

In this particular dispute the *lisudu* did not play a prominent role and was not carried very far, probably because at that time both parties expected better results from an appeal to the officers of government. In the past, however, *lisudu* competitions were obviously one of the principal means of diffusing tensions between prominent men aspiring for prestige and leadership. In my earlier book (*Himalayan Barbary*, p. 75) I argued that the *lisudu* served to maintain the equilibrium of Apa Tani society, and that from the point of view of the average villager it was not a bad thing if two men competing for prominence and leadership relieved each other of some of their surplus wealth. For the flesh of the slaughtered mithan was not wasted but distributed among a large circle of kinsmen and co-villagers. As mithan serve no other purpose than to provide meat, there was little harm in a holocaust when large numbers of Apa Tanis enjoyed a feast at the expense of two rich men who were likely to emerge from the contest with their wings considerably clipped. The *lisudu* played in this respect a role similar to that of feasts of merit among such tribes as Nagas and Chins, though competition between the givers of feasts of merit was not explicit and usually extended over considerable periods. The Apa Tanis too have rites of the feast-of-merit type, but the number of animals slaughtered on such occasions is not of the same dimension as the carnage which used to characterize some of the *lisudu*. Predominant was always the idea that the more wealth a man can destroy the higher his social prestige rises, and the support given by numerous affinal kinsmen was regarded as proof of his influence in a large social group.

Whereas the *lisudu* was the recognized means by which a man could vindicate his personal honour slighted by a fellow villager, disputes between members of different villages often led to the involvement of much larger numbers. There were two stages in the pursuance of such disputes and the attempts at settlement: a peaceful one known as *dapo-sodu* and one that involved the possibility of armed combat and known as *gambo-sodu*. In my earlier accounts of the Apa Tanis I dealt only with the latter because I was not aware of the distinct procedure of the *dapo-sodu* which I discovered only in 1978.

Let us take a hypothetical dispute of whatever nature between two men of Kalung and Tajang, two villages of the Büla cluster. One of the litigants would call all his relatives and friends to his house and explain his case. The assembled men would start a *dapo* and, forming a procession, go to other villages, and canvass for support. In such a procession the affinal kinsmen (*nyim-nyan* and *milobo nyan*) and ceremonial friends (*buning ajing*) play an important role. Thereupon the other litigant would call together his nearest kinsmen and friends and they would start a counter-*dapo*. Representatives from both sides, i.e. Kalung and Tajang, would then go in two separate groups to a neighbouring village, say Hija, and the people of that village would agree to have the case debated in their presence. This would happen on one of the assembly platforms, and those relatives of the members of the *dapo*-processions who lived in Hija, would provide some food and beer. The giving of food to a litigant's representatives signifies support for his cause. At such a first joint meeting the *buliang* and people of Hija might successfully mediate and the representatives of the litigants might then return to their clients and report to them the terms of the settlement and ask for payment of any fines which might have been imposed. The two litigants would prepare feasts called *gandu aping* for all those involved in the discussions leading to the settlement. They should also go to each other's houses to partake of the feasts, but this was not always done.

If no settlement could be achieved in Hija, the whole party of both sides accompanied by the Hija people would go on to Duta to discuss the dispute further, and if there no agreement was reached either, the whole group would go on to Mudang-Tage to solicit the mediation of the people of that village. In this way a growing crowd made a round of the whole Apa Tani valley, and if all attempts to reach a settlement were exhausted, the *buliang* of the whole valley came into action. They might meet anywhere and their decision should be unanimous. If such a decision was reached the *buliang* had the right to enforce their verdict. Thus they were entitled to cut through the palisades of a house in which one of the litigants was holding a prisoner and to free him. They even had the authority to seize a recalcitrant litigant and to tie him up. As nowadays the *buliang* can no longer take such forcible action they have lost much of their authority and are no longer effective.

In the past too the *buliang* sometimes could not achieve a settlement because they were unable to reach a unanimous decision. In such an event a critical situation arose, and the parties decided to stage a *gambu sodu*, an armed contest in which the supporters of both litigants turned out for an open fight. On the day fixed for the combat the men of both parties lined up and fought with long lances, bows and arrows, and sometimes even with swords. The men whose dispute was the immediate cause of the *gambu* usually did not take part, but confined themselves to marshalling their partisans. It was argued that they were not supposed to risk their lives because they were under an obligation to pay compensation for anyone wounded or killed in the fray.

The actual combat was governed by various rules and conventions, and there was no intention to inflict heavy losses on one's opponents. As soon as there were one or two fatal casualties on either side, the *gambu* was usually called off. It seems that no permanent enmity resulted from these pre-arranged fights and it may be argued that they served as a kind of safety valve through which pent-up ill-feeling between groups could be discharged with a minimum of harm to the tribal community as a whole. In the heat of the fight some damage was sometimes done to gardens and bamboo groves, but there was never any large-scale destruction of houses and granaries, such as occurred in the raids of Nishis on each other's settlements. The fighting in a *gambu* was more or less ordered and confined to long-distance arrow shooting and spear throwing. I never heard of a *gambu* which ended in a general mêlée where men fought with swords and knives for their lives. The description of a *gambu* by Ursula Graham Bower in *The Hidden Land* (pp. 120-127) shows that *gambu* do by no means always involve actual fighting but may consist only of an armed demonstration to exert pressure on a village. Her eye-witness account of a *gambu* in 1947 is all the more valuable as no other *gambu*, including the last *gambu* in 1972, has ever been described by an outside observer and all existing accounts are based on the testimony of Apa Tani participants and onlookers.

Two examples may demonstrate the types of quarrels which used to lead to such pre-arranged fights. In 1939 Hage Sa of Hari ambushed some Nishis of Linia who had come to trade with the Apa Tanis of Büla and killed one man and one woman in retaliation for the earlier killing of his brother by men of Linia. The people of Büla were infuriated by the attack on their trade-partners on their village territory, and they demanded that Hage Sa should pay compensation to Linia. When he refused, two of the constituent settlements of Büla declared a *gambu* against Hage Sa, who took up the challenge supported by the whole of his village. On the appointed day men of Büla and Hari lined up on an open field between the two villages. Numbers were fairly equal and the parties attacked each other with arrows and spears, while the women brought up reinforcements in the shape of new bamboo spears. Many were wounded, but after two men on each side had been killed the *gambu* was broken off. There was no formal peace-making, but the dispute was considered settled and both villages resumed friendly relations.

Another *gambu* in which Hari was involved resulted from the capture of two Nishi women visiting Hari on the occasion of the Mloko festival by men of Hang, who had nursed a grievance against their village. When they refused to release the guests of Hari, the latter village declared a *gambu* against Hang and was supported by Büla, Mudang-Tage and Michi-Bamin all of whom had a friendship pacts with the Nishi women's village. The men of these four villages marched to Hang and formed a long line on the fields in front of the village. The battle raged for some time inconclusively, watched by crowds of warriors from the neutral villages of Hija and Duta. Just when the men of Hari and their allies were on the point of pushing the Hang men back into their own village,

Celebration of Padi Yubbe's election victory (1978)

Guests at the feast given by Padi Yubbe (1978)

Priest chanting before a pig sacrifice at a yugyang (1978)

Priest reciting prayers before a cattle sacrifice (1978)

Preparation for a ropi *rite* (*1944*)

Procession during a ropi *rite* (*1978*)

Two mithan (Bos frontalis) (1945)

Priests on a lapang *during a sacrificial rite (1962)*

Woman weaving on a stretch loom (1962)

Woman shaping pots before they are fired (1962)

House with high fence in which prisoner is being held (1944)

A nago *shrine in Reru (1978)*

Morning parade at the Hapoli School (1978)

Children in the Hapoli School (1970)

Nishi of Jorum with his two wives (1962)

Nishi long-house in Jorum (1978)

the rumour spread that a son of Ponyo Tamar, Hang's most influential man, had been mortually wounded. The news sobered the Hari men, who realized the seriousness of such an incident, and they withdrew from the fight. The rumour was exaggerated and the boy hit by an arrow in the chest escaped with his life. On Hari's side two men were wounded, but there were no fatal casualties. Normal relations between Hang and Hari were resumed gradually without formal peace negotiations.

At the present time the causes of disputes have changed and it is no longer imaginable that Nishis coming as guests to the Mloko festival would be ambushed and captured, and even more that an Apa Tani village would have to take up arms in revenge for the killing of trade-partners by other Apa Tanis. But prestige and status are still values hotly fought for, and the last *gambu* staged in the Apa Tani valley arose from a quarrel over a matter lacking any material implications. A school was to be built outside Reru on cultivated land near Limpia, a colony of Tajang which together with Reru and Kalung forms the large composite settlement known by the collective term Büla. There was, it seems, no serious dispute over making the site available for the school-building but a violent argument arose over the name of the school. The people of Reru wanted it called "Reru School" because Reru is larger than Tajang and most of the pupils were likely to come from Reru, but the people of Tajang opposed this proposal tooth and nail arguing that the school was going to be built on Tajang land and should hence be called "Tajang School." Tempers rose to such a degree that the two villages decided to stage a *gambu*. On 22 February 1972 men of Reru and Tajang donned the dress of warriors and faced each other in long lines on open ground. There was possibly no intention to inflict any fatal casualties, but an arrow struck Nyilang Halyang of Tajang so unluckily that he died. The *gambu* was then broken off, and there is every likelihood that on that February day the long sequence of Apa Tani arranged village-fights—"mass duels" as I once called them—has forever come to an end. *Buliang, gaonbura* and panchayat members then resumed negotiations and on 23 March held a great formal debate. But it was not until may that a final decision was reached, which in true Apa Tani style was based on a compromise. The land in question was recognized as Tajang village-land, the school was to be built on another site and was called "Reru School." No compensation was awarded to the family of the Tajang man killed in the *gambu*, but 20 young men of Reru blamed for the killing were subsequently jailed by the administration.

To confirm the agreement reached each party to the dispute brought and slaughtered a mithan on the disputed land, and moreover each party brought one piece of old meat, as well as cooked rice and beer. Both parties sat together, exchanged some of the food and beer, and ate together. It is interesting that to my knowledge no comparable fraternization followed any of the many *gambu*, the circumstances of which I recorded in 1944 and 1945.

We may now pose the question to what a degree *lisudu* and *gambu* can be regarded as methods of social control. In a *lisudu* there was certainly coercion, but it was of a moral and not of a physical kind. The challenger did not destroy his opponent's property but forced him to undertake the destruction himself under the threat of a loss of prestige. One may well argue that the *lisudu* served a positive social purpose by curbing the pride and influence of two prominent men competing for a dominant position in their village, and at the same time effected a distribution of meat to many of the villages. Thus the *lisudu* may have acted as a device to check too great an accumulation of capital in the hands of a few prominent families. For if we may judge from the examples mentioned by my Apa Tani informants it was the wealthiest men who, being most sensitive to any slight to their honour and prestige, were most inclined to indulge in these expensive competitions.

Nishi and Miri society did not know any competitions comparable to the Apa Tani *lisudu*. There rivalry between co-villagers and even clansmen expressed itself in much cruder form, and a man feeling aggrieved and strong enough to stand up to an opponent would organize a raid or kidnap him or one of his dependants. Similarly Apa Tani *gambu* involve far less violence than a Nishi attack on a settlement which would often be wiped out with half of the inhabitants killed and the remainder captured and held to ransom. The casualties in a *gambu* were usually small, and it is surprising indeed that so often hundreds of Apa Tani warriors armed with bows and arrows, swords and pikes could advance on each other and go through the motions of a spirited fight without inflicting on each other very serious losses.

Our limited knowledge of the manner in which disputes were settled and criminals punished in past days tends to show that the preservation of social harmony and equilibrium was considered the supreme aim of all efforts on the part of the *buliang* and the com· munity in general. There was no doubt a lack of moral sense in a system which provided for the elimination by public action of the man or woman of low status who through the habit of petty theft had become a nuisance, while a rich man could pick a quarrel with an equal, capture and imprison opponents, and finally resolve the dispute by a *lisudu* competition. In the eyes of the Apa Tanis there is a subtle difference between common crime and certain acts of violence which are deemed not altogether disreputable, such as the imprisonment of an opponent in the course of a private dispute.

If a quarrel between two men of about equal standing arising from an accusation of theft or a similar crime could not be resolved by negotiation and the mediation of *buliang* and *gaonbura*, Apa Tanis used to resort to an ordeal, but this practice is now frowned upon by government officials. Each party in the dispute used to call a *nyibu* but such a priest was not to be an Apa Tani, for only Nishi *nyibu* were thought suitable for organizing an ordeal.

For the ordeal water had to be brought from one of the major rivers, such as Kamla, Khru or Panior, and the first step was to consult omens to discover the most appropriate water-course. When this had been done, water from the river indicated was boiled in a section of a large bamboo, such as Nishis grow. A small stone was put into the water and the person accused of the crime had to take the stone out of the boiling water with his bare hand. If the hand swelled he was deemed guilty, but if it remained unharmed he was declared innocent. During the ordeal both sides wore war-dress and both prayed to Doni-Polo (Sun and Moon), asking them to decide in their favour.

Sometimes a second ordeal was demanded. A piece of iron was heated in a fire and was then put on the accused person's palm which was protected only by three leaves of the *saro*-tree. The *nyibu* then examined the hand and if it was burnt the accused was considered guilty, but if there were no marks his innocence was proved. The man declared innocent could then fine his accuser.

The most recent ordeal was held in Hija. The dispute was over the alleged theft of a valuable necklace. But when the water into which the stone had been dropped began to boil the bamboo split, and thus the ordeal could not be completed. The by-standers and the two priests considered this as a sign that the man accused of the theft was innocent. Later events, however, created doubts in his innocence, for within a year his wife, his son and the Nishi *nyibu* whom he had called all died.

Ordeals were arranged when the parties involved in a dispute could not resolve their differences and the *buliang* or the representatives of public opinion were doubtful about the rights and wrongs of the case, and hence could not effectively intervene. Today there is in such cases a tendency to appeal to the officers of government and thereby break the deadlock in much the same way as an ordeal was essentially an appeal to higher powers and an acceptance of their judgement.

We have seen that the Apa Tanis have developed a system of social controls which aims at restricting the use of force as far as possible, and plays on the individual's sensitivity to social approval and disapproval. Ths Apa Tanis do not admire the strong and ruthless man to the same extent as their Nishi neighbours, but value skill in negotiations and the power of leadership in influencing the deliberation of a council of *buliang* and *gaonbura*. To attain one's aim by peaceful means was always considered preferable and more meritorious than to resort to violence, and if a dispute between two men of equal wealth and status had defied a negotiated solution, the adversaries tried to shame each other into submission by a *lisudu* competition. The fact that such moral pressure was effective seems indicative of a sensitivity to public opinion.

The Apa Tani's judgement of good and bad conduct relates to the degree of a person's conformance to the accepted standards of social behaviour. Unprovoked infliction of an injury to a fellow tribesman, murder, theft, cheating in trade deals, adultery, clan incest and the breach of undertakings such as failure to repay a debt are all considered bad, but the public attitude depends on the nuisance caused to the community. We have seen that an isolated case of theft arouses little comment, but that in the past a habitual thief was likely to be executed. A couple guilty of clan incest was driven out of their home village, but no objection to their union was raised by the inhabitants of any other village where they managed to settle.

The approval of their fellow tribesmen has always been of great importance to Apa Tanis, and the fear of being "shamed" is a powerful incentive to conformity. There is, on the other hand, no sense of "sin" and no corresponding desire to acquire "merit" in

Traditional Social Controls and Values 149

a system of supernatural rewards. Neither do the Apa Tanis ascribe to their gods a general interest in the moral conduct of man. The individual cannot conceive of right or wrong conduct other than as a response to the requirements of the society, and feels no responsibility to a higher power. Hence the lack of any sense of "guilt" or "sin" such as might be felt by those at variance with the values of a supernatural order. In their moral thinking and sentiments Apa Tanis remain always close to earth, and if they think of the fate that awaits them after death they think of it as a reflection of life on this earth, as we shall see in greater detail in Chapter 8.

SEVEN

Rituals and Ceremonies

AT A TIME when the Apa Tanis' world is being transformed
by profound changes in many sectors of their economic, social and
political life, there remains one sphere in which conservative forces
still prevail, and modifications of traditional procedures have been
confined to superficialities. This is the sphere of rituals by which
priests and seers establish contact with supernatural forces, and
laymen reinforce and make apparent the links which hold the web
of society together. The ability to be in touch with gods and spirits
is not acquired by accident, for unlike the deities of other peoples,
those of the Apa Tanis do not impose themselves on mortals sum-
moning them to their service. Priests, known as *nyibu*, have to learn
the art of communicating with the denizens of the invisible world
by a lengthy process of training. They do not belong to a special
class of people, but any patrician—though not a *guchi*—can acquire
the skill of invoking gods and spirits. This is usually done by ap-
prenticing himself to an experienced *nyibu* and by assisting him in
the performance of rituals and sacrifices.

There passes no day in the Apa Tani Valley without one or
another priest approaching gods and spirits on behalf of individuals
who seek their help in a personal crisis, be it an illness or an enterprise such as the construction of a house or the appeasement of
spirits after a fire which devastated part of a village. Indeed it is
common to find priests dressed in ceremonial robes reciting incanta-
tions on a public *lapang* or to hear their monotonous chants re-
sounding in the interior of a dwelling house.

There are no temples or shrines containing the images of gods,
and no special buildings where worshippers gather for the performance of rites. The open assembly platforms (*lapang*) are the venues
for public rituals and a special corner in dwelling houses, close to
the family hearth, is used as the seat of the priest whenever a private

rite is performed. Private rites are performed as parts of such cere-
monials as weddings or funerals, but far more spectacular are the
great festivals celebrated at certain seasons of the year.

The two main public festivals are the Morom and the Mloko
(also pronounced Myoko) both of which are associated with the
beginning of the agricultural season. Yet, unlike the Mloko which
every village celebrates once in three years together with the other
villages of the same group (described hereafter as Mloko group),
the Morom has not the character of a communal festival participation in which is compulsory for every household. It is rather a
festive season providing the framework for celebrations by individuals intent on increasing their prestige and status in the community by sacrificing mithan and feasting their kinsmen and neighbours.

The sacrificial rites performed within the context of the Morom
are of the nature of feasts of merit, and just like in the case of the
feasts of merit of Angami and Ao Nagas there are different grades
of Morom rites. The lowest of these grades involves only a modest
expenditure but the higher grades are of great complexity and their
performance can be very costly.

The distinction between the different grades of the feasts performed at the time of Morom is complicated by the fact that the three
groups of villages do not use the same terms for the individual rites.
There is little difference, however, in the purpose and the procedure
of the feasts.

The three grades of the usual Morom rites are:

Rung-sere, a simple rite which involves the sacrifice of only one
or two mithan, or a mithan and a cow. Their meat is distributed
only to the donor's agnatic kinsmen, who assisted in the rite, and
his *nyim nyan* (mother's brothers) and *milobo nyan* (father's
mother's brothers). There is no procession to other villages.

Takum-putu is a more complicated rite, requiring the sacrifice
of several mithan and involving a procession to the villages of
the donor's own Mloko group; for instance, in the case of a donor
from Reru village to Tajang, Kalung and Hari.

Rung-ti or *gyamo-pido* is a more superior and more expensive
rite and at its celebration the donor's procession visits all the
villages of the Apa Tani valley.

A generic term used for both *takum-putu* and *rungti* is *un-pedo*, and Apa Tanis use normally only this term when speaking of either. The ritual procedures for *takum-putu* and *rung-ti* (*gyamo-pido*) are nearly identical and the following summary of events applies to either of the two major rites, which are far more elaborate than the ritual performances at the *rung-sere*.

On the first day of any *un-pedo* the mithan and cows for slaughter are brought to the village and tied up at the *lapang* of the donor. There the officiating priest, standing on the *lapang*, invokes the gods. In the evening a special *mura*, formerly a slave of the donor, takes the mithan and cows to the latter's house where they are sacrificed.

On the second day the donor's ceremonial friends (*buning-ajing*) and affinal kinsmen (*nyan-mida*) and sisters' husbands and sons (*barma-obo*) bring rice and millet. All the grain is boiled in the house, and then the donor's family and the visitors prepare the rice millet for the making of beer. They work the whole night.

On the third day the helpers sleep most of the time. In the evening the moistened grain is filled into smaller vessels and stored in a granary for fermentation.

On the fourth and fifth day all the visitors and helpers stay in the donor's house and are fed by him. On the evening of the fifth day the beer is strained.

On the sixth day the meat of all the mithan and cows is cut into small pieces and filled into baskets. On the same evening the *buning-ajing* come, some of the meat is roasted and eaten and beer is served. Early next morning boiled rice is served.

On the seventh day, early in the morning, the *buning-ajing* of the donor fill the small meat pieces into baskets and take them for distribution to all the villages of the Valley if a *rung-ti* is performed and to those of the donor's Mloko group in the case of a *takum-putu*. The distribution is done by the *buning-ajing* from their respective villages where they know the exact number of houses and families. The meat has been cut into such thin slices that all Apa Tani households can get their shares. Later on the seventh day a procession called *un-pete-taling*, consisting of two priests in full ceremonial dress, and small as well as older boys carrying swords and bronze plates which they beat like gongs, makes a round of the valley. The course of the procession is determined by omens, which indicate also on which *lapang* the priests and boys shall stop and rest. They rest, however, only on the *lapang* of those villages which belong to their own *asso* (see Chapter 3) and only the people of their own *asso* entertain them with beer and rice. In each of the villages visited the members of the procession perform a dance, forming a long line and bending their knees as they brandish swords. All the boys are dressed in clean white cloaks and laden with all the ornaments their families could provide. As the procession moves across the fields from vilage to village, the two priests intone prayers and scatter husked rice, thus magically reinforcing the fertility of the soil.

Before the procession returns to the donor's village, a halt is made on a piece of pasture land, and there a long rod is rigged up on two posts, and the young men show off their skill in the high-jump. This is followed by a fertility dance of a few of the young men holding bamboo staves in the position of phalli. This dance is continued in the village of the donor for the benefit of women and girls watching from the platforms of their houses. The same evening the two priests are entertained in the donor's house, but later go to their own houses. The young men, on the other hand, spend most of the night in the festive house, drinking large quantities of beer and singing and dancing.

On the eighth day, the donor may want to perform some additional rite, and for this purpose he calls a priest and sacrifices a mithan for Morom-ui the god of the Morom. This rite is done for the general welfare of the donor's house. In the evening there is again singing and dancing. After the priest has been entertained with food and drink, he is given the present of a side of bacon, and this he carries to his house.

On the ninth day the helpers who prepared the beer give some to the people who cut up the meat, and the latter give some meat to the brewers of beer. This ceremonial exchange takes place in the donor's house. When they have had a meal they return to their respective houses.

After the ninth day there is a period of rest, during which no one goes to his fields.

On the fifteenth day all the people who participated in the ceremonies come to the donor's house. There they are entertained with beer, and after that they all go to his fields and work there for the rest of the day, mainly repairing dams and channels, and levelling the ground.

On the same day the donor's wife sows some rice in her seed-beds. She then brings back a small quantity of rice, pounds it and eats it roasted. With this ritual act, which links the Morom rites with the cultivation of rice, the celebrations come to an end. Only after the seed-beds of the donor or donors—in case of two men performing rites—have been sown will the other villagers begin to sow their rice. Those villages in which no Morom rite is being performed follow in that year the time-table of villages which held *un-pedo* or *rung-sere* rites.

For the performance of the *rung-ti (gyamo-pido)* four or five mithan are required because shares of meat, however small, have to be distributed to all households of the Valley. Those who cannot afford such a rite may perform a *takum-putu* rite, and for this only three mithan are needed, and only the inhabitants of the villages within the donor's own Mloko group receive the symbolical shares of meat.

Apart from the rites so far discussed, there were in past years two higher and more expensive grades of Morom feasts but some years have passed since either of them has been performed.

The rite ranking immediately above the *rung-ti* (or *gyamo-pido*) is called *pinko-pranye kedu*, and when this is performed each Apa Tani household in the Valley receives two pieces of mithan meat.

Even more expensive is a rite known as *yapu-yalung-pido*. At this feast each household in the Valley must be given one piece of mithan meat and one piece of bacon, the latter being much more expensive than beef. The donor must moreover kill two pigs for distribution to his relatives by marriage (*nyan mida*), and moreover large numbers of sides of bacon, up to two hundred, have to be bought, and each of these pieces may cost Rs 300-400. My informants calculated that at present prices the performance of a *yapu-yalung-pido* would cost Rs 30,000-40,000. Until about 1956-1957 quite a number of Apa Tanis held this feast killing 15 to 20 mithan; among them were Padi Lailang of Reru, Gyate Tadu of Hari, Hage Tamo and Hage Morthi, both of Hari. The last *yapu-yalung-pido* was performed by Mudang Laling in 1972. I was told that now such feasts are no longer given because people have become money-minded, and they prefer putting money into the bank rather than spending it on feasts which raise their prestige.

In some years there may nowadays be no one in a village who is willing to perform one of the Morom rites and in such a case the time of Morom passes without any celebration. In 1978 this happened in Mudang Tage, and in the same year only a *rung-sere* with the sacrifice of one mithan and one cow was held in Duta. In

Hang two men performed *rung-ti* rites, and in Michi-Bamin there were also two men performing the *rung-ti*. Similarly one man of Hija and one man of Reru performed *rung-ti*, and in Tajang there was a performance of the *takum-putu* rite with the sacrifice of two mithan and one cow.

Although my notebooks and diaries of 1944 and 1945 do not contain any positive statement regarding the frequency of the performance of Morom rites, I am under the impression that then there were in all villages annual celebrations of Morom rites. The fact that nowadays a year may pass when no one in a village performs such a rite may be due to the availability of other status symbols which compete with the Morom rites for the resources of Apa Tanis. If a man has the choice of either sacrificing five mithan at a *rung-ti* rite or buying a second-hand jeep, he may well decide on the purchase of such a vehicle.

The performance of one of the Morom rites still lends the donor a measure of social prestige, but does not invest him with any tangible privileges. Unlike a Naga who has spent part of his wealth on the performance of a feast of merit he can neither decorate his house with the visible insignia of a feast-giver nor don a special cloak or wear ornaments indicating his elevated status. The giving of one of the *un-pedo* feasts does not qualify an Apa Tani for any public office, and a man may be a *buliang* or *gaonbura* without ever having performed such a feast. Yet as the slaughter of mithan followed by the distribution of meat and the feasting of large numbers of friends and kinsmen with beer and rice are regular features of the time of Morom, there must be considerable speculation as to who would devote a portion of his cattle wealth to the common good, and wealthy men who have never performed a Morom rite may well be subjected to some public criticism. Particularly a *buliang* known for his wealth would be looked down upon as stingy if he had never spent some of his resources on the giving of an *un-pedo* feast. Among those who profit from the performance of any Morom rite are the *buliang* of the same *asso* group of villages, for the donor of the feast has to send special shares of meat to all the *buliang* of his own *asso*. A man who wants to display his wealth and generosity more than once can repeat the performance of one of the *un-pedo* rites after an interval of five years but not earlier.

The cooperation of numerous kinsmen, both agnatic and affinal, over several days in the preparation of beer, and the butchering and distribution of meat undoubtedly serve to knit together kingroups and demonstrate their size and cohesion to the village at large. Finally the sharing of the meat of the slaughtered cattle with the entire Apa Tani community reaffirms the sense of corporateness pervading the whole Apa Tani tribe, and the mechanism of this distribution invests the donor's *buning-ajing* with a specific and responsible role. Apart from the Morom rites' function of demonstrating and cementing social links there is of course also their function of providing the sheer entertainment of processions and dances which benefits the entire community, for any youth may take part in the processions and not only the kinsmen or ceremonial friends of the donor of the feast.

While the Morom is celebrated at the end of winter before the beginning of agricultural work, the second and far more important seasonal festival, the Mloko (or Myoko), coincides with the flowering of the fruit trees and indeed it cannot be begun before a certain ritually relevant plum-tree (*thakum*) has begun to flower, an event which usually happens in the middle of March. The Mloko is held by each village only once in three years, but an unalterable system of rotation assures that every year one of the village groups celebrates the Mloko. According to this system, Hang performs the Mloko one year, Hari, Reru, Kalung and Tajang the next year and the group comprising Haja, Duta, Mudang-Tage and Michi-Bamin in the third year of the cycle. Preparations for the festivities extend over many weeks and include the purchase of sacrificial animals, the collection and storing up of firewood, and above all the erection of tall poles known as *bobo*, which at the time of the Mloko—and at no other time—are used for a game of acrobatics performed on strong cane ropes attached to the top of these poles and anchored at some distance on the ground. By pulling on one of these ropes and making it swing, people get themselves propelled high up into the air and the sport is popular among young people of both sexes, though even older men and women sometimes show their skill in the game. Cutting these poles, sometimes nearly 100 feet high, in the forest, dragging them to the village and finally erecting them near a *lapang* requires great efforts on the part of the men of the *lapang* in question. As late as 1962 when I watched the performance of the Mloko in Hang, the rope-swinging game was an integral part of the celebration, and the Apa Tanis explained that it was played to amuse the gods who had been summoned to the feast. At that time young men, girls and young boys propelled each other into the air day after day, and in 1978 when Hari and Büla celebrated the Mloko I was surprised to see only a few young boys half-heartedly swinging on the ropes. I noticed too that many of the *bobo* poles had no ropes attached to them, and it was explained to me that there was the fear that those swinging on the ropes might collide with the electric cables which now extend between high masts rivalling the *bobo* poles.

The ritual side of the Mloko begins with its inauguration by the priests (*nyibu*) of the individual clans, each of whom performs a sacrifice in his own house. In 1978 I watched this inconspicuous inauguration rite in the house of a priest of one of the branches of the Hage clan of Hari. It was evening when the priest, assisted by his wife, prepared himself for the rite, which was to be performed near the hearth in the right back-corner of his house. He started by putting a second brass hair-pin through his top-knot, and attaching to it a small brass chain. He then covered his head with a stiff, embroidered square of cloth, and then draped himself in the heavily embroidered priest's clock worn on ritual occasions. Finally he hung a sword with a strap covered with cowry shells over his shoulder.

Dressed in all this finery he sat down by the fireplace and holding a staff in his hand began a long incantation of gods and spirits couched in an archaic language which even Apa Tani laymen do not completely understand. In this incantation which lasts about four hours, the priest summons gods and spirits to the Mloko, and at the end he sacrifices a small chicken and sees the omens from the intestines.

While the priest chants in the corner of his house, other clan members gather in their own houses and entertain visitors with beer and pieces of roast beef and pork. They pay no attention to the inauguration rite which is considered purely the priest's business.

The following day a rite is performed at each of the *nago* shrines. There is a special priest known as *Mloko nyibu* who places a monkey skull into the *nago* and offers a chicken and some eggs inside the shrine. Then all the men and boys of the ward of which the *nago* is the ritual centre form a procession, and carrying large leaves of a special kind chant as they make a round of the village. They finally assemble at the *nago*, where some of the leaves are then stuck into the mouth of the monkey skull; if these shake spontaneously the priest knows that the god of the *nago* has come. The rite ends with a dance in which mainly veteran warriors participate. Brandishing their swords they jump about with fierce facial expressions, dancing repeatedly round the *nago*. This dance resembles the dancing at the *ropi*-rite (see below) which used to be performed whenever an enemy was killed, and part of the head or a hand were deposited in the *nago*. It is not unlikely that the monkey skull now required for the rite inaugurating the public Mloko celebrations is a substitute for a human skull.

On the evening of the same day every clan erects a ritual structure (*agyang*) in a plot known as *yugyang* which serves as the ceremonial centre of the clan or sub-clan as the case may be.

The sacrificial rites of the next day, called *yugyang todu*, begin at dawn. They are the most important part of the Mloko festival, and we have seen in Chapter 4 that participation in these rites is a symbol of a man's or woman's status as fully privileged clan member, and that patricians married to *guchi* or members of other tribes are excluded from these important rites.

In the dim light of dawn the clan members carry their sacrificial pigs with the legs tied to a pole to the *yugyang*, and put them down wherever they find a free space. Unconcerned about the squealing pigs priests in ceremonial robes stand near the *agyang* and chant in the manner typical of all sacrificial rites. Their recitation deals with the history of mankind and particularly of the Apa Tanis. Sacrificing small chickens and tying them to the ritual structure they invoke the first ancestors of the Apa Tanis. Every time a chicken is sacrificed the priests scrutinize the liver for omens.

In the meantime women wearing new jackets of white home-woven cotton with broad embroidered blue borders arrive carrying vessels with millet beer and baskets with rice-flour and crushed slightly fermented rice. They are the wives of the men providing pigs for sacrifice, or in some cases the wives of the eldest sons of the families sacrificing pigs. Guided by the priests they pour millet beer on special parts of the ritual structure, and the chickens suspended from it, and then pour beer and scatter rice flour onto the pigs of their husbands and also on the pigs to be sacrificed by any of their husbands' agnatic kinsmen. Similar scenes take place at all the *yugyang* of the village, and after the women have sprinkled beer and rice flour on the sacrificial pigs, they go from house to house in the streets of the neighbourhood and distribute beer, and slightly fermented crushed rice mixed with salt and ginger to the people in the street and those standing on the verandahs. In this way all the villagers gain from the spirit of hospitality prevailing during the Mloko festival, and the generosity of families sacrificing pigs extends to visitors coming from other villages and even to Nishis who flock to the Apa Tani villages where the Mloko is being celebrated.

After the completion of the rites at the *yugyang* men carry the squealing pigs back to the houses, where they will ultimately be slaughtered. The priests go from house to house, accompanied by some old men who kill the pigs by cutting out the heart. The blood is collected in earthen pots, kept for a few days and then boiled till it becomes solid. It may also be mixed with rice and cooked in the same earthen pot.

People of *guth* class may not eat the blood of pigs sacrificed by *guchi* people, and vice versa. It is believed that any one eating of the blood prepared by the other class will die.

The pig is cut up in the sacrificial corner of the house where it has been killed, and part of the skin with the adhering fat is given to the priest. While a *guchi* gives the whole head of any pig he has sacrificed to his *guth* patron, a *guth* sacrificing a pig gives the head to the oldest man among his close paternal kinsmen. On the day after the rites at the *yugyang* and the sacrifice of pigs, a village celebrating the Mloko invites people from the same *asso* group to a singing competition known as a *khobo gyodu*. In 1978 the people of Hari invited singers of Duta, Mudang-Tage and Michi-Bamin. The number of singers invited is not specified, but usually some 30 to 40 people come. When they arrive the hosts select their own counterparts known as *khodo ajing* and take them to their houses. The relationship established in this way is the first step towards a *buning ajing* friendship. Each house invites only two singers and their hosts and guests compete in the singing of chants which consist of questions and answers the words being made up on the spur of the moment.

The arrangements for the invitations to singers are made by the *buliang* of the villages celebrating the Mloko, in order to avoid a clash of invitations. Thus the *buliang* would see to it that two villages of the same Mloko group do not invite at the same time singers from the same village. In 1978, for instance, the singers of Duta, Mudang-Tage and Michi-Bamin were divided into two groups, and one of them remained for the whole competition in Hari, while the other group went to Kalung.

The experienced singers of Hari and Kalung chose their own partners from among the visitors, took them to their houses and plyed them with beer and food. Then the singing started and went on most of the night. They sang about the legendary events of past ages and the history of the Apa Tanis, and doing this put each other's knowledge to the test. One of the singers would ask "Who was the ancestor of the Apa Tanis ?" and his partner would have to give the fullest answer possible. Though only a game, these knowledge quests were of high educational value. In a society without a script and a literature, the young listening to the singing learnt thereby of the traditional lore of the tribe and the memory of mythological events was kept fresh. Present-day school education is no substitue for such oral education, for the curriculum of the schools does not contain any reference to Apa Tani history.

This visit of singers from the other Mloko groups was terminated in a highly ceremonious manner. Four *buliang*, two of Hari and two of Kalung, went to Duta, Mudange-Tage and Michi-Bamin taking with them gifts of the best kind of beer to the *buliang* of those villages. In return they received presents of roast squirrel, an animal of high ritual importance, which stems perhaps from the distant past when Apa Tanis depended on the yield of the chase, and large squirrels were a favourite prey. The next morning those of the singers who had been entertained in Hari went to Kalung to bid farewell to the *buliang* of that village. There they were joined by those singers who had spent the night in Kalung, and both groups went to Hari to take leave from their hosts, and before they left the latter gave them small presents of foodstuff and beer. In years when it is not possible to invite singers from other villages because of epidemics or other emergencies, shares of meat are given to the *buliang* of the villages from which singers should have been invited.

After the ceremonial visits connected with singing competitions which are arranged on a village-basis, individual households invite their personal friends (*buning ajing*) from other villages to their houses. There they are entertained the whole day with drink and choice food, and when towards the evening they leave they are given presents of smoked bacon and rice-beer of best quality. They will reciprocate in the same fashion when it is their turn to perform the Mloko.

The various exchanges of shares of meat play an important role in the maintenance of social relations, and a complicated system regulates the distribution of meat to the *buliang* of the villages of other Mloko groups. Every ward of a village centred in a *nago* has certain ceremonial ties with corresponding wards of villages outside its own group, and the exchange of Mloko gifts occurs between such wards.

In the past perhaps more than today the ceremonial links of the *buliang* of one village with specific wards of another village served as channels for inter-village contacts, and negotiations for the settlement of disputes ran often along the lines of these permanent channels. The comparative peace and orderliness in the Apa Tani Valley, which contrasted so significantly with the turbulence among Nishis, may well have partly been due to the strength and durability of such ceremonial inter-village links which made up for the lack of any institutionalized tribal authority.

After the visits of the *buning-ajing* each household performs once more a domestic rite at which a priest worships Dani Tamu, Mei-ping, Metu and some other deities. Fowls and eggs are offered inside the house or on the verandah. This rite is followed by a period of *anyodo* during which it is taboo for the householders to go to the forest or any other place outside the Valley. As long as this *anyodo* is valid those who sacrificed pigs may not eat any meat other than the meat of the sacrificial animals, and they also do not eat potatoes and lentils, both of which are probably relatively novel items of food.

The main gods connected with the Mloko are Kiru-Kilo, a divine couple, invoked in most of the invocations of the priests, both public and private. On either the 15th, 17th or 20th day after the rite at the *yugyang* and the subsequent pig-sacrifices, each household performs a rite of farewell for Kiru-Kilo, and presents its priest with some pieces of meat.

The clan members who share one *yugyang* bring on that day fowls for sacrifice to their priest's house as well as eggs which are boiled and eaten by the children. This rite is called Ui-alodu "farewell to the gods." Immediaely after this the priest makes a round of the houses of his clients, and standing close to the ladder leading up to the verandah chants at each house for a few minutes.

The same day, about two hours before sun-set, the *lapang*, houses and granaries are surrounded with hoops made of bent slivers of bamboo, and this serves to keep evil spirits away. Priests in ceremonial dress chant prayers at each *nago*, but there are no more sacrifices. The priests address the gods (*ui*) to leave the village to which they came for the Mloko celebrations, and not to return until at the next Mloko, three years hence when "they will be offered large pigs and big chickens." The man chant as they surround the *nago* and *lapang* with bamboo hoops, until they are enclosed by a veritable thicket of bamboos. Later all the paths leading into the village are barricaded. After dark all the jaws of the pigs sacrificed during the Mloko are deposited in the *nago*. The jaws brought by each clan are put down in a special place within the *nago*, and in each jaw there must be a raw egg which the priest later breaks and eats.

On the following day each householder goes to his rice fields, gardens and groves and gives offerings of pork and eggs to the gods of the locality.

On the 29th day after the sacrifice of pigs the Mloko comes formally to an end with a ceremony in the course of which each of the householders who sacrificed pigs roasts some rice and offers it to his priest. On that day all the taboo restrictions on the villagers' movements are removed by the eating of a small piece of squirrel meat. Squirrels have become relatively rare and as they are required for many rituals their price has risen to about Rs 10 or one *enti-yage* basket of rice.

Apart from its function as a period of relaxation before the beginning of the strenuous work on the fields, which occupies the Apa Tanis for the subsequent seven months, the Mloko also serves to give ritual expression to the unity of the tribe. The way in which men and women of all villages join as visitors and guests in the celebration of one village-group cements friendly relations across village boundaries and counteracts tensions and jealousies between the inhabitants of different villages.

The Mloko was always an occasion for Nishis and Miris with friends among Apa Tanis to come to their villages and profit from the hospitality so generously dispensed to all comers. But the number of those who could safely travel as far as the Apa Tani Valley, and who felt sufficiently secure in a friendly village when they had still outstanding disputes with other Apa Tanis was never very large, and visitors from villages outside the Valley were hence no great imposition. This situation has now changed, for the general pacification of the Subansiri region has removed the hazards of travel and sojourn in villages outside people's home ground. Hence many Nishis and Miris come now to the Apa Tani Valley at the time of the Mloko, and in 1978 Hari and the three other villages celebrating the festival were crowded with visitors. Some of my Apa Tani friends did not hold back with their complaints about the strain these uninvited guests placed on their resources of food and drink. They said that they had never minded individual trade partners coming to their houses and asking for shelter and food, but that nowadays many Nishis abused their hospitality by bringing with them whole gangs of relatives and friends whom the Apa Tani hosts had never met. Nevertheless the rules of hospitality compelled the Apa Tanis to feed all those who had come, without any expectation of a return of their hospitality. For Nishis have no seasonal festivals comparable to Mloko and Morom, and they are not in the habit of inviting Apa Tanis even to their weddings. It may well be that the younger generation of Apa Tanis, many of whom have lived and travelled in parts of India where shelter and food has to be paid for by hard cash, will ultimately be less generous in the offer of hospitality to uninvited guests, but the older Apa Tanis retain the ideal of an openhanded hospitality provided to all those who cross their threshold whether invited or not.

The Apa Tanis have no other seasonal rites comparable in complexity and social importance to either Mloko or Morom. But in certain months minor rituals are performed by priests acting on behalf of individual villages. Thus in June or July a small pig, a dog and some chickens are sacrificed in the name of Potor, Met and Tamu, three deities believed to dwell in the earth, and in July or August a chick and eggs are offered to Yapun, the god of thunder, and to Mloru-Su, Punglo and Korlang, deities connected with hail and capable of warding off damaging hail-storms. For ten days after the performance of this rite no villager is supposed to go beyond the cultivated area or even to visit the other villages of the Valley, and it is believed that any breach of these injunctions would lead to hail-storms damaging the crops.

Another rite known as Myokun is intended to benefit the growth of the rice, and is performed before the transplanting. A priest acts on behalf of the whole village and offers chickens and eggs, at a ritual structure (*agyang*) situated at a site specifically set aside for this purpose.

A seasonal rite which used to be of relatively little importance but has now been transformed into a tribal festival is known as Dri. Each village always had a special *agyang* structure for the Dri rite, and there a priest used to sacrifice a dog and some chickens for the benefit of the crops at the time when the rice-seedlings were being transplanted.

Some years ago the educated students wanted to have one common festival to be celebrated year after year on the same date. Particularly some students of the Jawaharlal Nehru College at Pasighat had come in contact with Adis and other tribes who hold communal festivals celebrated by the entire tribes made propaganda for the establishment of a similar festival among the Apa Tanis. Through the Youth Organization they petitioned the Deputy Commissioner to aid the arrangements for such a celebration and he provided a grant of Rs 1,000. In 1965 a special fund was set up and contributions were collected. The 5th July was chosen as the fixed date for the festival and a site at Nenchanglya between Duta and Old Ziro was prepared as the festival ground. There is a committee to organize the festival for which in 1977 Rs 1,400 were spent in cash and kind. One mithan and one cow were sacrificed and all the Apa Tani villages contributed rice. The committee is entitled to five villages for non-cooperation and in one year Hari was fined Rs 400. Each of the villages delegates one priest to officiate at the ritual part of the festival. Even more prominent than this are the social events organized by the committee. There are games, various competitions as well as singing and dancing. The contribution by government is the outcome of a general policy which seeks to encourage social activities serving the integration of larger tribal units, and in pursuance of this policy a festival called Longte Yullo has been established to bring together the Nishis of the Khru and Kamla region.

Various rites are performed on the occasion of special emergencies. Thus after a fire which destroyed part of an Apa Tani village a rite known as *muchu* must be performed. This rite should preferably be performed by a Nishi priest, who is called from a neighbouring village, but if no such priest is available an Apa Tani *nyibu* may act. The priest must leave his house at midnight before performing the rite, and if he is an Apa Tani he may not re-enter his village for two days. While the *muchu* rite is being performed the village is closed and no one may go in or out. If the priest is a Nishi, and after performing the rite he enters another Apa Tani village he will be heavily fined; for it is believed that the misfortune which caused the fire will adhere to the priest. The *muchu* rite involves the sacrifice of a dog and several fowls to the *gunipan-ui*, a group of deities worshipped on the occasion of various disasters and misfortunes, such as for instance a serious illness.

Another rite performed on special occasions is the *ropi*-rite which used to follow the slaying of an enemy and is still being held wherever a leopard or leopard-cat has been killed. The first *ropi* I watched was held in Kalung in March 1944 when a man of that village had brought home the hand of a Nishi woman of Pemir whom he had killed in revenge for his capture by her kinsmen, and the last I watched was in April 1978 again in Kalung when a leopard-cat had been killed by men of that village. There were obviously differences in the mood the two events evoked among participants and spectators, but most of the ceremonies were performed according to the same traditional pattern.

The main purpose of the *ropi* is to prevent the soul (*yalo*) of the slain person or animal to come back to this earth and take revenge on the killer. It is invariably performed at the *nago* of the killer, and the importance of the *nago* is indeed derived from its function as a depository for the trophies from exploits in war and the chase.

When in the days of feuding an enemy was killed the slayer usually cut off one hand and secured the eyes and the tongue for disposal at the *nago* of his village. All these trophies were kept in the nago until the performance of the *ropi* when the hand was burnt; the ashes and the eyes and tongue were buried under a flat stone at the side of the *nago*.

On rare occasions not only a hand but also the head of an enemy was cut off and brought to the *nago*. Such an incident occurred in 1943, and was told to me in detail the following year. A man of Tajang going out to cut wood saw some suspicious footprints and thinking they might be those of Nishi raiders called the men of his village. Fully armed they followed the trail and found a group of Nishis sitting in the forest and drinking beer. Rade Takling hurled a spear and killed one of the Nishis; the others fled. The Apa Tanis cut off both the head and the left hand of the victim and deposited them in their *nago*. At the subsequent *ropi* rite tongue and eyes were placed into a bamboo vessel and buried, and then head and hand were burnt to ashes.

An alternative to the practice was the sacrifice of a dog, known as Talukiri, who symbolized the enemy. The tongue and part of the dog's heart were cut out, and buried in front of the *nago*. It is possible that this substitution was resorted to when in the heat of a fight there was no time to cut out the eyes and tongue of a slain enemy though a hand could be rapidly slashed off. But the idea behind either procedure was the belief that the burial of the enemy's or his substitute's vital organs would prevent his ghost from pursuing the slayer and taking revenge.

When burying the eyes and tongue in the section of a bamboo, the slayer used to take rice beer in his mouth, and spit it on to the stone covering the interred trophies. He and the priest then addressed the victim with an incantation containing the following sentences:

Go to your own place; we are sending you under the earth, we are closing the gate of the earth. It was your fate to be killed, do not be angry with us. For ten generations to come you shall be powerless to harm our descendants. You have been buried in the earth, and we have sent you off; do not come to us, but move away to other places.

After the disposal of the trophies, there were dances with the slayer leading a line of men in war dress, brandishing swords and spears, who danced round the *nago* and paraded through the village.

The *ropi*-rite performed after the killing of a leopard cat lasted also most of the day, and contained many of the details I had noted 34 years earlier. Several priests in ceremonial dress and wearing black hats made of palm fibre such as worn in war and hunting sat on the *lapang* besides the *nago* and chanted prayers. The skin of the leopard was hanging on a pole beside the *lapang* and a priest dressed in a white and blue cloth stood in front of it open sword in hand, and chanted. The young man who had shot the leopard wore a combination of modern and traditional dress and sported a gun.

He invited us to his house which was full of men drinking beer and eating boiled eggs. Women from related houses kept on bringing sides of bacon and boiled rice. All the kinsmen of the killer, both on his father's and his mother's sides as well as his wife's relatives, contributed in this way to the feast.

The priests sacrificed some chickens at a ritual structure erected by the side of the *lapang*, and then a procession of men carrying drawn swords and uttering war-cries moved in single file round the *lapang* and through the village. They wore fibre rain-shields and these were ultimately stacked on the *lapang*. Later they set out on a second procession and this time carried spears and bamboo-staffs.

The killer had to observe a taboo on agricultural work for ten days, and so had those participants in the rite who had been involved in the sacrifice of chickens. Other participants observed this taboo only for one day.

Ropi rites used to be performed not only in case of slain enemies and killed tigers or leopards, but also after the execution of criminal members of the Apa Tani tribe. On such occasions a mithan, bought by public subscription, was sacrificed during the *ropi*, and then men of the village where the execution had taken place danced and chanted as if they had been celebrating the victory over an enemy slain in battle.

Apart from the rituals here described there are many occasions when a priest is commissioned to perform a sacrifice aimed at propitiating the one or other god or spirit, and particularly in case of illness such appeals to supernatural powers are considered indispensable for effecting a cure.

EIGHT

The World of Gods and Spirits

In the view of the Apa Tani the world has two dimensions. One is the visible world made up of living people of various tribes, of animals and of the material environment from which men draw their sustenance, and the other world, invisible to the ordinary layman but familiar to priests, is a far more extensive sphere peopled by deities and spirits of many kinds and by the departed Apa Tanis. Though priests and seers claim to be able to see deities and spirits in their dreams, most Apa Tanis have only a vague idea of the invisible beings who surround them and may affect their welfare and health. He believes, however, that they are accessible to the approaches of men, and that their reactions to requests, offerings and promises are somewhat similar to those of humans. Although there are many categories of such supernatural beings, the generic term for all is *ui,* and this term is usually attached to the individual name. The same term *ui* is used also in connection of natural features in the spirit world of which the Apa Tanis have no direct experience.

Apa Tanis do not think of their gods as occupying hierarchically ranked positions in a pantheon, and there is no deity comparable to a supreme being of the type of the Konyak Nagas' Gawang. In recent years the cult of Doni-Polo ("Sun-Moon") has attained some importance, but this pair of deities did not seem to have figured at all prominently in traditional Apa Tani religion. Indeed the priests who told me about the various deities in 1944 did not mention Doni-Polo, and it was only among the Miris that I heard about the divine couple Doni-Sü ("Sun-Earth"). Now there is a Doni-Polo house in Hapoli, and this is used for some cultural gatherings sponsored by the administration. There is on the part of educated Apa Tanis a movement to propagate the worship of Doni-Polo as a

kind of high-god whose worship unites all the different tribes of
the Subansiri District, and such a cult is supported by the government as a counter-force to Christianity and perhaps also Buddhism.
The Apa Tanis whom I asked about Doni-Polo in 1978 told me that
the original Apa Tani version of the name is Dani-Pulu, and that
Dani-Pulu was one of a multitude of gods while Nishis and Adis
worship Dani-Polo as their principal god. Educated Apa Tanis, if
asked about their religion, tend now to say that they are worshippers of Dani-Polo in contrast to the adherents of Hinduism, Buddhism and Christianity.

There seems to be no consistency in the various myths which
explain how various features of the visible world came into being,
though I would not exclude the possibility that an intensive study
of Apa Tani myths with the help of a large number of priests might
reveal a comprehensive system comprising all the various stories
about the creation of sun, moon, earth, water, plants and living
creatures. So far no one has had an opportunity for such research,
and little more can be said than that two deities, known as Chantung and Didun, were somehow involved in the process of creation
and that a divine pair, Kilo and Kirung, emerged about the same
time. Another divine pair are Yapung, the sky, considered male,
and Dani, the sun, which is said to be female. Before any rite is to
be performed for the sun, omens have to be taken to establish the
type of acceptable victim and, according to the outcome, chickens,
pigs, a dog, a mithan, or a cow will be sacrificed.

The multitude of *ui* worshipped by Apa Tanis on various occasions is divided into three classes differing in their characteristics,
and it is said that one of these classes of *ui* is in opposition to the
other two.

The names and characteristics of the three types of *ui* are as
follows:

(1) Tigo-ui are gods connected with happiness and prosperity,
and are worshipped at the time of propitious ceremonies such
as those performed on the occasion of Morom, Mloko, Subu-
tado and wedding-rites. There are many different branches of this
class of Tigo-ui.

(2) Guniyan-ui, also called Chiching-ui, are connected with unfortunate events, such as illness or accidental fires. Thus we have

seen that after the gutting of houses by fire a sacrifice must be performed for Guniyan-ui.

(3) Yalu-ui are concerned with disputes and war; they are invoked before raids and on the occasion of *lisudu, gambu-sodu,* kidnapping and criminal cases.

As the Tigo-ui are deities of a benevolent nature concerned with happy celebrations, they should not be brought in contact with the fierce Guniyan-ui and Yalu-ui. Hence a priest engaged in a series of rites directed towards the Tigo-ui must not come near to the performance of a rite in honour of gods of the Guniyan-ui and Yalu-ui class. The latter two, both fierce and hence similar to each other, may come in contact with each other. Only married people may perform rituals connected with any of the Tigo-ui, for such joyous rituals are inappropriate for widowers, widows or single persons. The rites for the fierce deities Guniyan-ui and Yalu-ui on the other hand may be commissioned also by unmarried or widowed persons.

The three categories of Tigo-ui, Guniyan-ui (or Chiching-ui) and Yalu-ui do not exhaust the types of gods, but Apa Tanis seem to think of them as outstanding and somehow distinct from the host of other *ui,* such as a large group of *ui,* known as Hilo (or Yulo), who live in forest and hills, near but not inside villages, or even in the sky.

There are also some deities who are specifically associated with certain natural phenomena. Prominent among them are three deities collectively known as Korlang-ui and worshipped annually by a priest representing his entire village or even two neighbouring villages. Niri-Korlang resides in the sky and provides protection against hailstorms which are dreaded as a threat to paddy-crops; Tagung-ui, who also dwells in the sky, is propitiated to ward off thunderstorms and excessive rain, and Angura Korlang, who dwells in the lowlands, is believed to protect against disease those Apa Tanis who visit the plains of Assam. A rite directed to the Korlang-ui is performed before the commencement of the transplanting of rice, and as a site for this and other rites each village maintains a place on one of the communal grass-covered grounds outside the settlement. There a priest sacrifices a chicken and calls upon the spirits of lightning, water and earth, and certain local deities to ward off dangers from the young crop. This, as many other rites, is followed by two days of abstention from work outside the village.

Apart from deities associated with the forces of nature there are others who stand in a special relation to certain spheres of human activity. Thus the gods Ui-Kasang and Nia-Kasang are associated with war, and before Apa Tanis went on a raid they prayed to these deities to give them strength and courage, and afford them protection in battle. On such an occasion, which today no longer occurs, a dog, pig or mithan was sacrificed either at the *lapang* of the raiders or at a special ritual structure put up on a communal ground.

Also connected with the vicissitudes of war and today equally obsolete, are Pila and Yachu. They live under the earth and are believed to assist captured persons to escape from the bonds of their enemies. When a family learnt of the capture of one of its members, a fowl was sacrificed inside the house and a priest addressed himself to Pila and Yachu, begging them to help the captive to escape. And again when go-betweens were sent out to negotiate the prisoner's ransom, the same two deities were begged to make their mission successful. Further offerings were promised in the event of the captive's escape or release, and when the captive returned he himself offered the promised fowls to the two Yalu deities. Even if a mithan was stolen the same fierce deities were begged to enable the animal to break its ropes so that it could return to the grazing grounds of its owner.

Besides the gods known by individual names and associated with special activities or needs, there is a host of spirits inhabiting the surface of the earth, and most of them are worshipped only in connection with activities taking place in the locality where they are believed to dwell. When a new sitting-platform is constructed, for instance, the spirit of the site is invoked and fowls and dogs are sacrificed to gain the spirit's favour for all those who will use the *lapang*.

Unspecified *ui* are also credited with intervention in certain vital human processes. Thus Apa Tanis believe that when a child is still in the mother's womb its sex is decided by the *ui*. The *ui* also outline the child's fate: one child will become rich, one will be a great warrior, one a priest (*nyibu*), one a great orator, one will be blessed with good looks. If the *ui* do not grant a child such qualities even before birth, there is little hope for its future; the child's life will be undistinguished and steeped in poverty.

Although there is this belief in the intervention of gods in the life of individual men and women, it is doubtful whether the Apa Tanis see any of their gods in the role of guardians of the moral order. For a long time I failed to obtain any evidence which might have clarified this problem, for most of my informants disclaimed any knowledge about the gods' attitude to the moral conduct of men. There is, however, the expression *ui-kao* ("god-displease") and this was explained to me as having a meaning equivalent of that of the Hindi word *pap* (sin), and I was also given examples of what Apa Tanis considered *ui-kao*. Fratricide, adultery, telling lies, cheating were described as *ui-kao*, but there was no hint of the identity, of the god displeased, nor of any adverse result arising from such displeasure. One must also take into account that many Apa Tanis, particularly those with a modern education, are now familiar with the terms *pap* and "sin" and may unconsciously have developed an Apa Tani equivalent.

There are occasions when Apa Tanis address themselves directly to the gods, but normally a priest (*nyibu*) is required to act as mediator between men and gods. One Apa Tani described this role of the *nyibu* very succinctly: "The *nyibu* asks the *ui* to cure men, and he tells men to give offerings to the *ui*." Yet, a *nyibu* has to do much more than to be a mere go-between. He is the repository of the tribe's sacred lore, and must be able to recite and chant for hours invoking multitudes of gods and recalling mythological events, relevant to the nature of the ritual he is performing. Unlike priests and shamans of some other tribes a *nyibu* is not chosen by gods who force themselves upon him by making him fall into trance, but the selection for the profession of priest is based on rational grounds. If it is noted that a boy is good in memorizing and also has a tuneful voice, he is considered suitable for the work of a priest, and may be apprenticed to an experienced *nyibu* as whose assistant (*buo*) he learns the way to perform rituals and the traditional chants and recitations. As he learns more of the gods and spirits he is supposed to acquire also the capacity to enter in the dreams the underworld known to the Apa Tanis as Neli, which is the land of gods and spirits as well as of the departed. One of the most prominent *nyibu* of the 1940s told me then that he could see the houses and inhabitants of Neli but not clearly while most laymen believe that *nyibu* can see the *ui* and the departed in Neli in their dreams. Educated Apa Tanis with whom I discussed the problems of the *nyibu's* knowledge of Neli in 1978 were sceptical of the average *nyibu's* first-hand knowledge of Neli and said that a *nyibu* could discharge his priestly functions even without the ability to enter the underworld either in dreams or in trance. They insisted that it was not the *nyibu* who normally fell into trance but the *ui-in*, shamans who need not have the training and knowledge of priests, but could induce states of trance in which they were able to enter Neli and establish direct contacts with *ui*. Such shamans might be men or women, and in Reru and Tajang there were at that time several female *ui-in* but no men capable of trance experiences. The functions of *nyibu* and *ui-in* do not seem to be exclusive, for some *nyibu* would seem to have also the power to put themselves into trance and in that state set out to trace the whereabouts of a straying soul (*yalo*) and to prevail upon the *ui* holding the *yalo* in their power to release their victim and enable the *yalo* to return to its material body. While *nyibu* perform usually in public, normally holding sacrificial rites on *lapang*, *ui-in* operate in the secrecy of their houses, and are hence not easily observed.

The Apa Tanis' idea of the worlds beyond is very similar to that of their Nishi neighbours as well as the beliefs of several other Tibeto-Burman speaking tribes of North East India such as Nagas, Mizos, and Adis. They believe that the souls (*yalo*) of all those who died a natural death go to Neli, an underworld which looks very much like the Apa Tani valley with villages and long rows of houses. On the journey to Neli, about halfway between this earth and Neli, they come to a house called Hissing Nyato. There they are met by Nelkiri, the guardian of the underworld, and also by their parents, kinsmen and friends who had preceded them in death. Nelkiri and those gathered to welcome the *yalo* asks every new arrival about his exploits in his or her earthly life. A man is asked how many enemies he had slain or captured, how many mithan he has sacrificed and how many ferocious animals such as tigers, bears and wild boars he has killed. There is a scale for such exploits, and the reception of the departed by the residents of Neli depends on the extent to which he can impress them by his achievements in his previous life. These are reckoned by the number of *ikhang* he has accumulated. An *ikhang* is a symbol or tally for certain creditable deeds, and each is represented by a cane attached to the funeral monument of the deceased.

The following list of achievements each resulting in the gain of one *ikhang* demonstrates the relative value attributed to various meritorious deeds:

Killing one man; killing one woman (of hostile village); killing one tiger or leopard; killing one bear; killing one wild boar; killing any number of wild sows; killing any number of deer; killing one eagle.

Purchase of one slave; purchase of one mithan from Nishis or Miris (the purchase of cattle from Apa Tanis does not gain *ikhang*); purchase of one big rice field; purchase of several small rice fields.

Celebration of one *un-pedo* feast (either *rung-ti* or *takum-putu*); celebration of several *rung-sere*.

A woman who has remarkable achievements in the economic field also earns *ikhang*. The feats within the reach of a woman are the purchase of rice fields, of mithan (from Nishis) and of valuable Tibetan bells.

Those arriving at the half-way house on the way to the Land of the Dead who have many *ikhang* to their credit are received with honour and entertained with good food, but a man who has aquired none or only few *ikhang* will be ashamed and too shy to speak to any of the prominent departed. Whatever their ranking in terms of *ikhang*, the *yalo* of all departed go to the same place in Neli, but in the same way as on this earth there are rich and poor. A man who was rich in his previous life will be rich again, and a slave will serve his master. When the son of a rich man of Hang died and a few days later a slave of the same house also died the family expressed satisfaction that the son of the house would be served by the slave in Neli. There a man also finds the cattle which he sacrificed during his lifetime; but those animals which passed to his heirs or which he gave to his sons in his lifetime are lost to him.

Apa Tanis also believe that every woman who dies after her husband returns to him in Neli, and vice-versa. Those who died unmarried can find spouses in Neli, and even beget children. Life in Neli is similar to life on earth; people work and grow crops, and ultimately they die and go to another Land of the Dead. Though Neli is believed to be under the earth and is thus a real underworld, it has no gloomy associations, but is considered a pleasant place. The fact that according to the accounts of priests and shamans the departed share Neli with numerous gods and spirits, is not often mentioned, and does not seem to be much on the Apa Tanis' mind.

Another Land of the Dead is situated in the sky and to this

abode, known as Talimoko, all those repair who died an unnatural
or inauspicious death. Men who were killed by enemies or by lightning, and women who died in childbirth go to this celestial region.
There is no suggestion that the fate of those in Talimoko is one of
unhappiness and suffering, but it would seem that life in Talimoko
is not considered a continuation of life on earth to the same extent
as the existence of the *yalo* in Neli. Yet, *ikhang*, the tallies of success on earth are useful also for those who go to Talimoko, for
among the inhabitants of this sky-land there are also many who respect the successes a man achieved on earth.

Both those in Neli and in Talimoko are believed to return at
times to the dwellings of the living but their visitations are not welcome. Men in Talimoko sometimes fall in love with beautiful
young women on this earth, and then make them die by an unnatural death, such as in childbirth, in order to be able to take
them to Talimoko. If a beautiful girl dies an untimely death, people
will therefore say: "Some one came from Talimoko and has taken
her away." The souls who have gone to Talimoko are not known as
yalo but as *igi*, but there seems to be no appreciable difference
between the two types of departed souls. The involvement of such
an *igi* with a beautiful young woman, whose life is threatened by
his unwanted attention, can be counteracted by the sacrifice of a
mithan.

The departed kinsmen or forefathers who are supposed to be in
Neli, but capable of visiting their descendants or relatives on earth
are known as *ayo-asi*, and if there is any suspicion that the *ayo-asi*
are not happy and draw attention to themselves by troubling their
surviving kinsmen with the one or other affliction, a rite known as
ayo-asi mendu is performed to placate the ancestors. This rite is
performed also when a family's rice-crop is not sufficient to feed
the household for the whole year. For it is believed that the bad
harvest may be due to the displeasure of the *ayo-asi*, and every
effort is made to reconcile them.

It is far more serious if a *yalo* returns from Neli in the form of
a *yaj-yalo-ui*, a ghost liable to make people ill. In such an event a
nyibu is called and commissioned with the placation of the troublesome spirit. The *nyibu* invokes the help of Nelkiri, and tries to
buy off the ghost by promising him sacrifices and food offerings.

We have seen already that the *igi* of a slain man and women is
prevented from returning to earth by the performance of the *ropi-*

rite, and Apa Tanis are confident that this rite is fully effective and capable of warding off any danger from the soul of the killed man or woman.

Unlike many other Indian tribes Apa Tanis do not have the idea that the human personality splits up after death, and its different elements proceed to different places. Yet, there is the idea of the detachability of the *yalo*, the soul, from the body even while the body is still alive. While a man is asleep his *yalo* may leave his body and roam about the world, and dreams are interpreted as the experiences of the *yalo* on his wanderings. But there is a risk in such escapades. Many of the *ui* who inhabit Neli side by side with the *yalo* of the departed are ever avid to draw straying *yalo* into their sphere. If they succeed to kidnap a wandering *yalo* the person whose *yalo* is kept captive and prevented from returning to the body, will fall ill and may fail to regain consciousness. In such an event it is necessary to employ a shaman who will try to ransom the *yalo* with the sacrifice of an animal, and if the *ui* accepts the offer and releases the *yalo* the patient will regain consciousness and recover.

It appears that the *yalo*, which has already a separate existence while a man is alive and can detach itself from the body, is the permanent element in man, which survives after death and will lead another and similar life in the underworld. Apa Tanis are vague about the more remote Land of the Dead which lies ahead of those who die in Neli, for they say that shamans cannot penetrate to this underworld beyond the region of *yalo* and *ui* with which they are familiar.

One could argue that the idea of an interminable series of underworlds and the inevitable death of a person after a span of life in any such Land of the Dead is comparable to the successive existences in a chain of rebirths as postulated by Hindu ideology. The difference between the two concepts lies in the fact that Apa Tanis think of life in each underworld as a replica of the life in the previous existence, whereas the Hindu idea of *karma* involves the belief that it is within the powers of man to influence his fate in his next existences by his conduct in the life on this earth.

In recent years the Apa Tanis' ideas about the after-life have been thrown into some confusion. Many Apa Tani children go now to mission schools in Assam, and some young people are studying in Shillong. Though only a few have become Christians, ideas of heaven and hell have spread not only among such children but also among some of their parents who may have seen naive pictures of heaven with angels and saints among the clouds. These pictures must have appeared to them like representatives of Talimoko which is also set in the clouds. Hence Apa Tanis have begun to wonder whether Talimoko may not be a better place than Neli so easily identified with the subterranean hell of Christian eschatology.

There is as yet no sign of any spread of Christian—or indeed Buddhist or Hindu—ideas of rewards for morally commendable acts in the next world nor conversely any fear of punishments for crimes in the life after death. The value attached to deeds of valour symbolized by the accumulation of *ikhang* is, of course, in the nature of a translation of success achieved in this life into benefits in the next world, but there is no trace of any idea that morally reprehensible acts such as incest, the murder of kinsmen, theft or cheating would render a person liable to punishment in the Land of the Dead. The nearest allusion to morality in connection with the Apa Tanis' beliefs in the after-life was a *nyibu's* brief comment that in Neli good people will be good again, and bad people bad. This does not mean that Apa Tanis lack any sense of moral values, but only that they see no connection between the moral conduct of men and women and their fate in the next world. In short, as life in Neli is a reflection and—despite the change of scene—a continuation of the personality's existence the aim of all conduct is of necessity "this worldly" and tribal morality lacks the "other worldly" dimension and incentives of ideologies such as Buddhism, Hinduism and Christianity.

NINE

Interaction with Neighbours —
Past and Present

THE APA TANIS constitute a very compact but numerically relatively small ethnic group surrounded by far more populous but less well organized tribes. Those to the south, west and northwest used to be known as Daflas and this is the tribal name by which they were described in the literature up to the 1960s including B.K. Shukla's book *The Daflas of the Subansiri Region* (Shillong, 1959), while the people inhabiting the hills to the east and north were described as Hill Miris. Already in my *Ethnographic Notes on the Tribes of the Subansiri Region* (Shillong 1947) I pointed out that the distinction between "Daflas" and "Hill Miris" was largely arbitrary and suggested to replace the Assamese name Dafla which meant "wild man" with the term Nisü, the name by which the Eastern Daflas referred to themselves in their own language. In recent years the educated young men of the people known to the Assamese as "Daflas" objected to that term because of its derogatory implication and declared that they were Nishis and should be described as such. This term is derived from the word *ni* which means "human being." The term Nishi (or Nishang) is now being used in official publication, but although the Hill Miris are sometimes described as Mishang the old term Miri has still greater currency, and I shall continue to use it in the following pages.

The relations between Apa Tanis and Nishis as well as Miris have undergone a profound change since the entire Subansiri region has been brought under the control of the Government of India. The resultant pacification has put an end to the numerous feuds which used to divide the various tribal groups and often even the individual villages within the same group. In the 1940s when I first entered the area the Apa Tanis' relations with their Dafla and Miri neighbours fluctuated between intensive trade contacts involving frequent reciprocal visits and periods of hostility punctuated by kidnappings, raids and killings. At first I was puzzled by the discovery that villages linked by traditional trade-contacts were often also hereditary enemies, but I soon realized that the Nishi and Miri villages which figured in the Apa Tanis' accounts of raids and feuds were usually those with whom the tellers of these stories had the closest barter and trade relations. Yet, on reflection I began to understand that friction arises more frequently between tribesmen pitching their brains against each other in deals of buying, selling and lending than between casual acquaintances whose interests are seldom in conflict. The pattern of tribal trade necessitated moreover concentration on a limited number of trade partners. As there were no markets and no shops the trader, intent on selling his wares in villages two or three days' walk from his home, had to have friends in whose houses he was sure of a welcome. Such friends and trade-partners were prepared to guarantee their visitor's security to the extent that they regarded any attack on him as equal to an attack on a member of their own household. The Apa Tani partners reciprocated by doing their best to protect their Nishi friends when they visited their villages, and in the past several conflicts between Apa Tani villages arose from the outraged sense of responsibility of an Apa Tani whose Nishi guests were attacked by Apa Tanis of another village.

Formal friendship pacts between Apa Tanis and Nishis or Miris were relatively rare, but there exists a recognized mechanism for the conclusion of such pacts, and occasionally this is used even nowadays. The potential partner who wishes to conclude such a pact sends a messenger (*potun*) to the other partner and asks whether the formalization of the relationship is desired. If the latter agrees the initiator of the move takes a mithan decorated with bamboo-shavings in procession to his partner's house, and on this mission he and the *potun* are accompanied by their wives and members of their family, and the whole party moves solemnly to the sound of chants. In the partner's house they are entertained with food and drink. A ceremonial friendship thus created is called *gyotu-bosudu*, and the two friends are subsequently called *gotu-arang*. Apart from such individual pacts, Apa Tani villages, moreover, used to conclude treaties (*dapo*) with leading men of neighbouring Nishi or Miri villages in order to safeguard as far as possible the safety of the men and women visiting such villages in the pursuance of trade. When I arrived in the Apa Tani valley in 194- the *dapo* between Hari village and a group of Miri villages had broken down, and I subsequently spent much time trying to get the parties together and to persuade them to restore the treaty and with it the flow of trade, but it was not until April 1945 that this mediation was crowned with success (see *Himalayan Barbary*, pp. 107, 108, 117, 225).

The choice of trade-partners was by no means haphazard but followed a course laid down by tradition. Each of the Apa Tani villages had traditional trade ties with certain Nishi or Miri villages, and with few exceptions these were the villages whose land bordered on the hunting grounds of the Apa Tani village concerned. Thus Hang, which lies at the southern end of the Valley, maintained trade relations mainly with the Nishis of Leji, Pochu, Mai and Jorum; Duta and Hija were both oriented towards the west and trade with Talo, Nielom, Likha, Licha and Linia. The area of influence of the villages of Reru, Kalung and Tajang extended mainly to the north-east of the valley in the Miri villages of Dodum, Taplo, Pemir, Rakhe, Bua and Chemir.

An Apa Tani could trade with Nishis or Miris of a village not included in the group of traditional trade partners only if he had matrilateral or affinal kinsmen in one of the Apa Tani villages habitually trading with the Nishi or Miri village in question. An Apa Tani without the rights derived from such kinship ties risked upsetting and antagonizing those of his neighbours on whose sphere of commercial interest he was encroaching. In the event of a conflict with his legitimate trade partners he was therefore not free to switch over to a village traditionally trading with other Apa Tanis. A complete suspension of trade between an Apa Tani village and all its Nishi or Miri trade-partners, such as periodically occurred when feuds reached a degree of high intensity, resulted for the Apa Tanis concerned in real hardship. Hostile feeling had to run very high before all individual trade contacts were abandoned, usually because the danger of being kidnapped or killed was just too great. There were innumerable cases of Apa Tanis continuing to barter with Nishis who to all intents and purposes were at war with other clans of the Apa Tanis' own village. In the days of slavery it was sometimes also possible for slaves to go backwards and forwards between hostile villages without any great risk of capture.

The mutually beneficial relations between trade partners could be disturbed in many different ways, but it would seem that unpaid trade-debts, the shelter given to escaped slaves and violent self-help of those feeling cheated in trade-deals were among the most frequent causes of disputes which subsequently gave rise to kidnappings, raids and counter-raids.

When I arrived in the Apa Tani country in 1944, several clans of Hija and Duta had fallen out with their traditional trade-partners of Licha, a Nishi village some two days' walk to the east. A large number of cattle thefts and captures of men committed by the warriors of Licha had raised the Apa Tanis' temper to white heat. They claimed that within the previous three years the men of Licha had extracted from them a total of 92 mithan, 15 cows and bullocks, 58 Tibetan bells, and 38 swords. Some of the mithan had been lifted from the forest, but most of the animals and valuables had been paid in the form of ransoms for Apa Tanis captured by Nishis of Licha. When it came to surprise attacks in the forest Apa Tanis were no match for Nishis who were adept at ambushing men out wood-cutting or hunting. They could have mounted a massive raid on Licha, but the political organization was unsuited to the rallying of large numbers of men and working out a strategy for subdueing a determined and resourceful enemy, who would avoid any pitched battles and rely on guerilla tactics. Alone Hija village could easily have put five times as many men into the field as all settlements of Licha together, but there was no one to marshal all able-bodied men and lead them in a raid on Licha. Those clans of Hija who had not suffered from Licha's depredations were indifferent, and there was not even sufficient support for a general boycott of Licha which would have cut it off from supplies of Apa Tani rice. Hence some poor men of Hija, unattractive to Nishis interested in large ransoms, would continue to visit Licha for the sake of petty trade.

The people of the composite village of Büla (Reru, Kalung and Tajang) had suffered equally from the depredations of the men of Licha and they told me of the following attacks on members of their community. Though they are tediously repetitive I am listing herewith some of the incidents about which the Apa Tanis of Büla complained:

(1) Milo Nia and Milo Taram had gone to the forest to collect the edible pith of a tree-fern. Two men of Licha, leading a gang of altogether eight, captured them and kept them for two months in

stocks, demanding ransom. Two men of the Nishi village of Linia acted as negotiators and the two Apa Tani brothers were ransomed for a payment of two mithan, three Tibetan bells and numerous minor valuables and textiles.

(2) Milo Yubbe, a slave of Milo Dübo, went hunting and was captured by Gem Pumbo of Licha. He was kept in stocks for two years and was at last released on payment of two Tibetan bells. The deal was negotiated by a go-between of Hija, and the period of captivity was so long because Gem Pumbo started by asking a price much too high for a slave.

(3) Rubu Tupe and Rubu Tapo, two *guchi*, went hunting and were captured by several men of Licha. They were kept in stocks for three months, and ransomed with the help of two Nishis of Linia as go-betweens. The ransom for both brothers amounted to one mithan, one Tibetan bell, and several minor objects.

(4) Rubu Mudu, a *guchi*, went hunting and was captured by Licha Laling, who kept him for two months in stocks. Two Nishis of Linia acted as go-betweens, and arranged a ransom of two mithans, four Tibetan bells, and several minor valuables.

(5) Rubu Sa, a *guchi*, went hunting and was captured by Licha Taka and kept in stocks for two months. A Nishi of Linia arranged a ransom of one mithan, one Tibetan bell, one bronze plate and one sword.

(6) Doliang Takar, *guth*, worked on his rice field when Licha Taka and four other Licha men tried to carry him off. As he resisted they killed him and cut off one of his hands.

(7) Nyilang Tari, a *guth* went hunting and was captured by Licha Taka, and kept in stocks for two months. A Nishi of Linia arranged his ransom for two Tibetan bells, two cloths and two swords.

(8) Nyilang Paiyang, a *guth*, went to the forest to see his traps; Licha Taga and seven men captured him. He was kept in stocks for one month. Two Apa Tanis of Hija arranged to ransom him for two mithan, one Tibetan bell, two bronze plates and several minor articles.

(9) Rade Guro, a *guth*, went to the forest and was captured by Licha Tagur. He was kept in stocks for two months and released for a ransom of one mithan, one Tibetan bell, one bronze plate and minor articles.

(10) Tago Rade, a *guchi*, went to his fields early in the morning and was captured by Tajo Chaliang of Licha, and kept in stocks

for two months. A Nishi of Talo arranged his ransom for two Tibentan bells, one Tibetan sword, and one Nishi cloth.

(11) Tage Murne, a *guchi* girl, went alone to Licha to barter rice for cotton. She was captured by Licha Tai, and after two months was ransomed with the help of a Nishi of Linia.

This list of attacks by Nishis of Licha on Apa Tanis went on with few variations, and in most, though not all case the negotiators who arranged for the ransoms were Nishis of Linia, a village then on good terms with both Licha and Büla. All negotiators were paid fees by the kinsmen of the victims, usually one Tibetan sword and one cloth.

In most, though not all, such kidnappings there was no loss of life, and captured persons had a very good chance of regaining their freedom within about two months. Custom demanded that captives held to ransom must be fed well, and though a heavy log of wood attached to one of their legs impeded their freedom of movement, they were usually well treated and shared the house and meals of their captors.

The procedure followed in the negotiations for the release of a captive ran usually according to the same pattern. If the capture occurred in an ambush of several Apa Tanis some of whom could escape, the identity of the captors was likely to be known, but even if a man was captured while he was alone in the forest, his kinsmen had usually not much difficulty of learning from friendly Nishis where he was kept prisoner. The captors themselves had no interest in concealing their deed, for they wanted the victim's kinsmen to initiate negotiations for a ransom.

As soon as the missing man's kinsmen had discovered his whereabouts, they secured the services of an experienced go-between (*ghondu*), who could be either an Apa Tani or a Nishi from a friendly village. If an Apa Tani was chosen as *ghondu* he usually asked some Nishis of a neutral village to accompany him on his mission. The principal negotiator usually took some valuables with him and his status as envoy assured that he would not be attacked or robbed. The captors tended to hold out for as high a ransom as they thought their prisoner's kinsmen were likely to be able and willing to pay, and the go-between's skill lay in beating down these demands. Sometimes several trips of the *ghondu* and his helpers were required, and they had all to be compensated for their trouble and loss of time. If the prisoner was a man of status or his kinsmen known to be rich, as much as two or three mithan and several articles of value had to be paid, but the ransoms for poor people were much lower.

To Apa Tanis it was not only a matter of sentiment, but also of prestige, to ransom any kinsman or dependant who had fallen into captivity, but the feeling of injury on the part of the man who had to yield to the extortions of a kidnapper perpetuated the chain of acts of violence. For as soon as his kinsman had been released he contemplated how to redress his grievance, and if possible secure the person of a kinsman or dependant of his rapacious opponent.

Considerations of prestige induced Apa Tanis even to ransom captured cattle, and there were many instances of men paying for a mithan a ransom far in excess of the animal's market value.

Relations between traditional trade partners sometimes remained in an uneasy state of mutual distrust for years with only a reduced volume of trade maintained by poor men and slaves rather than those normally prominent in trade but vulnerable to kidnappings because of their known wealth.

Despite the frequency of incidents of violence involving Apa Tanis and Nishis there was a good deal of traffic between villages in traditional trading relations, and in the 1940s quite a few Nishis were living in Apa Tani villages partly voluntarily and partly as slaves of Apa Tanis. It was then quite a normal thing for Nishis who had run into some difficulties in their own village to come to the Apa Tani Valley, begin by buying rice on credit and, when they saw no possibility of an early repayment, settle down as the dependants and farm servants of their creditors. When such a Nishi bond-servant absconded without settling his debt, the Apa Tani creditor naturally felt aggrieved, and attempted to recoup his losses by capturing and holding to ransom a kinsman of the defaulter. Today the number of Nishis living in Apa Tani villages is negligible, but at the time of festivals many come to enjoy the hospitality of Apa Tani friends.

Though it seems that Apa Tanis were on the whole more peaceful and restrained than Nishis, and certainly more often the victims than the perpetrators of kidnappings, they were not incapable of organizing large-scale raids leading to much loss of life. Thus in the early 1940s Apa Tanis of Reru undertook a raid on the Nishi village of Dodum which resulted in the killing of thirteen men and the sale into slavery of seventeen captive women and children. Yet,

Apa Tanis as well as Nishis never attacked unless they were confident of taking the enemy by surprise, and a raid was usually a rapid action at dawn when those taken unaware had little chance of successfully fighting back. Casualties on the part of the attackers were usually not heavy, and I never heard of a pitched battle fought in day light between Apa Tanis and Nishis. Though the mounting irritation of a drawn-out feud sometimes culminated in a raid in which no quarter was given, normally Apa Tanis and Nishis did not think of their disputes in terms of a war which must end in total defeat of either side. Neither Nishis nor Apa Tanis had any intention of occupying their neighbours' territory, and the survival of their temporary opponents was essential for the eventual resumption of trade vital to their complementary economies. It thus lay in the nature of the relations between the Apa Tanis and their Nishis and Miri neighbours that periods of hostility had sooner or later to be followed by the conclusion of new peace-treaties.

All this belongs to the past and today Apa Tanis, Nishis and Miris can freely visit each other's villages without any need for peace-treaties or individual friendship pacts. They mingle in the bazaar of Hapoli, meet in the corridors of government offices and crowd into the same buses when they travel to North Lakhimpur or Itanagar. Apa Tani and Nishi students attend the same classes in the high school at Hapoli, in mission schools in Assam, and in the universities of Gauhati, Shillong and Dibrugarh. The Apa Tani Speaker of the Arunachal Pradesh Legislative Assembly has many Nishi villages in his constituency, and political parties extend across tribal boundaries. In 1978 there were already several Apa Tani administrative officers posted in circle headquarters situated in Nishi villages and Apa Tani teachers and members of technical government departments were also serving in Nishi villages. Though intermarriage between Apa Tanis and Nishis is still rare, its frequency will inevitably increase as a result of all these new contacts.

The changes in the pattern of trade between the Apa Tanis and their Nishi and Miri neighbours have already been mentioned in Chapter 3, and here it will suffice to outline briefly some of the development in Nishi villages bordering on the territory of the Apa Tanis.

The most striking development is the enormous increase in the population of some of the nearby Nishi villages. In Talo, which lies west of the Apa Tani country, for instance, there were in 1945 less than 40 houses. In 1978 their number had grown to 176, the number of hearths (each used by one family) was 1,077, and the total population 2,076. The men of Talo told me emphatically that this spectacular growth was due entirely to the increase in the families of the original residents, and that there were no new settlers who had moved to Talo from other localities. While I have no reason to doubt this statement, it is likely that there was a considerable influx of women born in other villages, for the men of Talo were rich and could marry wives from other places paying high bride-prices. Even in 1945 Toko Tekhi, for instance, had nine wives and his son Höli had five wives. Polygamy on such scale naturally led to rapid growth, if it was no longer balanced by the heavy loss of life which in the old days was the inevitable result of the many internecine feuds between different Nishi families belonging sometimes even to the same clan.

It seems that notwithstanding the enormous growth of the population of Talo, there is as yet no shortage of land. The construction of irrigable terrace-fields has greatly increased, and such terraces as well as maize plots near the houses and bamboo groves are private property. There is still a great deal of communal land suitable for slash-and-burn cultivation. While many hill-slopes have been denuded of forest, there are still wooded slopes, and it seems that Nishis can cultivate even plots where only some scrub was left after the previous period of cultivation.

Although the Nishis of villages such as Talo have greatly expanded the cultivation of wet rice, and are hence no longer dependent on bartering supplies of Apa Tani rice for their pigs and mithan, they have not lost interest in animal husbandry. The total number of mithan owned in 1978 by people of Talo was estimated as about 1,000, and while rich men owned an average of 30 mithan, even poor people had two or three mithan, and often also some cows. Many pigs were roaming about freely, and unlike Apa Tanis the Nishis of Talo are keen on breeding pigs. This continues to be a profitable business and a big pig can be sold for between Rs 300 and Rs 400. Many cows are brought from the plains of Assam, but Nishis do not buy chickens in North Lakhimpur because they fear that infected fowls may spread disease among their numerous home-bred chickens. In this respect they are more careful than the Apa Tanis who import large numbers of fowls for eating and use as sacrificial animals.

The most striking change in the outward appearance of a Nishi village is the introduction of the Apa Tani variety of bamboo, grown in numerous groves occupying the space between the clusters of long-houses. The Nishis have realized the advantage of growing bamboos in groves, and the rapid increase in the number of new house has undoubtedly necessitated the development of new sources of building material.

Like Apa Tanis many Nishis have derived considerable profits from the construction programme of the government. New roads such as the road to the Palin Valley, which branches off from the road between Kimin and Hapoli, have been built and are being maintained by labour-forces including a considerable Nishi element. Some Nishis work also as contractors.

Recruitment to the army and various government services has also contributed to the modernization of the Nishis, and education is making progress. Thus alone from Jorum, a village of 83 houses, 16 men went into the army and three men were in 1978 in government service; 14 boys and three girls were in the high school at Hapoli.

The progress of education among both Apa Tanis and Nishis as well as their involvement in economic development stimulated by government initiatives and funds will inevitably blurr tribal differences, and the traditional relations between individual Apa Tani and Nishi villages, alternately friendly and hostile, as they existed a generation ago will then be a thing of the past, remembered no doubt in tribal legend and individual family histories, but no longer of great social or economic relevance.

TEN

Recent Social and Political Developments

THE APA TANIS' traditional system of social controls was based on the general recognition that there existed no centre of authority capable of laying down the law and in the last resort enforce compliance with a code of conduct by the exercise of irresistable force. *Buliang*, as the leading men of individual clans, could debate and counsel and if they were *all* agreed on a course of action also apply certain sanctions, but unanimity was not easily attained when powerful groups, each represented by a set of *buliang*, were adamantly opposed to each other. Resort to such devices as *gambu* with the inevitable use of a measure of crude force was then the only way out of an impasse, and the pressures of expediency overruled any call for impartial justice.

Since the establishment of the Indian administration in 1947 all this has changed, not suddenly for certain, but by a gradual introduction of such institutions as a magistrate's court, a police force, village headmen (*gaonbura*) appointed by government, and ultimately a system of grass-root democracy in the shape of village-*panchayat* and district councils. The climax of this development came with the elections by adult franchise of the members of a Legislative Assembly for the whole of Arunachal Pradesh in March 1978. The thirty-one years separating these two dates saw a merging of old and new social controls, a process during which some features of the former system became obsolete or inapplicable while others survived in a new guise, and the rules and practices brought in by the new administration had to be adjusted to local conditions.

The first victim of the new regime was the authority of the *buliang*. Under the eye of the Deputy Commissioner and other district officials installed in their offices in Hapoli they could no longer take such punitive actions as the execution of criminals and their influence was undermined by the fact that even in civil cases any party dissatisfied with a decision of a council of *buliang* could appeal to the Deputy Commissioner. There was on the part of the government no deliberate policy to curtail the authority of *buliang* but with the rise of men more open to new ideas and developments, officials preferred to deal with such persons and many of them were appointed as *gaonbura* ("village-elders") and invested with the red cloth of office. This is a survival from the days of the British Raj when in the Naga Hills and the administered parts of the North-East Frontier Agency chiefs and village-headmen were granted recognition by government and given red cloaks which made them stand out from any group of villagers. Already in 1945 such clothes were distributed also in the Subansiri, region, and I invested myself several promineat Apa Tanis as well as some Miris of the Kamla valley with this type of red cloth, signifying thereby as well as by entering them in a register of *gaonbura* their recognition as spokesmen of the local population. At that time only *buliang* were granted such recognition, but the system was clearly somewhat haphazard and suitable only to a very loose administration which left the tribesmen to run their own affairs with little interference by government officials.

It seems that during the years following the establishment of the district administration in Hapoli government officials appointed very many Apa Tanis as *gaonbura*, but only few of them were also *buliang*. The respective functions of these two types of dignitaries were never clearly defined, but in fact the *gaonbura* had a greater say in the settling of disputes and more regular access to government officers. They were recognizable by their red coats supplied . by government, but unlike *builang* they had no right to shares of the meat of animals sacrificed at the annual festivals. A view which many Apa Tanis expressed in 1978 is that the *buliang* have become ineffective and are reduced to ceremonial functions.

The situation was further complicated by the introduction of *gram panchayat* in 1967. The members of these bodies were to be elected on the basis of 100 adults electing one *panchayat* member. In practice this ratio was not strictly observed and the members of one ward (*lapang*) elected one man by a show of hands. These elections were usually not contested and it seems they did not arouse a great deal of interest. Thus in Hang, Reru, Duta and Michi-Bamin the elections were not contested in 1971, and in Mudang-Tage they were not contested in 1975. Out of the *gram panchayat* members of a village one man is elected as member of the *anchal samithi* and this is a much more important body dealing with matters of local government such as the control of markets, certain taxes, bus schedules and similar items of local interest. The person elected as member of the *anchal samithi* also acts as chairman of the *gram panchayat*. The 25 members of the *anchal samithi* elect in turn two members of the *zila parishad*, a body on which all *anchal samithi* of the district are represented.

In the absence of an official definition of the respective functions and powers of *buliang, gaonbura* and *gram panchayat* members disputes are usually discussed in gatherings attended by all these dignitaries and the aim is to achieve consensus without putting any proposal to the vote. This is a time-honoured procedure similar to that adopted by the gatherings of *buliang* in the pre-administration days.

In order to regularize the cooperation of *buliang* and *gaonbura* in the running of the villages, the government revived parts of the Assam Frontier Regulation 1945, para 5, and established Village Councils by an order of the Deputy Commissioner dated 21 July 1977. The members of such councils were appointed by the Deputy Commissioner from among the *gaonbura* and *buliang*, and in each council there was to be a chairman, a secretary and an assistant secretary. The duties of the officers of such a council consist in the reporting of all crimes, voilent deaths and serious accidents occurring within their jurisdiction. The council has jurisdiction over all cases of a civil nature and cases of theft, including theft in a building, mischief (not by fire or explosives), simple hurt, criminal trespass, house trespass and assault.

The duties of the village councils, specified in the order of the 21 July 1977, confirm and in some way duplicate the general duties of the *gaonbura* to "assist the Government in maintaining law and order, apprehend offenders, report to the nearest administrative centre any crime, movement of suspects and undesirable persons, to assist the Government in development work, and look after the general interest of the public, and cooperate with other gaonbura."

From the following compilation it will be seen that the composition of the various village councils was by no means even, and that in some the number of *gaonbura* greatly exceeded that of *buliang* while in others these two categories were more equally matched:

Hang (Nyiti sector): *Buliang* 9, *gaonbura* 21, *buliang/gaonbura* 1; chairman and vice-chairman are *buliang.*

Hang (Nichi sector): *buliang* 4, *gaonbura* 20; chairman and vice-chairman are *gaonbura.*

Hari: *buliang* 21, *gaonbura* 33, *buliang/gaonbura* 2; chairman is *buliang,* vice-chairman is *buliang/gaonbura.*

Reru: *buliang* 22, *gaonbura* 38, *miha* 1; chairman and vice-chairman are *buliang.*

Tajang (upper sector): *buliang* 4, *gaonbura* 6, *anchal samithi* member 1; chairman and vice-chairman are *buliang.*

Tajang (lower sector): *buliang/gaonbura* 5, *gaonbura* 7, *buliang/ anchal samithi* member 1; chairman and vice-chairman are *buliang/gaonbura.*

Kalung: *buliang* 5, *gaonbura* 18, *buliang/gaonbura* 3; men who are neither *buliang* nor *gaonbura* 3; chairman and vice-chairman are *buliang.*

Hija: *buliang* 31, *buliang/gaonbura* 10; chairman and vice-chairman are *buliang.*

Duta: *buliang* 6, *buliang/gaonbura* 14; chairman and vice-chairman are *buliang.*

Mudang-Tage: *buliang* 13; *gaonbura* 8; *anchal samithi* members 2; *gram panchayat* members 3; chairman and vice-chairman are *buliang.*

Michi: *buliang* 6; *miha* 1; *gaonbura* 11; chairman is *buliang,* vice-chairman is *miha.*

Bamin: *buliang* 3; *miha* 2; *gaonbura* 11; chairman is *buliang;* vice-chairman is *miha.*

The most striking feature in this list is the difference in the composition of the village councils of Hang and Hari, on the one side and Hija and Duta on the other. Whereas in the former villages the *gaonbura* greatly outnumber the *buliang,* in Hija and Duta none of the council members are just *gaonbura,* but are either *buliang* or men combining the positions of *buliang* and *gaonbura.* A likely explanation is the fact that Hija and Duta are the most conservative villages which have made relatively little contact with the administration. Hence the *buliang* continued in their dominant position and even when *gaonbura* were appointed by government officials, only men who were also *buliang* were of sufficient prominence to appear eligible for such a position. In three villages there are also *miha* among the members of the village council; these are assistants of *buliang* and are sometimes also described *ajang buliang*.

Whereas on paper the organization of village government leaves nothing to be desired in practice the village councils do not seem to be very effective and their ability to deal with offenders against tribal custom or breaches of the peace was doubted by most of my informants. The mere fact that there is a higher authority, namely the Deputy Commissioner, within walking distance and easily accessible detracts from the authority of the village dignitaries, and I heard of several disputes which had ultimately reached the magistrate's court because *buliang*, *gaonbura* and members of the village council failed to produce a settlement.

During the early years of Indian administration government interpreters (*kotoki*) were of considerable importance. These were Apa Tanis who had learnt Assamese—and in some cases also some Hindi—and who provided a link between the tribesmen and the officials few of whom understood any tribal tongue. Such *kotoki* not only acted as interpreters but assumed also the role of mediators between litigants and in some cases gained considerable influence. With the increase in the number of Apa Tanis fluent in Assamese, Hindi and even English the need for interpreters in the pay of government is gradually dwindling, and there is the intention to fade out the institution of *kotoki*. I have heard Apa Tanis say that *kotoki* and *gaonbura* are obsolete, for as *gaonbura* themselves bring cases to the magistrate's court, "what is the use of *gaonbura*?" Disputes may nowadays be settled according to customary law or according to the Indian Civil Code. The former are not registered by the police, but there is no clear procedure determining the manner of deciding a case, and the police sometimes takes up cases already decided according to customary law. I was told, however, that most Apa Tanis are only satisfied if their disputes are settled according to the principles of customary law. Nevertheless those who could not win a case before a traditional forum often succumb to the temptation of taking their quarrels to a magistrate who may be more sympathetic or decide in their favour on procedural grounds. There is also the difficulty that criminal proceedings may be instituted against persons involved in a dispute which has come up for settlement before a tribal council adhering to customary law. Thus some participants in the *gambu* fought by Reru and Tajang were jailed presumably on account of the killing of a Tajang man though as a matter of fact all participants in the mass duel bore probably an equal share of the responsibility for the death of one of the participants, and had certainly voluntarily exposed themselves to the danger inseparable from such a contest.

In some cases government officers referred disputes back to village councils for settlement, but it seems that despite efforts on the part of the authorities to encourage tribal councils to adjudicate in disputes involving only Apa Tanis the response to this policy has not been very positive, and I have heard officials complain about the litigiousness of Apa Tanis. Their inability to deal effectively with their own judicial affairs is a novel phenomenon, for in 1944 and 1945 I was struck by the difference between Apa Tanis and Nishis in their attitude to any outside authorities. While then officers of the British administration, though newcomers in the Subansiri region, were soon overwhelmed by Nishis clamouring for their intervention in disputes with other Nishis, Apa Tanis kept their disputes entirely to themselves and never encouraged any intervention in their internal affairs, even though in 1944 they had appealed for military assistance against neighbouring Nishis who threatened their security. This spirit of independence seems to have evaporated and Apa Tanis have learnt to litigate in the magistrate's court at Hapoli.

Another novel phenomenon, which is difficult to understand, is the prevalence of murder among Apa Tanis often for trivial reason. The most notorious and also most inexplicable murder case was the recent killing of Kago Bida, one of the most prominent *buliang* of Hija (see *Himalayan Barbary*, Fig. 10, p. 80) by his own younger brother Tajo. It seems that one of Kago Bida's *guchi* dependants, who was under an obligation to give the head of any animal he killed in the chase to his senior patron Bida, secretly gave the head of a deer to Tajo. When Bida heard of this by chance, he rushed in a fury to Tajo's house, and as he did not find him at home, he drove Tajo's wife out of the house. Later Tajo returned and when he heard of his brother's unprovoked assault on his wife, he went to Bida and upbraided him. Bida flew into a rage and the two brothers quarrelled violently. In the course of this quarrel Tajo stabbed Bida to death. He was arrested and sentenced to life-imprisonment. The pleader who defended Tajo in an appeal told me that in the past few years there had been several murders among Apa Tanis, some as a result of trivial disputes connected with land or business transactions. This is a new development, and one wonders whether it may be due to the virtual abolishment of such traditional safety valves as *lisudu* competitions or the capture and temporary imprisonment of an opponent for the purpose of extracting a ransom.

Violence there has always been, but killings were usually only in feuds between Apa Tanis and Nishis or Miris, but not between Apa Tanis except in the course of an organized *gambu*, and then in full view of hundreds of other warriors. But the murder of a rival or opponent in a business deal would seem to be a new and ominous development for which I lack any satisfactory explanation.

Apa Tanis as Politicians

The formation of *gram panchayat* and the election of men to serve on these bodies, often, uncontested, did not introduce any new element into village society, for the *panchayat* rarely intervenes in the normal activities of the inhabitants of a village, and the *panchayat* members have rather less influence than the *buliang* of the traditional village community used to wield. The picture changes however, when we consider the role of *anchal samithi* and *zila parishad* in Apa Tani social life. Membership of these bodies can be a stepping stone to a political career leading to office outside the confines of Apa Tanis society, and hence it is desirable in the eyes of men with political ambitions. Without being a member of the *anchal samithi* it is not possible to become a member of the *zila parishad,* which is a body of 27 representatives of Apa Tanis, Nishis and Hill Miris, and the two Apa Tani representatives are elected by all the members of the *anchal samithi* from among their own numbers. The members of the *zila parishad* elect in turn their own vice-president who is the highest elected office-holder in the district, and as such is favourably positioned for election to membership of the Legislative Assembly of Arunachal Pradesh being already well known in the district. Gyati Takhe, the predecessor of the present incumbent of this office, did not stand again for the vice-presidentship because he planned to contest the election for the Legislative Assembly. In the end he stood in the elections of 1978 as an Independent and came second after Padi Yubbe, the successful candidate of the Janata Party, w o had already been an MLA and Deputy Speaker of the Assembly. Gyati Takhe is believed to be one of the richest Apa Tanis, with extensive business interests, and being also well educated he continues to rank among the most active politicians. The Congress candidate, Tasso Gryayo, came third, being a man of modest means though of considerable political experience. He had been active in the Youth Movement and was determined to stay in politics. The fourth candidate was Hage Hale, a prominent business man, who stood for the People's Party which did rather badly throughout Arunachal Pradesh. While Padi Yubbe was of Reru and the son of the influential *buliang* Padi Lailang, all the three remaining candidates belonged to Hari village, and this undoubtedly diminished their chances as none of them could profit from the loyalty of his co-villagers, the Hari vote being hopelessly split.

Apa Tanis are not very concerned about national politics, and the success of candidates depends mainly on their local standing, and the support of clansmen and above all affinal relatives they can rally. Such support has to be rewarded after a successful election campaign, and I was fortunate to be invited to a feast Padi Yubbe gave to his supporters and party workers.

The election had been held at the end of February 1978, but as many of the polling booths were in remote places the results were not declared until 10 March, and Padi Yubbe's election as speaker of the Assembly occurred only towards the end of March. So it was not surprising that the celebration of his victory on his home-ground had to be delayed until the middle of April, by which time the Mloko monopolizing the attention of many Apa Tanis had also come to an end.

The arrangements for the feast were elaborate. It was being held at Old Ziro where Yubbe has built a modern house as well as a large house in Apa Tani style. In front of the former there was a long table with two microphones, and loudspeakers were righed up on a tree and on the house. Numerous planks had been placed on the ground between the two houses to serve as benches for the guests. As Padi Yubbe's constituency included many Nishi and some Hill Miri villages not only Apa Tanis but also many Nishis and Miris had been invited. The colourful crowd which occupied the benches and milled around the ground in between the various events consisted mainly of Apa Tani and Nishi men, but there were also a few Nishi women. Apa Tani women worked largely behind the scene preparing the feast. The red coats of the many *gaonbura*, both Apa Tani and Nishi, provided most of the colour, but there were also bright blues, reds and yellows among the modern shirts of young helpers. Nearly all the Nishis were in traditional dress and headgear, wearing cane hats adorned with the beaks of hornbills and various feathers, but only the older Apa Tani men wore traditional clothes. Padi Lailang, the host's father, wore the same woollen vest and black shorts which he used to wear at home, but the younger Apa Tanis were in clean and well-ironed shirts.

The political part of the gathering began with speeches by Nishis and Miris, for the Apa Tanis had the courtesy to give precedence to their guests from distant places. There was a platform party of men sitting on chairs behind the table. It consisted of Bamin-Kano, Secretary of the local Janata Party and Vice-President of the *zila parishad*, who acted as chairman, Hage Babi, *anchal samithi* member of Hari, Nani Chatung of Reru, Assistant Secretary of the local Janata Party, Hage Hale of Hari, Tage Takhe, *anchal samithi* member of Hang, Padi Roza, the brother of Yubbe, and Taliang Bakhang of Kalung. Padi Yubbe sometimes also sat among the members of the platform party, but most of the time he was busy with arrangements.

One after the other the Nishi *gaonbura* held forth, using the microphones as if amplification were a common feature of tribal discussions. The training Nishis and Apa Tanis get in such debates stand them in good stead in political meetings of this kind, for none of the speakers ever faltered or stopped even for a moment to catch his breath. There were speakers from Nishi villages south of the Apa Tani valley, such as Jorum, Talo, Leiji, Pei and Yazuli, and next came Nishis from the villages to the north, i.e., Dodum, Tago, Linia, Tado and Rech-Taring in the Palin valley. Each spoke in his own language, the various tribal dialects being understood throughout the constituency. Thirty years ago many of the families here so peacefully assembled were sworn enemies, and would never have dared even to pass through each other's territories. Seeing the men of Dodum I could not help remembering the stories of the Apa Tanis' successful raids on that village in the 1940s.

The Apa Tanis were no less vociferous in their speeches than their Nishi guests, and many grabbed the microphone to congratulate Yubbe on his victory at the poll. They also reminded the audience how hard they had worked in the election campaign and admonished them not to relax their efforts to promote the cause of the Janata Party and to bring progress to the region. Some harped on the backward state of the local people, not realizing presumably that villages such as Hari are far more progressive than the majority of tribal villages in most other parts of India and educationally much more advanced than many Hindu villages in states such as Bihar or Andhra Pradesh.

While the speeches were still going on special guests, including some officials and businessmen of Hapoli, who were seated on chairs on the verandah of Padi Yubbe's house, were served rice-beer, rice with eggs baked in bamboos, and finally boiled mithan meat, of which a Marwari and a Nepali understandably did not partake.

Bamboo vessels, freshly cut by a team of young men, were then distributed to all the other guests whose number I estimated as about 500. While this distribution was still going on, Padi Yubbe held the final speech, partly in Apa Tani and partly, perhaps for our benefit, in fluent English, and thanked his supporters and also the helpers at the feast.

Next rice-beer was brought in red and blue plastic buckets—a major innovation—and boiled rice in baskets. Earlier large leaves had been distributed to the guests to serve as plates, and rice, eggs and meat were heaped onto these plates. Finally rum, jokingly described as "red tea", was offered to the more prominent guests while all the others were again served rice-beer. By the time the joyous gathering dispersed, and Nishis from the more distant villages sought the hospitality of friendly Apa Tani houses, many of the guests were in high spirits having consumed large quantities of beer.

Even ten years ago such a gathering with all the trappings of political meetings such as microphones and loudspeakers would have been unimaginable, and the peaceful meeting of so many Nishis from previously hostile villages also showed that a new era of inter-tribal and inter-village relations has dawned.

Apa Tanis play a new role in the political system not only as elected members of such bodies as the Legislative Assembly of Arunachal Pradesh, the *zila parishad* of Subansiri District and, on lower levels, as the *anchal samithi* and *gram panchayat*. Many have entered government service both in the reletively elevated positions of gazetted officers, and in a large number of non-gazetted posts. With the steady increase of young men and women possessing academic qualifications recruitment of Apa Tanis to executive posts in government departments is also growing.

In April 1978 there were already 15 Apa Tanis in gazetted posts serving in a variety of departments and, except for four, outside the Apa Tani valley. The latter posted at Ziro acted as Youth Coordinator, Medical Officer, Veterinary Surgeon, and Field Publicity Officer. Three Circle Officers were posted in the Subansiri District at Raga, Damin (Huri) and Nyapin, situated respectively in the Lower and Upper Kamla valley and the Khru valley. One worked at Itanagar in the Judicial Department; one as Transport Superintendent at Khonsa in Tirap District; one as Managing Executive of All India Radio in Dibrugarh; one as Statistical Officer in Shillong; one was a Revenue Officer at Tezu; one served as Flying Officer in the Indian Air Force and one as Second Lieutenant in the Indian Army.

The number of Apa Tanis in non-gazetted government posts was 342, and of these 115 were posted in the Apa Tani valley, the majority being peons and employees of the Public Works Department. Many worked in other places in the Subansiri District, such as Daporijo, Kolariang, Raga and Nyapin, but there was also a considerable number of Apa Tani government employees stationed at Itanagar. The remainder were dispersed over other districts of Arunachal Pradesh, and a few worked in Shillong and in towns of Assam.

After only 34 years of contact with government and an even shorter time when any kind of education was available to Apa Tanis this substantial share in government posts of various types is indicative of a rate of development and educational progress not matched by many tribal populations of India. This development is cumulative moreover, for men in government employment have usually both the possibility and the incentive to send their children to school, with the result that in the next generation even more Apa Tanis will be qualified for posts demanding a measure of higher education.

Quite apart from the psychological and political advantages derived by Apa Tani society from this substantial share of government employment, the economic benefits for the community as a whole are also considerable. The salaries of gazetted officers ranged in 1978 between Rs 550 and Rs 1300 P.M. and officials such as Circle Officers had an average income of Rs 750 P.M. The pay of non-gazetted government employees ranged between Rs 225 and Rs 560, and an appreciable part of these earnings were injected into the

economy of the Valley, because even those who served outside
their homeland tended to send part of their pay to their families.

Education

The opportunities in government service for qualified persons
no less than the successes of businessmen capable of operating in an
economy involving a measure of paperwork have impressed the
Apa Tanis with the advantages of modern education. Facilities for
obtaining an education irrespective of parental means have been
good ever since the late 1950s and in more recent years parents
capable of raising cash have sent their children also to fee-paying
schools outside Arunachal Pradesh. As a result of all these factors
educational progress has been rapid and literacy is relatively high.
In the early stages of the educational development there was some
confusion over the medium of instruction. At first Assamese as the
foreign language best known to Apa Tanis was advocated as the
most practical medium of education and the first primary schools
established in the Valley started teaching in Assamese. Efforts were
also made to produce primers in Apa Tani, which is a Tibeto-Burman
tongue. Subsequently the government decided to change over to
Hindi and this switch undoubtedly slowed up progress for children
already under instruction. The attempts to produce reading material
in Apa Tani, however, were continued and school books composed
with the help of the linguists in the Research Department of the
North-East Frontier Agency were printed in Devanagri script and
distributed to primary schools. It seems that there were not sufficient teachers capable of teaching in the tribal language and that
the Apa Tanis themselves were at that time not very enthusiastic
about books in Apa Tani. The experiment was hence abandoned.

A further change occurred when under the pressure of student
organizations the Legislative Assembly of the Union Territory of
Arunachal Pradesh decided that all education, beginning with the
primary schools, should be in English and, of course, in Roman
script. The main motive of this move was probably the wish to
educate young people in a language which they would need if they
wanted to join universities and other institution of higher education, and to be well prepared for competitive examinations required
for entry into government service. Those who had travelled in
other parts of India also knew that in many places English was more
useful than Assamese or Hindi. What was probably not realized

was the disadvantage of English for those children who went only for three or four years to school during which time they did not acquire a serviceable knowledge of English, while instruction in Apa Tani would have made them literate in their own language and the teaching of Assamese would have given them greater facility in the bazaar language useful on trading trips to North Lakhimpur or Itanagar. Adult education carried on by voluntary workers has of late experimented with the teaching of Apa Tani in Roman script, particularly to girls and young women, and the results seem to be encouraging, for the pupils attending evening classes held at Hang learn to write simple letters in Apa Tani within a period of four to five months.

The enrolment of pupils, both Apa Tani and others, in schools in the Valley was in 1977 as follows:

	Apa Tanis		Others		Total
	Boys	*Girls*	*Boys*	*Girls*	
Hapoli Primary School I	178	90	9	75	352
Hapoli Primary School II	76	22	2	11	111
Hang Primary School	136	35	0	0	171
Süro Primary School	35	17	2	1	55
Michi-Bamin Primary School	128	41	1	1	171
Duta Primary School	67	33	0	0	100
Tajang Primary School	114	41	0	0	155
Hija Middle School	196	70	0	0	266
Reru Middle School	166	51	0	0	217
Hari Middle School	174	149	0	0	323
Ziro Higher Secondary School	221	35	66	28	350
	1491	584	80	116	2271

The puplis other than Apa Tanis are mainly children of government employees stationed in Hapoli except in the Ziro Higher Secondary School, where there are also some Nishi boarders. In the primary schools there is a high drop-out rate, and only a small percentage of the children enrolled in the first form read up to the fifth standard.

Apart from the Apa Tani children who go to schools in the Valley, there are also children enrolled in schools outside the Subansiri District. The schools most favoured by Apa Tani parents are Christian mission schools in North Lakhimpur and Tezpur, but there are also some Apa Tani children in the Rama Krishna mission school in Along, Siang District. No official figures for children studying outside the Subansiri District are available. Some of my Apa Tani informants calculated that their number must exceed 100, but others thought this figure too low. Educationalists in North Lakhimpur familiar with Apa Tanis gave me the following approximate figures, which I was not able to check by visiting the individual institutions:

North Lakhimpur College	1 boy
Subansiri Seva Samithi Ashram	36 boys, 10 girls
John Firth Mission (Baptist)	4 boys
Collegiate High School, North Lakhimpur	4 girls
Saboti Mission School (St. Mary, Roman Catholic), North Lakhimpur	30 boys, 16 girls
Don Bosco Mission School, Tezpur	20 boys
Various Schools in Shillong	circa 20 boys

Most of the Mission schools charge fees but some special facilities, such as remission or reduction of fees are granted to many tribal children. Yet, it is believed that it costs parents about Rs 2,000 per year to send a child to a fee paying school outside the Valley, and this sum includes fares and some pocket money. The estimate is probably on the conservative side in so far as schools beyond North Lakhimpur are concerned. Apa Tanis believe that mission schools provide a better education than government schools and are, on the whole, not interested in what religious instruction the children receive. One of the unsuccessful candidates in the 1978 Legislative Assembly elections told me jokingly that his son, who attended the Rama Krishna Mission School, was a Hindu, his daughter a Christian, and he a believer in Dani-Polo, the tribal deity whose cult is being advocated by educated members of several of the Subansiri tribes as a kind of "national religion." Education is considered so good an investment that many Apa Tanis sold part of their land to pay for the schooling of their sons. I was told that in many cases such expenditure proved highly advantageous for the sons on whose behalf it was incurred. They prospered in business or obtained well-paid government posts, and in time were able to purchase twice as much land as their parents had sold in order to pay school fees and boarding expenses.

Study outside Arunachal Pradesh does not depend entirely on private initiative for the government of Arunachal Pradesh provides some grants for tribal students attending courses in educational institutions outside the Union Territory. No breakdown of the figures showing the number of Apa Tani award-holders is available but the following table relating to tribal students from the whole of Arunachal Pradesh gives some idea of the variety of facilities available:

Sainik School, Goalpara, Assam	7 students
Sainik School, Imphal, Manipur	14 students
Sainik School, Rewa	1 student
Rama Krishna Mission, Purulia, West Bengal	2 students
Rama Krishna Mission, Narendrapur, W. Bengal	1 student
Vanasthali Vidyapith, Jaipur	1 student

This list suggests that there is a pro-Hindu bias in the selection of the schools favoured by government.

In 1978 there were moreover six students holding Central Government scholarships for study in colleges outside Arunachal Pradesh, and nine students holding Arunachal Pradesh stipends for study outside the Union Territory, but no data on their respective location or even their tribal affiliations were available in the records of the Directorate of Public Instruction, Arunachal Pradesh.

Information on Apa Tani graduates obtained by personal inquiries is fortunately much fuller, and I am quoting it here in tabulated form because of the light it throws on the educational progress of the Apa Tanis in general and individual villages in particular.

Name	Village	Degree Obtained	University	Further Career
Padi Kani	Reru	B.A., LL.B.	Gauhati U: N.E.H.U. Shillong	Draughtsman (Judicial) Secretariat, Itanagar
Kuru Hindu	Reru	B.A.	Gauhati U.	Inspector, Agricultural Census, Bombdi La
Khoda Pasang	Reru	B.A.	Gauhati U.	Field Publicity Officer, Ziro

Padi Tana	Reru	B.A.	Gauhati U.	Superintendent, A.P. Transport, Khonsa
Duyu Randa	Reru	B.A.	Gauhati U.	Assistant, Secretariat, Shillong
Khoda Roja	Reru	B.A.	Gauhati U.	Sub-Inspector, Statistics, Govt. of A.P., Shillong
Nani Mali	Reru	B.A.	Gauhati U.	Postgraduate Student
Nani Challa	Reru	B.A.	Gauhati U.	Graduate Teacher Reru
Duyu Pusang	Reru	B.A.	Gauhati U.	Statistical Officer Shillong
Lod Koji	Kalung	B.A.	Gauhati U.	Youth Coordinator, Ziro
Rubu Tana	Tajang	B.A.	Gauhati U.	Graduate Teacher, Loth
Rubu Koyang	Tajang	B.A.	Gauhati U.	Graduate Teacher, Reru
Dani Tamu	Hija	V.B. Sc.	Gauhati U.	Veterinary Surgeon, Ziro
Pura Tado	Hija	B.A. M.A.	Gauhati U. Delhi Univ.	Managing Executive, All India Radio, Dibrugarh
Tage Moda	Mudang-Tage	B.Sc.	Dibrugarh U.	Announcer, All India Radio, Dibrugarh
Michi Butang	Michi-Bamin	B.A.	Gauhati U.	Circle Officer, Nyapin
Michi Tatum	Michi-Bamin	B.A.	Delhi Univ.	Public Relations Officer, Tezu
Gyati Sula	Hari	B.A.	Calcutta U.	Circle Officer, Raga
Tasso Bida	Hari	B.A.	Gauhati U.	Circle Officer, Huri
Hage Tatum	Hari	B.A.	Gauhati U.	Graduate Teacher, Palin
Hage Tatung	Hari	B.A.	Gauhati U.	Graduate Teacher, Hari
Hage Khoda	Hari	B.A.	Gauhati U.	Postgraduate Student
Hage Batt	Hari	B.A.	J.N. College, Pasighat	Postgraduate Student at N.E.H.U
Hage Taya	Hari	B.A.	Gauhati U.	Postgraduate Student
Hage Lase	Hari	B.A.	Gauhati U.	Postgraduate Student
Hage Challa	Hari	B.A.	Gauhati U.	Postgraduate Student
Hage Kojin	Hari	B,A.	Gauhati U.	Postgraduate Student
Miss Hage Yappa	Hari	B.A.	Banastali U.	Postgraduate Student
Dr. Hage Loder	Hari	M.B.B.S.	Bangalore U.	Junior Medical Officer Ziro

*North Eastern Hill University.

The above list, based on the position in April 1978, when many Apa Tani students registered in universities for degree courses expected to appear for their final examinations within a few months, evinces a remarkable imbalance in the educational progress in different village. Hari is clearly in the lead with 12 graduates, and Reru with nine graduates is a close second. Tajang, Hija and Michi-Bamin lag far behind with only two graduates each, and Kalung and Mudang-Tage can boast of only one graduate each, while Duta and the large village of Hang, so near to Hapoli and the Ziro Higher Secondary School, had no graduates among the young people. The prominence of Hari in the educational field is not easily explained, for it is neither very large nor particularly rich in land. I have heard Hari men say that in the early days of Indian administration the village fell foul of the district authorities and that after an armed clash, which resulted partly from misunderstandings due to faulty translation, the villagers decided that they could only get justice in future if they were educated and could convincingly put forward their case. This explanation has a certain plausibility though one wonders whether a whole community could really carry out such a long-term plan for the betterment of their position. Whatever the reason may be Hari is far ahead in the number of educated young men and in the share of its men in government employment. I mentioned already that in the last elections three of the four candidates were from Hari, while the winning candidate was from Reru, the village only slightly less progressive in the educational field.

Both Hija and Duta, villages which in 1944 and 1945 were foremost in their endeavour to establish good relations with government, and at that time profited most from incipient trade-relations with the plains of Assam, have been left far behind in education as well as in trade and politics. Equally Hang, at one time the one Apa Tani village, known by name in the plains of Assam, has kept a low profile and lacks prominence in most of the activities by which Apa Tanis have moved into the forefront of the economic and political life of the Subansiri District.

What are the future prospects for those progressive young Apa Tanis who are now studying for postgraduate degrees in the universities of Gauhati and Shillong? Their preference for political science, modern history and law and their relative lack of interest in such practical subjects as engineering, agriculture and indeed most science subjects suggests that they are looking to political careers rather than to activities connected with the development of the natural resources of their homeland. They can hardly be blamed for their political aspirations for one has only to compare the high prestige enjoyed by not only those members of Legislative Assemblies who attain ministerial rank, but also to the difference in status and power between a Deputy Commissioner heading the administration of a district, and even the most expert official in charge of a technical department.

The aspirations of educated Apa Tanis aim at political prominence, advancement in prestigious government posts, and thirdly success in trade and business. The latter is most closely related to the traditional talents of Apa Tanis, and it is perhaps significant that even young officers, who have done exceedingly well in such prestigious services as the Indian Air Force, are seriously considering an alternative career in commerce. If the exploitation of the allegedly rich mineral resources of Arunachal Pradesh should ever reach a stage where the economy receives from that side new impulses the Apa Tanis with their flexibility and spirit of enterprise should be well posed to make a contribution to the industrial development of the region.

The Youth Organization

Ever since young Apa Tanis went for higher education to institutions outside the Valley students played a role in local politics. For a time they were the only members of the community who were fully literate and had a grasp of conditions in the modern world. It is not surprising therefore that they looked at their society with new eyes and were critical of some of its features. Initially they objected mainly to practices which had caused them embarrassment in places such as Gauhati and Shillong where their heavy face-tattoo and even more the black nose-plugs of girls had made them objects of curiosity and sometimes ridicule. Later they also became aware of some customs which seemed to them inappropriate for a people seeking integration into the society of modern India. Thus they objected to *lisudu* competitions with their apparent waste of valuable resources and also to the prejudice against inter-class and inter-tribal marriages.

In 1973 several students formed an association which they called the Apa Tani Youth Association, and subsequently there was during vacations a large meeting in the Community Hall of Hapoli at which plans for a campaign for social reform were discussed. The first practices to be abolished were tattooing, the wearing of nose-plugs and child-marriage. It was decided, however, to proceed slowly and to tolerate child-marriage for the time being and concentrate on the two other issues. One of the leading spirits and first president of the Youth Association was Tasso Gryayo of Hari, who later became active in politics and stood as candidate in the 1978 elections to the Legislative Assembly of Arunachal Pradesh.

In 1974 the members of the association drew up a constitution, the more important parts of which read (in the original English) as follows:

> *Preamble:* We the youth of the Apa Tani Community have solemnly resolved to constitute an "Apa Tani Youth Association" in order to bring about integration and foster fraternal understanding among the young generation and thereby bring about unity among the youth of the Apa Tani community, to exploit the energy of young spirits for the greater interests of the community and to preserve, promote and protect our CULTURE and TRADITION, and to drive out all forms of SOCIAL EVILS and BAD PRACTICES from our society and thereby to bring a NEW LIGHT for our community, do hereby enact this CONSTITUTION for the APA TANI YOUTH ASSOCIATION this day, the 19th May, 1974.

The following are the important resolutions passed by the Association [quoted in extracts]:

> (I) The Association will have two youth clubs one at Ziro, and the other at Hapoli which will provide all sorts of facilities for indoor and outdoor games.
> ....
> (IV) The Association will conduct cultural touring, and a social service camp once a year to preserve our Culture and Traditions. The objects. . .will be as follows:
>
> (1) To abolish the puncturing of the nose and the tattooing of the face.
> (2) To discourage the use of (cane-) tails.

(3) To discourage the wearing of unnecessary heavy necklaces.

(4) To modify the hair-dress of the young generation.

(5) To encourage inter-caste marriage.

(6) To abolish child marriage.

(7) To encourage the use of traditional dress by both boys and girls. (This refers to hand-woven clothes worn as cloaks.)

(8) To encourage cultural and fashion shows annually.

(9) To encourage the community dance.

(10) To improve the use of the Apa Tani dialect.

(11) To encourage the use of the Roman alphabet as Apa Tani script.

(V) Development aims and objects:

(1) To ban begging on the Apa Tani plateau.

(2) To ban gambling and illicit sale of liquor and prostitution on the Apa Tani plateau.

(3) To ban goondas, thieves, dacoits and sales of smuggled goods on the Apa Tani plateau.

(4) To ban black marketing and check prices in shops and bazaars on the Apa Tani plateau.

(5) To check corruption/bribing in the society.

(6) To educate the illiterate people and to encourage them to send their children to schools.

(7) To help our illiterate people during famine, and epidemics and to teach them how to keep their houses clean.

(8) To educate illiterate adult people of the villages by conducting night adult classes.

The constitution also laid down detailed regulations regarding the number of office-bearers and their functions, the mode of electing office-bearers, and the financing of the Association by subscriptions (graded according to status) and by contributions from bodies such as the bazaar committees.

The resolutions passed at the same time as the articles of the constitution condemned also certain social practices, and laid down that "a fine of Rs 50 will be imposed for the puncturing of noses and the tattooing of the faces of Apa Tani children." It was decided moreover that fines of Rs 900 would be collected from anyone who challenges an opponent to a *lisudu* competition and procedes with the slaughter of mithan and cows in pursuance of his challenge. Soon after the passing of these resolutions the members of the Youth Organization began to enforce the prohibition of tattooing and nose-piercing. Though their rules had obviously no legal force, their enforcement surprisingly met with little resistance. The students formed groups of investigators, called jokingly C.I.D. (i.e. Criminal Investigation Department) who went to the villages to bring to light cases of recent tattooing and nose-piercing. Senior members of the Organization accompanied by *gaonburo* who, again surprisingly, lent their support and authority to the movement, then went to the houses of those who had offended against the new rules, by having their children tattooed or by piercing the noses of small girls. The amount of fine money which the offenders seem to have meekly paid totalled Rs 6,000. This sum was at first kept by the Youth Organization, but in response to public criticism it was later put into a fund from which the expenses of the Dri festival are met (see Chapter 7).

The Youth Organization also campaigned against the habit of Apa Tani women to leave their breasts uncovered in warm weather, but this attempt to set a new fashion met with little success, and as late as 1978 many women went about the villages without covering their breasts though when visiting Hapoli bazaar they usually wore blouses.

Another cause the Youth Organization took up without achieving much success was the right of women to inherit property. The organization agitated for a more equitable system of inheritance, suggesting that all sons should inherit identical shares irrespective of age, and that girls should also receive a share of the parental property. It does not seem that this agitation has so far met with much success.

There were, on the other hand, several occasions when the intervention of young men of the youth organization was successful in stopping a *lisudu* competition such as, for instance, the four-partite *lisudu* between Kago Bida and Nada Bakhang on the one side and Koj Nibo and Koj Goru on the other. We have seen above that on that occasion already many mithan and cows had been killed (see Chapter 7) when the students of the Hapoli High School, who had been in no way involved, prevailed on the opponents to stop the holocaust.

While it has not been practicable to give effect to all the elaborate rules about office-bearers and their elections, the Youth Organization remains a force in the social life of the valley, and so far the declared policy that the Association should not involve itself in political quarrels has remained effective. Hence the Association did not canvass in favour of their president Tasso Gryayo when he fought the 1978 election for a seat in the Legislative Assembly.

ELEVEN

Prospects for the Future

THE RAPID PROGRESS which the Apa Tanis have made in the fields of commerce and education, and the general sense of prosperity pervading the whole valley should not blind us to the fact that in the foreseeable future this very progress is likely to create a number of social problems. Anthropologists are neither cast in the role of prophets nor in that of planners. But as one who delights in the beauty of the Apa Tani valley, transformed by its inhabitants into a veritable garden, and who admires the skill of the Apa Tanis in ordering their social affairs with a minimum of dissension as well as their flexibility in adjusting themselves to the sudden contact with the modern world I cannot help speculating on the fate which may be in store for this vigorous and talented people.

The most serious problem looming on the horizon is the growth of the population in a strictly limited habitat. Even in the absence of precise figures for the recent increase in the number of Apa Tanis, it is evident that all the villages in the valley are expanding, with new clusters of houses occupying any available land. As irrigated rice-fields will never be readily sacrificed by being turned into house-sites these new habitations encroach mainly on land which could have been used for dry cultivation. In Chapter 2 we have seen that within the main valley and the few newly opened side valleys all arable land has already been taken under cultivation and that there is little scope for any further expansion of the farming area. It must also be remembered that the development of communications and the construction of government buildings occurred largely at the expense of land previously available for cultivation. The aerodrome alone, which is now hardly ever used, occupies a large expanse of land which used to be covered by fields, vegetable plots, and groves of bamboo and pines, and the road cutting across the whole valley is taking up a considerable amount of irrigable land.

In view of the fact that there exists as yet no cadastral survey of the valley, the exact acreage of cultivated land lost by Apa Tanis because of the construction of roads and government buildings cannot be assessed with any certainty. So far no attempt has been made to undertake such a survey and hence there is no record of the landholdings of individual Apa Tanis. The task of measuring the arable land and issuing documents confirming ownership would seem to be one of considerable urgency. In the past years, when all claimants to land lived in tightly organized village-communities, there was no need for any record of land rights. The ownership of individual plots of land was hardly ever in doubt and a system of go-betweens witnessing every transfer from one owner to the other was an adequate safeguard against disputes about rights to land (see p. 41). Today the situation has changed. Many Apa Tanis spend long periods of time outside the valley and are not present to watch the ongoing process of shifting bunds and minor irrigation channels, and of altering thereby the shape of fields and terraces. Disputes may therefore arise if any owner returns from a prolonged stay outside the valley and claims that those cultivating his land either as tenants or share-croppers have shifted boundaries to his disadvantage. Similarly questions of compensation for land acquired for public purposes can be equitably solved only if there is an official record of the precise landholdings of every individual Apa Tani. It is well known that population pressure in rural communities is conducive to litigation about land, and in the Apa Tani valley such pressure has been steadily mounting. If the colonization of the high-lying Tale valley materializes—a prospect which is by no means certain—the population surplus could be accommodated for some time to come, but climatic conditions at an altitude of some 2,000 feet above the Apa Tanis' present habitat would necessitate a complete change in cropping patterns.

In the relatively sparsely populated Nishi country there would probably be room for some Apa Tani colonies, but as the Nishi population is also increasing such colonization would almost certainly cause frictions and hence not be a long-term solution. Even the concentration of Apa Tanis in Itanagar and the nearby site destined for the new capital of Arunachal Pradesh has aroused the opposition of local Nishis claiming the area as their tribal territory, and in 1978 an unexpected outbreak of the old enmity between the two tribes led there to the burning of some Apa Tani houses by Nishis.

There remains the fringe of the Assam plains where years ago such small groups of Apa Tanis as the emigrant communities of Seajuli and Kakoi settled and obtained land for cultivation. Of all the states of India Assam suffers least from pressure on land and such excellent cultivators as the Apa Tanis would probably cause fewer problems than the many immigrants from Bangladesh who have already settled in Assam. Yet cultural differences between Apa Tanis and the Assamese peasantry might be a bar to the peaceful coexistence of compact groups of Apa Tanis and the local plains people.

There is, of course, no inherent reason why Apa Tanis in excess of the numbers of families that can make a living in their traditional habitat should continue to rely mainly on agriculture. Apa Tanis have a proven flair for trade, and many have already become wealthy by engaging in business and commerce. As none of the other ethnic groups of the Subansiri region can rival the Apa Tanis' skill as traders there may be a future for a great many Apa Tanis in the development of trading establishments throughout the district. In this sphere too local jealousies may cause difficulties, but as inter-tribal contacts increase and even inter-tribal marriages become acceptable, Apa Tani shopkeepers and merchants should be able to settle in most of the administrative centres where the presence of grovernment employees, some of them Apa Tanis, has already led to the growth of multi-tribal communities.

Related to the problem of the general population pressure in the Apa Tani valley is the future of the educated elite. We have seen that in the past ten years many young Apa Tanis have received higher education. So far all those who obtained university degrees experienced little difficulty in finding suitable employment, mainly in government service and within Arunachal Pradesh. Prospects for absorption in government departments are limited, however, particularly as all those recently recruited are young and not likely to retire for several decades to come. Future generations may therefore find it harder to obtain jobs commensurate to their expectations. These expectations are on the whole highly pitched because the first Apa Tani graduates succeeded so easily in settling in prestigious and profitable careers. In trade there will certainly be scope for educated young men, and as many of those who went to universities come from relatively wealthy families there is also the possibility that they will combine some local business with the development of inherited land. In other parts of India educated men of rural background have discovered that by farming their land with modern techniques they can secure a higher standard of living than by entering government service, but whether this applies also to Apa Tanis remains to be seen. The cultivation of rice is probably already so highly developed that substantial improvements are unlikely and the terrain does not lend itself to mechanized agriculture. But in horticulture, dairy-farming and stock-breeding there should be possibilities for those with trained minds capable of understanding and applying scientific methods.

The role which those educated outside the Apa Tani valley are likely to occupy within the traditional village-society may well pose some problems. As long as such men hold positions in government service and visit their villages only on the occasion of feasts and ceremonies, they do not compete with the established tribal leaders. But if members of the new elite were to settle in their villages, engaging there in business and improved farming, rivalry between them and the prominent *buliang* and *gaonbura* may easily develop.

The prestige and status of the traditional leaders of Apa Tani villages rested largely on their ability to organize labour and by doing so build up wealth. Such wealth was used not so much for their own consumption, but for lavish distribution at the time of feasts of merit and other ceremonial occasions. Thus the prominent Apa Tanis resemble in this respect the "redistributor chiefs" of Melanesia and owed their prestige to their roles as "great providers." The larger the amounts of meat, rice and beer with which they entertained their guests and which they distributed among a wide circle of kinsmen and friends, the greater was their glory and the respect their co-villagers paid them. Even the *lisudu* (see p. 135), which resembles so closely the American *potlatch*, evinced some of the features of competitions involving the lavish giving away of wealth by which "big men" in the Solomon Islands used to build up their prestige and power. Yet, we need not look so far to find examples of the distribution of wealth as a means to gain status and renown. The Sherpas of Nepal too are in the habit of distributing large quantities of food as well as considerable sums of money to hundreds of guests, invited and uninvited, on the occasion of memorial rites for deceased kinsmen.

We have seen that among the Apa Tanis the scale and the importance of feasts of merit have declined in recent years, and that the greatest of these feasts, the *yapu-yalung pido*, which might now cost Rs 30,000 to 40,000, has not been performed since 1972 (see p. 154). Although the Apa Tanis' general standard of living has risen, the use to which wealth is being put has changed, and one could well imagine that members of the new elite would hesitate to build up their social position by competing with the traditional leaders in the conspicuous distribution of food. The closest modern approximation to an old style feast of merit was the entertainment offered by Padi Yubbe to celebrate his victory in the elections to the Legislative Assembly of Arunachal Pradesh (see p. 195), but this feast was a special and probably atypical occasion. It seems that educated Apa Tanis prefer to spend their money on personal consumption, housing, schooling of children and occasionally even on travel. None of these types of expenditure benefits other villagers directly, and it is doubtful whether a member of the modern elite who does not provide lavish hospitality on the occasion of feasts and rituals can command the same respect and loyalty as the traditional leaders used to engender.

The slaughter of animals and the distribution of meat and beer were usually connected with the performance of rituals, and these involved the belief in supernatural beings to whom the power to intervene in human affairs was attributed. So far there has been no noticeable erosion of the beliefs and practices of traditional Apa Tani religion, though we have seen that some of the educated young men are promoting the worship of Doni-Polo as a counterpart to the deities of religions they heard about in educational institutions outside Arunachal Pradesh. Looking ahead one cannot easily visualize the shape which religious ideas will take. The traditional tribal world-view is not likely to satisfy indefinitely the intellectual aspirations of those who have studied in universities and other places of higher learning. Yet, none of the religions with which such men and women came in touch has made a strong impact on their thinking. There are a few pupils of mission schools who claim to have become Christians, but there is no indication that the practice of Christianity has been established in the Apa Tani valley. Hinduism, propagated by some schools of the Rama Krishna Mission, would

require Apa Tanis to give up their two favourite and most prestigious types of meat, namely beef and pork. Apa Tanis are great
meat eaters, perhaps knowing instinctively that as a source of
protein the flesh of animals is physiologically far more efficient than
any food plant, and it is highly unlikely that in the foreseeable
future they would accept a complete change in their diet. Quite
apart from the differences in food habits there is also a wide gulf
between the ideologies of Apa Tanis and Hindus. The Apa Tanis'
attitude to life—like that of many Westerners—is pleasure-oriented.
They treasure above all conviviality, enjoyment of sex, ceremonies
and festivals bringing together large groups and involving singing
and dancing. The ascetic and puritanical aspects of Hinduism must
be incomprehensible to Apa Tanis who think of life in the world
beyond as a repetition of this life, and have no concepts comparable to the Hindu *karma*. Self-denial and abstention from pleasur-
able activities must appear to the Apa Tani as pointless, for no
benefit for oneself and others appears to result from such practices,
and those who deny themselves sensual pleasures are in no way
rewarded in the after-life. It is possible that individual Apa Tanis
living outside Arunachal Pradesh may in future desist from beef-
eating purely for reasons of social conformity, but it is inconceivable
that Apa Tani society as a whole would voluntarily give up the
eating of beef and pork and the enjoyment of alcoholic drinks. In
1978 any such suggestion was ridiculed even by politicians who had
hinged their fortunes to the Janata Party, which in the rest of India
stands for total prohibition and the ban on cow slaughter. The
relations between Apa Tanis and Islam are not a problem, for few
Apa Tanis have had any close contact with Muslims, and their love
of pork no less than their belief in a multitude of gods and spirits
would certainly militate against the acceptance of Islamic principles.
Some Apa Tanis have had some superficial experience of Buddhism, for there are Buddhist members of the Legislative Assembly and
at the time of my last visit a Buddhist was Chief Minister of Arunachal Pradesh. Of all historical religions Mahayana Buddhism might
be most congenial to Apa Tanis, for adherence to its doctrine
would not necessitate the abandonment of essential aspects of their
life-style, though animal slaughter would have to be divorced from
ritual performance as it has been in Tibet. Yet, so far the Buddhists
of Arunachal Pradesh have made no efforts to proselytize Apa
Tanis or any other tribe of the Subansiri District.

Certain outward symbols of religions other than their own have penetrated into the Apa Tanis' thinking in a rather haphazard way, but it would be premature to see in these any indication of future conversions. Thus it has become fashionable to combine the traditional ephemeral grave monuments consisting of slanting bamboos and cane tallies of *ikhang* (see p. 173) with tomb-stones constructed of cement and engraved with the deceased's name and sometimes an inscription in English. Great value seems to be attached to such inscriptions and Padi Lailang, the father of Padi Yubbe MLA, begged me to compose a suitable inscription for his eventual tomb. His idea of the tomb in which he hoped to be laid to rest had been inspired by the Taj Mahal, one of the monuments he had been shown on a tour for tribal leaders organized by government. Though Apa Tanis do not use coffins but bury their dead wrapt in a cloth and a mat, Padi Lailang wanted for himself a coffin, preferably covered in silver. This coffin, rather like the cenotaph in the Taj Mahal, was to stand on the first floor of a modern building to be constructed for the purpose. Yet, Padi Lailang's acute business sense did not allow him to suggest wasting the groundfloor, and so he thought that one of his sons might use this as premises for a shop.

The merging of ideas and practices from various cultural backgrounds could hardly be better demonstrated than by this craving for a suitable funeral monument by one of the most prominent, most successful and most lovable Apa Tanis of the older generation.

If the Apa Tanis were as numerous as Nishis or Adis they would undoubtedly develop as one of the dominant ethnic groups of Arunachal Pradesh, but their insignificant numerical strength— below 15,000 out of 467,511—makes such a development impossible. However, their talents and determination may enable them to play the role of a specialized group, comparable perhaps to such numerically weak but yet important communities as the Kayasths, the Parsees or even the Kashmiri Brahmans in an all-India context. The fact that English and not any of the languages of the major tribes is the official language of Arunachal Pradesh is to the advantage of the Apa Tanis. For no preference is given to any of the tribal languages and the Apa Tanis as well as anybody else can learn English, and indeed it is noticeable that Apa Tanis with academic qualifications speak rather better English than Assamese students of equal educational standard. For being literate only in English they have to rely on English reading materials whereas Assamese students read also Assamese papers and books and converse outside the class-room mainly in Assamese. No doubt many educated Apa Tanis speak also Assamese or Hindi, but these languages take second place after English, a tongue in which they can communicate easily with other hill-people be they Nagas, Mizos or Khasis.

The future development of the Apa Tanis as a distinct group will largely depend on their ability to retain their tribal cohesion and their self-image as a dynamic community proud of having created by their own efforts the most closely integrated economy among all the tribes of Arunachal Pradesh. So far the only identifiable social movement, embodied in the Youth Organization, has tended towards modernization and the eradication of traits and practices believed to lower the Apa Tanis' image in the eyes of other Indian populations. Initially the aims of this movement were therefore predominantly reformist, but there were in the youth movement also some traces of concern for the retention of certain valuable cultural elements such as the wearing of specific clothes of Apa Tani manufacture. The movement has been successful in the achievement of some of its negative aims, e.g. the abolishment of tattooing, and as contact with other tribal groups intensifies it is to be expected that a movement which started with the aims of reform will gradually veer round to a more traditionalist stance and work for the preservation of the Apa Tanis' cultural identity. These are early days for the crystallization of any common attitude towards other communities, but the advocacy of inter-tribal marriages by some of the leading figures of the youth movement indicates a growing feeling that Apa Tanis can profit if instead of adopting a policy of social isolation they break down the barriers separating them from other tribes. Underlying such ideas may well be the belief that by creating kinship-links with other tribes the Apa Tanis can gain influence within a much larger group and hence secure political advantages beyond the reach of a small tribe of barely 15,000 souls.

A problem which in future is likely to become a debating point both in Itanagar and in Delhi is the continuation of the Inner Line policy which has proved so successful in protecting the tribal people of Arunachal Pradesh from being swamped and exploited by outsiders such as has been the fate of many of the tribes of Peninsular India. Apa Tanis of the present generation, both traditionalist and modern, fully support this policy, and there are no indications that they would welcome the lifting of the protective barrier which interferes in no way with the movements of Apa Tanis and other tribesmen but keeps out potential exploiters. It is difficult to imagine that in the foreseeable future Legislative Assembly of Arunachal Pradesh, composed overwhelmingly by tribal representatives, would agree to open the territory to an uncontrolled influx of populations from the plains. It may thus be safe in predicting that for a long time to come the Apa Tani valley will remain a heaven for a self-contained society unsurpassed in its skill to utilize the natural resources of its environment and to invest life with a *joie de vivre* such as few Indian societies can rival.

Glossary

Agyang: Ritual structure made of bamboo and leaves, and used as a kind of altar for sacrifices.

Anchal samithi: Regional council for an area comprising several villages.

Anyodo: Taboo, period of ritual abstention from work.

Ayo-asi: Spirits of the departed ancestors.

Asso: Section of Apa Tani society comprising several villages.

Bobo: High pole erected in village at the time of the Mloko festival.

Buliang: Clan dignitary; village councillor.

Buning-ajing: Ceremonial friend.

Buru: Legendary aquatic reptile.

Dao: Sword-like weapon, used also as universal cutting implement.

Dapo: Peace treaty.

Dapo sudu: Peaceful demonstration.

Dujo-mudu: Commission paid to mediator in trade-deal.

Enti-yoge: Measure of capacity taking 35 kg of unhusked rice.

Gambu, gambu-sudu: Prearranged fight between villages, mass-duel.

Gaonbura: Assamese term for village elder.

Ghondu: Go-between in negotiations about ransom.

Gram panchayat: Statutory village-council.

Guchi: Commoner, member of the lower class of Apa Tani society.

Guth: Patrician, member of the upper class of Apa Tani society.

Halu: Patrilineal clan.

Hipro: Illegitimate child.

Ikhang: Tally symbolizing meritorious deed.

Ipo: Yeastlike substance used in beer-brewing.

Jhum: Hill-field made by cutting forest or shrub and then burning it.

Kiri-dun: Go-between in trade-deal.

Kotoki: Government interpreter.

Kūmar: Castrator of domestic boars.

Lapang: Wooden assembly platform; also village-ward surrounding such a platform.

Larsudu: Betrothal presents; confirmed engagement.

Lemba: Village.

Lisudu: Competition between litigants involving slaughter of cattle.

Maji: Bell without clapper used by Nishis and Apa Tanis as currency for ritual payments.

Mida: Wedding.

Mite: Patrician; term interchangeable with *guth.*

Mloko: Spring festival performed in each village once in three years.

Morom: Festival-time when individuals perform feasts of merit.

Mura: Slave: term interchangeable with *guchi*.

Nago: Wooden shrine serving as ritual centre for group of clans.

Neli: Subterranean land of the dead.

Nyibu: Priest.

Patang: Labour gang of young people working permanently together.

Patta: Title deed for land (Indian revenue term).

Pattadar: Landowner holding *patta*.

Ropi: Rite performed after killing an enemy, tiger or leopard.

Rung-sere: Feast of merit.

Rung-ti: Feast of merit involving the sacrifice of 4-5 mithan.

Takum-putu: Feast of merit involving sacrifice of 3 mithan.

Thakum: Plum tree of ritual importance.

Talemoko: Celestial land of the dead.

Tulu: Sub-clan.

Ui: Deity, spirit.

Ui-in: Shaman, seer.

Un-pedo: Feast of Merit.

Uru: Lineage.

Yalo: Soul.

Yugyang: Ritual clan-centre where sacrifices are performed at the Mloko.

Zila parishad: District council.

Bibliography

Barthakur, J.K., *Census of India 1971*, Series 24, Arunachal Pradesh, Part II, General Population Tables.
———, *A Portrait of Population. Arunachal Pradesh, Census of India*, 1971, Delhi, 1975.
Betts, U., "The Village Duel in Apa Tani Society," *Man in India*, Vol. 28, 1948, pp. 163-69.
Bower, U. Graham, *The Hidden Land*, London, 1953.
Dalton, F.T., *Descriptive Ethnology of Bengal*, Calcutta, 1872.
Das, N.K., "Agricultural Economy of the Apa Tanis," *Indian Farming*, Vol. 8, 1947, pp. 294-98.
Dubey, S.M., *Modernization and Elites in Arunachal Pradesh, Census of India*, 1971, Delhi, 1975.
Duff, B., *Report on the Miri Country and the Operations of the Miri Mission*, Simla, 1912.
Dunbar, G., *Other Men's Lives*, London, 1938.
Elwin, Verrier, *Myths of the North-East Frontier of India*, Shillong, 1958.
———, *Democracy in NEFA*, Shillong, 1958.
———, *A Philosophy for NEFA*, Shillong, 1959.
———, *India's North-East Frontier in the Nineteenth Century*, Bombay, 1959.
Fürer-Haimendorf, C. von, *The Naked Nagas*, London, 1939.
———, "Agriculture and Land Tenure among the Apa Tanis," *Man in India*, Vol. 26, 1946, pp. 20-49.
———, "Notes on Tribal Justice among the Apa Tanis," *Man in India*, Vol. 26, 1946, pp. 181-95.
———, *Ethnographic Notes on the Tribes of the Subansiri Region*, Shillong, 1947.
———, *Exploration in the Eastern Himalayas*, Diaries of Travel in the Subansiri Region 1944 and 1945, Shillong, 1947.
———, "Anthropology and Administration in the Tribal Areas of the North-East Frontier," *Eastern Anthropologist*, Vol. 3, 1949, pp. 8-14.
———, "The After-Life in Indian Tribal Belief," *Journal of the Royal Anthropological Institute*, Vol. 83, 1953, pp. 37-49.
———, *Himalayan Barbary*, London, 1955.
———, *The Apa Tanis and their Neighbours*, London, 1962.
———, *Himalayan Traders—Life in Highland Nepal*, London, 1975.
———, *Return to the Naked Nagas*, London and Delhi, 1976.
Izzard, R., *The Hunt for the Buru*, London, 1951.

Luthra, P.N., *Constitutional and Administrative Growth of NEFA*, Shillong, 1971.

Mills, J.P. "Tours in the Balipara Frontier Tract, Assam," *Man in India*, Vol. 27, 1947, pp. 4-35.

Pandey, B.B., *The Hill Miris*, Shillong, 1974.

Shukla, B.K., *The Daflas of the Subansiri Region*, Shillong, 1959.

Simoons, F.J., *A Ceremonial Ox of India. The Mithan in Nature, Culture and History*, Madison, 1968.

Stonor, C.R. "Notes on Religion and Ritual among the Dafla Tribe of the Assam Himalayas," *Anthropos*, Vol. 52, 1957, pp. 1-23.

Index